Geography
for Today's Children

Geography
for Today's Children

LINNIE B. JAMES
University of Pittsburgh

LA MONTE CRAPE
Butler County Community College

New York APPLETON-CENTURY-CROFTS
Division of Meredith Corporation

Copyright © 1968 by
MEREDITH CORPORATION

G
74
.J27

6117-1

Library of Congress Card Number: 68-12128

PRINTED IN THE UNITED STATES OF AMERICA
E 47980

preface

It is the right of every American child to know the geography of his own land and how geography has influenced its development. It is also his right to know how dependent upon each other are all of the nations of the world, including his own. We believe that every child should be able to see for himself the part that environment plays in accounting for man's activities, and that he should be able to understand how geographic relationships affect his life. He must be able to see all parts of the world in his mind's eye, and he must come to understand how geographic conditions are contributing elements in many of the problems of the world.

Many children are denied their right to geographic literacy and understanding because they have teachers who are inadequately prepared to teach geography. As we have taught our college classes, we have reached the conclusion that part of the reason for poorly prepared geography and social studies teachers is that there simply are too few methods texts in geography which tell, in forthright fashion, how to teach geography properly and how to make use of geographic facts. Furthermore, too few teacher-trainees and teachers in service have the geographic background necessary to teach relationship geography so that geography has meaning.

There are few subjects which offer so many opportunities to help children to develop the ability to think and to reason as does relationship geography, yet there are still many teachers who, because they know of no better way, teach geography in the same way in which they were taught— read, recite, test. As a result, geography becomes a subject despised by most of their pupils. It is with these teachers in mind that we have tried to show how relationship geography is developed, how geographic concepts are introduced, and when geographic tools may be used effectively. We have also provided geographic information which elementary teachers must know if they are to teach geography as a separate subject, or as a part of the social studies.

Where we have carefully outlined methods, it has been done with the intent of *suggesting* a method that *works*, one which should be used by the teacher until he is able to develop a successful one of his own. We believe that teachers should not use trial-and-error methods, to the detriment of their pupils, in any of their teaching. To experiment with pupils in the classroom is to rob them of a part of the short time in which they must prepare themselves for life. The tested methods which we suggest will help the inexperienced teacher get the feel of the subject and of *teaching* geography. Once he is at home with geography *and* with his pupils, he will be more likely to have success with his own methods and with his adaptations of the methods of others.

We hope that our text will be a useful guide for teachers in service who wish to bring additional life to their geography teaching techniques, and that teachers in training will find it informative and clear.

We wish to acknowledge our indebtedness to the following persons and publishers who have given us permission to quote from their works: Mr. Warren E. Preece and the *Encyclopaedia Britannica*; Dr. Herbert H. Gross and *The Journal of Geography*; Mr. Alex Fraser and J. B. Lippincott Company; Mr. F. G. Vosburgh and the National Geographic Society; Mr. J. K. Cordy and Clarendon Press, Oxford; Dr. S. H. Steinberg and *The Statesman's Year-Book*; Mr. G. Raponi and the Food and Agriculture Organization of the United Nations; Mr. A. Mazaud and the Publications Board of the United Nations; and Mr. Luman H. Long and *The World Almanac*. We also wish to express our appreciation for the work of Mrs. La Monte Crape in compiling the index for the text.

L. B. J.
L. C.

contents

PREFACE   v

INTRODUCTION   1

1   Discover geography   5
2   Teach relationship geography   16
3   Become world minded by using the globe   33
4   Become world minded by using the globe, continued   55
5   Make maps indispensable   76
6   Make maps indispensable, continued   98
7   Use all available tools   129
8   Use all available tools, continued   170
9   Plan your work   187
10 Teach a readiness program in the primary sequences   215
11 Test with a purpose   221
12 Make your program active   230
13 Factors to which some of man's activities are related   245

Appendix A   Types of climate   259
Appendix B   Climatic regions   261
Appendix C   Climatic data   264
Appendix D   Teaching the concept of rainfall—intermediate
             sequences   266
Appendix E   Growing conditions, special requirements, and
             production figures for selected crops   268
Appendix F   How vegetation is affected by elevation in the low
             latitudes   272
Appendix G   How vegetation is affected by elevation in the middle
             latitudes   272
Appendix H   Crops are determined by latitude, elevation, and
             rainfall   272
Appendix I   Leading producers of essential products   274
Appendix J   Land use data for selected countries   280
Appendix K   Population and area of selected countries   281

BIBLIOGRAPHY   283

INDEX   287

Geography
for Today's Children

introduction

Attention Teachers

You, as a teacher, conduct your children on an exciting world tour. It is a tour which begins in kindergarten, where they study their own community, and ends in high school with a detailed study of the whole world. You cannot expect to show them everything on their tour, but you can show them the meaning of those things which they will see. Pointing out important relationships en route will help develop their insight and their understanding of the problems which exist among peoples, and how people are forced to make the best of what they have in their environment.

Your journey with the children will be much more rewarding if you are able to use geographic "tricks of the trade," and if you try out new methods in attaining your goals. There will be times, of course, when you will be tempted to take excursions which do not pertain to the actual relationships or concepts which you are attempting to develop. At times like this you must remember that too many details cause "mental fog." It is then that you must be content to teach less but to teach well! You will learn to hang new knowledge on old pegs of experience, and you will make your teaching a "doing" program. Children remember very little of what they hear, but they seldom forget experiences in which they have had a part.

Make the landscapes of the countries in which the children visit live! Help your pupils feel the heat of the tropical deserts, the chilly dampness of the marine climate, and the apprehension of traveling at dizzy heights over high mountain roads. Enable the students to people the various countries with human beings who become tired and hungry just as we do, and who have different standards of living from ours, not through choice, but because of circumstances. By having the students try to imagine themselves in the environment which they are studying, you will help them to develop concern for the people of other countries and, eventually, bring them to a better understanding of the problems of others.

We sometimes forget that not all of our pupils are as interested as we are in the subject. You will need to plan unusual motivations and vary the procedure in your lessons every day. Dramatize more! You need to dramatize in order to make your lessons more alive, more interesting. It may take nothing more than a change in the pitch of your voice or the rapidity with which you speak, or the wave of your hand to illustrate a point, to capture the interest and arouse the curiosity of less interested students. Challenge your pupils often and leave the challenge unanswered so that the pupils' feeling of frustration will lead them to seek knowledge. Of course, continued frustration without release can lead to serious problems; one has to use good judgment and consider the lessons he has learned in his study of educational psychology. Nevertheless, good teaching demands that the pupils be left something to discover for themselves. Plan always to do good teaching!

Good teaching means that you will teach the truth about places, people, and conditions. Picture the places as they really are. You will find that keeping up-to-date with what is going on in the world is a prime necessity. Changes are taking place daily. There are probably some teachers who are teaching that all Eskimos live in igloos, that the wooden shoe is the typical footwear of the Netherlands, and that a tropical rain forest and a jungle are identical. Why? Undoubtedly, part of their misinformation is due to a lack of proper training, but certainly some of it is the result of not keeping pace with the times. Be always on the alert for inaccurate generalizations which children are likely to make without sufficient information. Do not be guilty of contributing to their misinformation for a similar reason.

You and your class will have many exciting adventures as you travel. What the children traveling with you get out of the journeys and out of the work they do depends upon you, their guide. Nothing is accomplished without enthusiasm. As their guide, then, be enthusiastic about the trip!

As you read this book you will undoubtedly discover that there is much about geography which you either never knew well, or have forgotten. It is possible that you are, for some reason, "antigeography," or indifferent to it. Whatever your present attitude may be, one of the purposes of this book is to broaden your knowledge about geography and to strengthen your understanding of it.

Professional geographers devote years of their lives to the study of intricate relationships between man and land. As they have studied, they have created branches of geography which are highly specialized and perhaps beyond the immediate understanding of the teacher with a limited geographic background. Yet every teacher is capable of understanding, appreciating, and teaching simple geographic concepts and skills. A second purpose of this book is to acquaint you with these concepts and skills in such a way that you will truly appreciate geography and be enthusiastic about it as you teach it.

Not only can you learn as you read, but in the following chapters you will find teaching suggestions and techniques for the development of skills and concepts which will make your teaching more effective. The methods suggested are not the only ways to develop certain concepts and skills, but they are methods which will work until you develop your own techniques. You cannot learn for the children, but you can show them the way to learn. By presenting information in a logical, orderly, step-by-step manner, which will lead them to the correct conclusion, you will be developing their ability to think; and teaching children to think is, after all, the primary purpose of the teacher.

Educators who are trying ungraded curriculums often divide the subject matter into "sequences" or "levels" instead of "grades," permitting pupils to proceed as fast as their ability and interest allows them. This is as it should be. Geographic concepts and skills should be introduced when needed to make the work more meaningful regardless of so-called "sequences" or "grades." You will find the work in this book presented in sequences rather than grades. Although the words may seem synonymous to many of you, there is a hint of an artificial barrier if the term "grade" is used.

And now, try out some of the methods mentioned, plan new activities, and use the suggestions to vitalize your work. Teach the children all their inquiring minds will hold about the world and its people. Do not be afraid to go out on a limb; that is where you will find the fruit. And may you have a wonderful harvest.

1

Discover geography

Have you discovered what geography really is? No doubt you have learned that "geo" is a root word having something to do with "earth" and that "graphy" has to do with "writing." Geography is, apparently, simply writing about the earth.

A simple definition, such as this one, is desirable, but it is, unfortunately, incomplete. Before one can write about the earth, he must first gather information about it. He must observe the kinds of environment found on and around the earth, as well as the many varieties of life which the earth sustains. These observations must then be organized and evaluated. In so doing, certain patterns or hypotheses emerge which can be tested. As fundamental truths develop, the knowledge which they afford can be applied for the benefit of mankind. Since the study of geography involves these particular aspects of learning, we may safely say that it is a scholarly and scientific pursuit devoted to the orderly study of man, of his environment, and of their interrelationships, for the purpose of stimulating and maintaining the continuing improvement of humanity.

Geography, defined in these terms, is neither man centered nor earth centered. It is, instead, relationship centered, with the implied notion that the knowledge which geography generates shall be both understood and used. There are many facets to geography as a discipline, and the goals of the professional geographer and the teacher of geography in the elementary school are somewhat alike. Only their approaches differ.

The professional geographer is interested in both the collection of facts and their interpretation in terms of principles or truths, and the *immediate* application or use of those truths in the service of people. The elementary school teacher is primarily concerned with the development of lasting concepts, skills, attitudes, understandings, and appreciations which his pupils can *eventually* use effectively as adults.

The many ways in which professional geographers study the earth's surface and the several fields from which geographic facts are taken give rise to the two main branches of geography, physical geography and human geography. Social, cultural, and political geography, and demography, are all subbranches of human geography, just as oceanography, climatology, cartography, biogeography, and the geography of soils and hydrology are subbranches of physical geography.

Economic geography, which is the study of how man attempts to satisfy his needs, draws its knowledge from both of the main branches of geography, i.e., from physical and human geography. Principles and facts from *all* of the subbranches are embraced in regional geography, which devotes itself to the study of a particular region or area wherein the features of the landscape are very similar. Regional geographers consider, quite correctly, that the complete geography of the region or area is influential in the development of the economic and cultural life of the people of the area. One must remember, however, that economic and regional geography are only two of the theoretical approaches available for the study of geography.[1]

The professional geographer is concerned with these content areas which are the special branches and subbranches of geography. The elementary school teacher must also know the content of geography, but in addition, he must be aware of how children develop and the techniques he must use to bring about learning. Geography, as it is taught in the elementary grades, should include a combination of both physical and human geography, with the principal emphasis on human geography, and it should be taught by someone who fully understands child development and the principles of learning. If geography is to be of interest and value to our pupils, it must be about people and it must be taught by teachers well acquainted with both its content and the techniques for teaching.

Why is the teaching of geography necessary at all? We Americans, as a whole, are geographically illiterate in comparison with the people of many other nations. Does this matter? Where does our geographic illiteracy show itself? We show it in the opinions we hold and in the remarks we make about foreign lands and peoples. Because we live in a land of plenty and

[1] Because most students have had introductory geography courses, definitive statements regarding each of the subbranches of geography are not necessary in this work. For definitions, the student should consult Preston E. James and Clarence F. Jones, eds., *American Geography: Inventory and Prospect* (Syracuse, N.Y., Syracuse University Press, 1954), or any other general work on geography.

opportunity, we cannot always appreciate the problems of other lands. We read in the newspapers about other countries and our relations with them, but we seldom have the background necessary to fully understand what we read. For example, when we hear about foreign aid, we are often opposed to it because it affects our purse strings. Following World War II, some people objected to the economic assistance which the United States gave to foreign countries. In discussing economic aid for Italy, a wartime enemy, many of our citizens shrugged off their responsibilities with a remark such as, "Why should we help them?" A knowledge of several simple geographical facts and an understanding of a few basic relationships might have forestalled such a remark. Did those who felt this way know that Italy is a small country, about the size of Arizona, which must support a population of fifty million people? That only one-fifth of Italy's land is in plains, some of which are marshy and cannot be cultivated? That much of Italy is in that part of the world where the rains come chiefly in the winter, and what this means to the millions of people who make their living from the land? That nearly two million farmers had only about one acre of land apiece at the close of the war? That it is difficult, if not impossible, to make a living from so little land? That the annual income for the people of southern Italy was then about one hundred fifty dollars, while in northern Italy it was three hundred dollars? A knowledge of geography, particularly relationship geography, would have helped American taxpayers understand the economic and political problems of Italy.

We show our geographic illiteracy by our attitude toward other lands and people and by our lack of honest respect for them and their ways of living. If we know very little about a country, we are inclined to judge its people by our own standards. We do not take the time or trouble to learn how people in other countries use what they have and how they make adjustments in order to survive. We look at pictures in magazines. Perhaps we see a Hausa village in the high Nigerian plateau. We notice the mud houses with thatched roofs, the fences of guinea corn and the people busy with the never ending tasks of daily living. With a glance at the picture we think, "Just a primitive village of people living in Africa," and turn the page. How much real understanding do we have of conditions found in this tropical grassland? We do not stop to consider the ingenuity of these people in making homes of materials which are at hand, or of the many problems these excellent farmers and skilled craftsmen face in order to live. Their lives have been greatly influenced by their environment and many of their problems can be traced directly to the geography of the land where they live. This is a region with scattered trees, and grass which often grows to a height of five to twenty feet. The climate is too dry half the year and too wet the other half. Farmers have to grow all their food and also special cash crops such as cotton and peanuts to bring in money to supply other needs. But the weather does not always cooperate. Droughts, long heavy rains, and insects may destroy the crops. The solution of these problems requires knowledge of irrigation, water storage, soil conservation, and crop requirements as applied to their environment. It is evident that we can better understand other peoples if we are fully aware of the geographic influences which affect their lives.

We show our geographic illiteracy when we think that the customs of foreign countries are amusing. The Chinese have a saying, "The more you know, the less you think queer." How true this is! Different customs and ways of living are not queer. They are natural and the outgrowth of existing conditions, many of them geographic. Our geographic illiteracy makes it difficult to understand "foreigners," but it is just as difficult for people of foreign countries to understand us. It would be interesting if we could see ourselves through their eyes. Perhaps we would seem to be the "queer" ones!

We show our geographic illiteracy when we are quick to make generalizations without sufficient information. We often assume too much and are inclined to accept as general truth such statements as these: the East Indians wear white cotton clothing; the Chinese eat rice; Japan has a warm, sunny climate and has no need for substantially built houses. How wrong these statements are! Each of them might be true of one part of the country referred to, but most countries, like our own United States, are very complex, and conditions in them vary according to topography and latitude. Geography teaches us not to make general statements until we have all of the information. Then, and only then, can we draw correct conclusions and state generalizations.

Businesses and industries cannot be managed by the geographically illiterate. Geography is helpful in analyzing a considerable number of industrial problems such as the location of new factories, transportation patterns, availability of labor, power costs, water supply, availability and cost of raw materials, and the purchasing power of people in other nations, all of which are related to the natural conditions of the land. Businessmen frequently need geographic information for which they must consult geographers on a fee basis. Much of the information for which they pay is based upon material that our pupils should learn in their geography classes.

We show our geographic illiteracy in our lack of understanding of world affairs. Our distorted views of life in foreign countries can no longer be afforded or tolerated. We dare not act as though what happens in other countries does not concern us. Everything concerns us. Our country is now in a position of global leadership. The lasting effectiveness of our leadership depends greatly upon the ability of our people to think in global terms. Too often foreign and domestic policies are determined by emotions rather than facts. To a certain extent, our people control policies through our elected officials. Intelligent action by our officials is directly related to their geographic literacy, and our judgment of their actions depends upon our own geographic literacy. Foreign and domestic policy formulation should be based, in part, upon clear, geographical thinking. We cannot know what lands our pupils may visit during their lifetimes. Our military forces, for instance, are located in many parts of the world. Certainly, these young men should be as well prepared as their leaders for what they will find in foreign lands. None of them can afford to be geographically illiterate.

Our enjoyment of daily life is diminished by a lack of geographical background. Did you take a trip last summer? How much did you get out of it? Did you see only trees, hills, and a long, blank stretch of concrete? Or were you able to "read" the landscape and grasp its meaning? Had the part of the country through which you travelled once been covered by the sea? Had the streams cut wide valleys? How was the land used? What differences in the amounts of rainfall could you detect? Could you account for the types of industry located in the towns through which you passed? Teaching our pupils to "read" landscapes is part of geography. We want them to see when they look at any landscape. How much more enjoyment all of us would be able to obtain from our leisure time reading of books and magazines, and from pictures, if we could visualize them in their geographic settings!

Where and when do we lay the foundation of geographic literacy? It begins in the geography readiness program in the primary grades and continues through the elementary grades and the junior high school into the senior high school. It cannot be done with a little geography here and there; that is, through geography programs which lack continuity. Geography has definite techniques and its own language. It takes time to build geographic concepts through relationship study, and it takes time to practice and acquire geographic skills. All of these must be developed, step by step, slowly and thoroughly, within whatever curricular framework exists in the school setting.

Of the several types of curricular framework developed for the elementary school, the core curriculum, the correlated curriculum, and the experience or child-centered curriculum are most frequently found in use. Geography, happily, can provide an ideal and logical focal point for each of them, since all of these curricular designs have certain common characteristics. The unit of work, or problem solving activity, is common to all. Each kind of curriculum mentioned cuts across the traditional subject-matter lines. The immediate interests of the individual child are considered in all of them. Every one of the designs encourages pupil participation in choosing the topic for study and in the planning of the learning activities connected with the topic. The topic chosen occupies the major portion of the time allotted for all learning activities in each. They all encourage both individual and group work of a purposeful nature, and, finally, they all consider man and his environment—social, cultural, and physical—as central to the problem or theme that is being considered.

Geography, related as it is to every discipline known to man, and contributing to all disciplines, is well suited for the task of providing initial and basic relationships for the study of any topic chosen by the teacher and pupils. Whether the problem to be considered is economic or social, cultural or political, man-land relationships will be found basic to the study, understanding, and solution of it.

Geography is a "tool" subject for us and our pupils. That is, in the same sense that a tool enables us to do a task more quickly and better than we could do without it, so a knowledge of geography contributes significantly to a fuller understanding of the world and its people, and helps to determine whether or not we function effectively as individuals and as citizens of our nation.

Have you discovered the contribution of geography to social studies? Of all the social sciences included in the social studies, geography has been the most neglected, probably because too few teachers have the necessary background to teach its concepts and skills.

Geography can provide a unified structure for social studies, giving the work continuity. It can provide interest and challenge as the pupils study the problems of other people. Social studies, which include instructional material from geography, history, economics, anthropology, social psychology, political science, philosophy, and sociology, is one example of a unified program. Each discipline contributes to the problem under study, and the task of the teacher is to relate them to each other, or "fuse" them so that a unified picture emerges. One thing which all teachers of social studies must recognize in trying to fuse geography with history, for instance, is that the geography of the land during the period being studied was far different than it is today. The pupils, in order to get meaning from their history, must learn that events were related to the geography of the land as it was at that time. If you are teaching social studies, do not confuse the geography of earlier times with that of the present day. Develop the geographic relationships which will help to explain the activities of the people of an earlier day, but do not cheat the pupils of their right to understand today's world.

Frequently, social studies textbooks will give a few facts about a region without explaining the relationships which exist. Consequently, there is little meaning and almost no thinking involved. The social studies teacher needs to have background in several social sciences but he especially needs a geographic background, so that he will be able to supplement the meager amount of textbook material, thus enabling the pupils to understand the relationships that may be suggested. Otherwise, the work descends to the level of memorization and becomes dull and meaningless.

Sometimes textbooks will suggest locating places on a map or tracing a route as if the mere mention of a globe or a map indicates the use of geography in social studies. Location is only one facet of geography. Much more must be added to explain the reason for the location and the relationship of all other factors to the location. To illustrate, let us assume that a class is beginning the study of the western states. In teaching the pupils about the settlement of the West, there is a need for map work. We must make the work meaningful and we must encourage thinking. On a large outline map, have the Oregon Trail plotted exactly.[2] Then, with a physical map, find the relationship between the route and the topography of the land. Find where the passes in the mountains were, where the mountain slopes were very steep, and where the region being traversed would provide flat areas and ease of travel, and protected areas upon which to rest and camp. Then, a study of the rainfall and natural vegetation maps, together with the physical map, needs to be made to help re-create the experiences of the migrants as they traveled through various parts of the western states. Help the pupils to "read" the landscape suggested by the physical map and picture it as they might have seen it if they had been with the settlers making the trip. Until the pupils know about the physical features of the land at the time of the Oregon Trail, they cannot possibly understand the hardships of the trip. Next, contrast that landscape with what the pupils would see today if they traveled the same route. Have them give the relationships which would explain the present highway pattern, the land use, and the growth of several cities and towns. Notice how much more is necessary to make this work mean something to the pupils than merely placing the Oregon Trail on a map.

Social studies often misses its mark, primarily because of poor teaching. Good teachers make social studies work, but good teachers are thoroughly grounded in all of the disciplines. Social studies ought to be a study of relationships, beginning with relationships in geography. The study of geographical relationships provides training in thinking and teaches pupils how to attack and solve problems. Social studies should not merely be a study of what; it should be a study of why and how, as well. Its aim should be to develop the understanding of the pupils, not their ability to memorize. It must involve practice in solving problems, not memorization of the solutions that others have found for similar problems. When the teacher lacks the ability to point out interesting geographic relationships, to develop concepts and skills, and to use geographic tools, the pupils are not taught how to understand, they will have had little or no opportunity to practice thinking, and they will eventually develop a distaste for social studies, in general, and geography, in particular. The wise teacher, the geographically literate teacher, realizes the importance of geographic relationships to the social studies curriculum and knows that, whatever the region being studied, geographic relationships help pupils to understand what is going on there today as well as what went on there in the past.

[2] For the exact route, see Ellen Churchill Semple and Clarence Fielden Jones, *American History and Its Geographic Conditions* (Boston, Houghton Mifflin Company, Riverside Editions, 1933), p. 215.

Discover the importance of geography as a "tool" subject in the interpretation of current events. The study of current events can be made an exciting adventure by pointing out the geographic factors which may have triggered them, by showing their relationship to the events of the past, and by considering the reactions of the people involved in them. Every day newspapers, magazines, radio, and television, make us aware of important happenings in different parts of the world. Some of these events may be the result of natural forces at work, such as floods, storms, and earthquakes. Others may deal with man's activities in some part of the world in relation to his environment. Invariably, children seek to discover the reason why the event occurred. A knowledge of geography is essential to the understanding of current happenings, and conversely, current events give reality to the study of geography. Many times a partial explanation of why the event occurred can be found in the geography of the country in which it took place.

Seldom are the geographic implications of current events pointed out by the news media which report them. It should, then, be the work of the teacher to guide his pupils, by means of map study and a review of geographic relationships, in an attempt to account for the cause of the event and to evaluate its importance to them and the world. If this is done, pupils will form the habit of looking for the "geography behind the news" in their attempt to find an explanation for it.

One way to stimulate interest in current events is to place a large map of the world on the board and, as the clippings telling about important world events are brought to class for enrichment or study, have the pupils attach them to the board beside the map. With a colored string, connect each clipping to the place where the event occurred. This draws the attention of the pupils to the news-making regions of the world and should make them curious about the geographic implications of them. (The *Daily Geographic News* is another device which will also promote interest in current events. For a description of this activity, see page 237.)

What we know about geography and geographic relationships influences our appreciation and understanding of the fine arts. For example, we cannot fully appreciate or understand the periods of Van Gogh's life and his surroundings as they are portrayed in his paintings unless we know something about the geography of the Netherlands and its influence upon the Dutch. Here nature has decreed that a large population must wrest its living from a small area of arable land. The business of living becomes serious when a nation must constantly fight the sea for fields in which to grow food. When nature has failed to provide enough mineral resources with which to engage in trade, then the land must be made to produce marketable products not easily available in other lands. If such production is limited, an improved standard of living may be obtained by transporting the produce of others. Livelihood comes to depend upon commerce more heavily than upon production. Buying, selling, and tranporting goods is not for frivolous people. It takes concentration to survive, and it was these serious people, and their surroundings, who were the first subjects of Van Gogh. And, later, how vividly he portrayed the poverty of the Belgian miners in his painting, "The Potato Eaters." Here, nature provided a mineral, but mining is injurious to health and it leaves little time for food production. Geographic relationships and conditions created the subjects of the painting who, in their turn, influenced the painter. The paintings done by Van Gogh during his sojourn in southern France clearly reflect the change in latitude made by the artist and the differences in the lives of the people living there when compared with the lives of the people in Belgium and the Netherlands. The brilliant colors and seemingly carefree abandon of the artist in his works executed there, both prior to his mental breakdown and after it, illustrate the influence of geographic environment upon a painter's work. The alert teacher can discover many such examples to be pointed out to his pupils.

In literature, certainly the dreadful sameness of the plains of northern Mississippi and the difficulty of providing a living have influenced the lives of the people and of William Faulkner who wrote about them. Nor can the influence of geography, and events occurring as a result of geography, be denied in Bret Harte's tales of the California Gold Rush. There would have been no Tom Sawyer or Huckleberry Finn without a lazy Mississippi River and the caves and islands left by it as it cut through the land. Marguerite Henry could not have written the tale of *Misty*, the horse of Chincoteague Island, had there been no island, no storm, or wrecked ship. And is it possible to imagine Heidi with all of her honesty and simple directness in any other place but the Swiss Alps? With a knowledge of geography the reader is better able to visualize the setting of the story and to account for the activities of the characters.

The character of the music of such composers as Sibelius, Grieg, Tschaikowsky, even Gershwin (to mention only a few), has been determined, in part, by the geographical characteristics of their homelands or native regions, and the temperaments of their compatriots, whose folk melodies arise from their respective environments.

It is neither stretching the imagination nor straining credulity to look for, and find, geographic influences in the art, literature, and music of any group of people. Although critics may differ as to the degree to which geography has influenced creativity in the arts, none will deny that such influence exists. Therefore, it is both wise of us, and profitable for our pupils, to recognize the influence of geography in the creative arts.

If geography is taught, if it is taught well, and if it is taught by an enthusiastic teacher, it will take its proper and proportionate place in any curriculum plan, and our pupils will like it.

But many of our pupils do not like geography. Why don't they like it?

It may be that geography is not interesting to them because it consists of meaningless drill and memorization of names or facts, or that their teachers, lacking background in geography, have not discovered what a dynamic subject today's geography really is.

If our pupils are to learn geography and like it, we must discover how different relationship geography is from the meaningless rote learning of unrelated facts and lists of products and chief cities. We need to rid ourselves of the old "read-recite-test" routine, with its fragmented learnings, and build an entirely different concept of geography. Once we are aware of the potentials of relationship geography and use this approach in our teaching, we will become geographically literate and enthusiastic to learn about the world on which we live, along with our pupils.

What do we want our pupils to get from their study of geography? What behavioral changes can we hope to see in them as a result of their learnings? Let us consider for a moment what our objectives would be in teaching an actual unit, since units are basic to almost all curricular patterns.

In teaching a unit on Brazil we want our pupils to be able to picture the landscapes in the different regions of that nation, such as the hot, humid, Amazon lowlands covered with rain forest vegetation, the undeveloped savanna lands of the interior, the beautiful harbor of Rio de Janeiro with its statue of Christ the Redeemer standing majestically on the top of Corcovado, and the vast areas of rolling lands where the many coffee *fazendas* can be found. We also want them to understand the relationship between the activities of the people and the physical conditions where they live. We want our pupils to become acquainted with the Brazilian people, to be concerned about their problems, and to appreciate how much these people do with the little they have, as well as to understand the hopes and ambitions of those Brazilian children who must spend much of their time at work on the coffee *fazendas*, farms, or in the crowded areas of the cities. Our pupils should be aware of Brazil's importance in world trade, know to what extent we are dependent upon Brazil, and be able to understand the reasons for Brazil's position in the Organization of American States (OAS). Most important of all, we want our pupils to be able to do logical thinking about Brazil's current problems and to begin to form a background, with the help of which they may be able to suggest practical solutions for some of them. We also want them to understand how solutions have been worked out by others.

Could we hope to achieve these objectives for the study of Brazil by having our pupils memorize facts, or lists of products and cities? Of course not! Our pupils must understand why the facts presented are true. This can only be accomplished through a study of relationships. The study of relationships requires logical thinking, and the pupils must do the thinking themselves. They must also acquire skill in the use of such geographic tools as maps, pictures, graphs, and statistics. Through personal discovery the pupils learn to be self-sufficient. They will increase their power to work out relationships and to interpret maps. Through relationship study, geographic concepts are enlarged with the study of each new country or region, and the ability to use geographic skills is increased, regardless of the curricular pattern in which we teach.

Let us, then, acquire an understanding of geographic relationships and how they are taught.

2

Teach relationship geography

What Are Geographic Relationships?

The world around us is a world in which people and their activities, ideas, and problems are more important than places and commodities. The lives of people are influenced by many things. Some of them are cultural heritage, technological advances, and natural environment. Geography is always the study of the relationships existing between human affairs and physical conditions.

In some parts of the world man has adjusted his activities to the natural environment. In others he has adapted the environment to his needs. It is necessary for our pupils to have a basic understanding of the natural environment, and man's use of it in every part of the world, so that they can understand the problems created by these factors and the effect of new technological developments upon them. We want our pupils to have respect and sympathy for the people of less fortunate countries of the world. They need this background of geographic knowledge to enable them to draw conclusions and to form opinions and desirable attitudes about their own and other lands. They can then see that geography is a dynamic subject, not a static one.

How can we make this dynamic subject more meaningful to our pupils? Teaching a list of geographic facts will not do it, but developing geographic relationships inductively will. To teach that the Hawaiian Islands grow pineapples, or that iron ore is brought from Venezuela to Morrisville on the Delaware River, may lead to factual geographic learning, but these facts are not geography in themselves. To make these descriptive facts geography, relationships must be shown. Relationships explain why the facts are true.

Let us show the two facts, just given, as relationships:

1. Pineapples, which require a frost-free climate, are grown on the higher elevations of the Hawaiian Islands where there are regions of low rainfall. Thus, we see that the growing of pineapples is related to frost-free climate and light rainfall on some of the higher elevations.

2. The steel mills at Morrisville on the Delaware River use iron ore which has been transported from Venezuela.

Here we see that the making of steel at Morrisville is related to the ease with which iron ore is brought from Venezuela by boat.

Relationships explain why people live where they do in a certain region or country, and why they make their living as they do. Even the development of certain customs with regard to food, clothing, shelter, and travel can be better understood through a study of relationships. In other words, relationships include all the ways in which human items are related to natural features or conditions.

Our environment is made up of two main groups of elements. Natural elements, or *items,* are those which nature has given to us. They include rivers, wild animals, forests not planted by man, mountains, minerals, insects, and so on. Cultural or human items are those pertaining to man, his activities, or the result of his activities. Cultural items include roads, farms, and cities, as well as features in the landscape which have involved human activity, such as a field of wheat, or a stand of timber planted and cultivated by a lumber company. When we give the *reasons* for the natural or cultural descriptive facts dealing with man and his environment, we have relationships.

There are three kinds of relationship: relationship between natural items, relationship between cultural items, and relationship between cultural and natural items.

Relationship between natural items (N–N) is shown in the following two statements:

1. The earthquake caused a huge tidal wave to speed toward the coast.

2. Sodium nitrate deposits occur in the Atacama Desert of northern Chile because it seldom rains in the region more frequently than once in every decade.

To help pupils understand a natural-to-natural relationship (N–N), one must make them aware of cause and effect in a natural setting. A tidal wave is a *natural* result or effect of a sudden *natural* displacement of a portion of the earth's crust beneath the ocean or near the seacoast.

Natural mineral deposits are not leached or washed away from the soil if *natural* rainfall is a rarity in the vicinity of the deposits.

Relationship between cultural items (C–C) is shown in these statements:

1. Cotton is grown in the South and made into cloth in the large mills.
2. Vegetables grown in many truck gardens around Philadelphia partly supply the demand for food in retail stores.

As the preceding examples indicate, the cultural-to-cultural relationship (C–C) involves activities carried on wholly by man. Cotton, cultivated by man, is made into cloth by man. Vegetables, grown near a large city by man, are consumed by the residents of the city. Man's production and consumption of goods is shown in a cultural-to-cultural relationship.

The relationship between cultural and natural items (C–N) is the most valuable geographic relationship because it shows how man's activities are often related to his environment. The natural environment is never the sole cause or reason for any human activity because human characteristics and cultural heritage often exert their influences. Consequently, we say that a study of relationships between man and his environment, cultural-to-natural (C–N), helps to explain man's activities. Examples of cultural-to-natural relationships are:

1. The rolling land, natural pastures, and cool, moist climate help to make dairying a leading industry in Wisconsin.
2. Sugar cane can be raised in large quantities in Cuba because there is no frost.

In working with relationships, it is helpful to use the "arrow" statement. The symbol ⟶ can be read "is related to," or "can be partly explained by." Often, in order to see the relationships, the sentence needs to be rearranged or transposed. For example, suppose that the relationship reads, "Cotton can be grown in the South because it requires a 200-day growing season to mature (C–N)." Transposed, and expressed in an arrow statement, it would read:

"The growing of cotton in the South ⟶(is related to) the 200-day growing season."

Another relationship might read: "In the rain forest of South America, the temperature is high throughout the year and the rainfall is very heavy. As a result, a great tangled mass of trees and vines covers the land (N–N)." Transposed, and expressed in an arrow statement, this relationship would read:

"The great tangled mass of trees and vines ⟶ the high temperature and heavy rainfall."

Relationships are written in sentence form when formal work in geography has begun, usually in the fourth sequence. (See page 29.) After the pupils gain ability in expressing relationships in sentence form, they can be written in two columns:

The great tangled mass ⟶ 1. high temperatures.
of trees and vines   2. heavy rainfall.

The relationships discussed thus far are one-step relationships; that is, only one set of reasons is needed to explain a natural or cultural item. As relationship study broadens their understanding, children can be taught to expand these one-step relationships into two-step or three-step relationships. Two-step and three-step relationships provide children who are rapid learners with opportunities to make finer distinctions between the causal and resultant aspects of a relationship. The illustrations of one-, two-, and three-step relationships which follow are purposely broad and quite general. Study of them by teachers and prospective teachers will reveal how specific applications of two- and three-step relationships can be made.

One- , Two- , and Three-Step Relationships

ONE-STEP

Chief work, kinds of ⟶ outstanding conditions of surface, rainfall, temperature, and height of the noonday sun.
food, clothing, and shelter, means of travel, and many items of culture

TWO-STEP

Density and distribution of people ⟶ outstanding ways of living and earning a living, and cultural factors ⟶ outstanding conditions of surface, rainfall, temperature, and height of the noonday sun.

THREE-STEP

Relative importance of the region in world affairs ⟶ density and distribution of people, standard of living, cultural assets of people ⟶ outstanding ways of living, distribution of various types of work ⟶ outstanding natural factors.

Why Teach Relationships?

The study of relationships in geography makes sense. It gives meaning to the facts learned and encourages learning in depth. It creates an inquisitive attitude on the part of the pupil, which in turn gives purpose to his work. It provides a standard method of teaching from kindergarten through college.

Teaching relationships increases reasoning ability. The challenge presented by working out relationships helps to form the habit of logical thinking on the part of the pupils. They find it necessary to reason in order to arrive at the conclusions needed to complete relationships. Seeing relationships is thinking. This is the greatest value of the study of geographic relationships.

Teaching relationships also helps to create a better understanding of facts. We know that facts which are memorized without understanding why they are true are soon forgotten, but pupils must apply facts when they are needed to help solve a relationship. The geographic concepts of the pupils are often revised and enlarged because different aspects of learned facts have to be considered in each new relationship. For example, dairying in Switzerland will be much better understood in the sixth or seventh sequence if the pupil has been taught the relationship of dairying to natural conditions in Wisconsin during the fifth sequence. Even though there are other factors involved in the relationship, understanding will come more readily as a result of the pupil's prior acquaintance with the basic relationship.

An additional benefit to be derived by the pupils from the teaching of relationships is that they help the teacher to promote pupil initiative. Teachers will all agree that one of the best ways to maintain pupil interest is to let the pupils work out some problems for themselves. The teacher can state a cultural descriptive fact and refer his pupils to maps, pictures, or reading materials, asking them to find the natural and cultural items which explain the fact given. Textbook assignments will be much more interesting and worthwhile if pupils are asked to complete relationships which they may find on a particular page of the text.

While there are many ways a teacher might direct his pupils to write out the arrow statements which we call relationships, one of the best methods is to have the pupils fold a sheet of lined paper in half vertically. The part of the relationship to be explained is then written on the left half of the folded paper. The number of explanatory facts which the teacher wishes the children to find can be indicated by numbering the lines of the right half of the folded paper. Such a paper would appear thus:

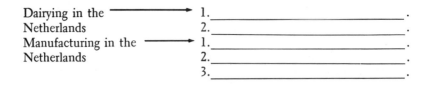

You are not teaching geography unless you are teaching relationships. This method of teaching does require thinking and background because you need to know more geography than your pupils in order to guide the reasoning needed in relationship study. But background can be acquired if you plan your work ahead and do supplementary reading. If you wish to teach geographic relationships you cannot limit yourself to the textbook, nor can you confine your thinking to what goes on within the classroom alone. You are shaping the mental processes of your pupils. The responsibility is staggering. Teach relationship geography to increase the pupils' ability to think and their geographic understanding.

The Use of Relationships

Much class time can be wasted in teaching material which may be interesting but which does not contribute to the major understandings of the country or regions to be studied. It is wise to plan the relationships you want your pupils to understand before you start the work. The amount of material to be covered and the particular relationships to be developed depend upon the maturity of the pupils. The list of relationships becomes an outline of content to be developed regardless of the teacher-pupil planning which may change the order of presentation.

To illustrate, suppose the problem suggested in the motivation of the work on Brazil is "Why should the United States send aid to Brazil? In what form should this aid be given?" You might suggest that your class pretend to be an investigating committee sent by the State Department to survey the needs and problems of Brazil. A project such as this would necessitate a thorough study of Brazil. You, the teacher, would need to work out a set of relationships which would give your pupils sufficient background with which to solve the problems. One of these relationships might be:

The sparse settlement of the rain forest in Amazonia ⟶
1. high year-round temperatures.
2. heavy rainfall from 60 to 100 inches.
3. soils of low fertility.
4. difficulty of building roads and railroads.
5. difficulty of carrying on agriculture.
6. shifting agriculture.
7. no large stands of one particular kind of tree.
8. low level of economic development.

Relationship study can be used in the development of lessons, in summarizing them, in application work, and in testing. The advantage of using relationships in testing is that they eliminate rote memorization of facts and emphasize to the child the importance of reasoning.

Let us see how a lesson can be built around a relationship, showing how to develop the different parts of it. Suppose that the introductory work on Brazil has been done and that Amazonia and the east coast have been studied. The pupils are ready to learn about the East Central Plateau and the importance of coffee in Brazil. Your lesson plan might develop as follows:

TEACHER'S PLANNED RELATIONSHIPS

The importance of the ⟶ coffee industry in Brazil

1. the elevation of the land in East Central Brazil.
2. the rolling land which gives air and water drainage.
3. the frost-free season.
4. sixty inches of annual rainfall.
5. terra roxa soil.
6. labor available on the *fazendas*.
7. rail and roadways which connect the coast with this region.
8. world and domestic market for coffee.

SPECIFIC OBJECTIVE

To teach why coffee is of so much importance to Brazil and how it affects the lives of millions of Brazilians.

MOTIVATION

1. "What did you have to drink for breakfast? *Milk, cocoa.* Which of these is produced in our country? Cocoa comes from tropical lands, doesn't it?

2. What do your mother and father drink for breakfast? Why don't they want you to drink coffee? *Coffee is a stimulant and it is not good for you until you have your growth.* Adults in the United States drink a very large amount of coffee. Coffee, like cocoa, doesn't grow in our country and so we import nearly three billion pounds a year.

3. Look at this world map while I draw circles around some of the countries which send us coffee." Brazil, Colombia, Mexico, Guatemala, Kenya, Ethiopia, Ecuador. "There are many more than these which send us coffee but these are the large producers.

4. What do these countries have in common? *They are nearly all in the same latitude.* Brazil, alone, produces nearly half the world's coffee. It is Brazil's chief export. Why do you suppose that coffee is so important in Brazil?" Children's responses:

1. *Maybe Brazil has a better place to grow it.*
2. *Maybe it's because Brazil is nearer to the chief importer, the United States.*

3. Maybe they have more people to do the work.
4. Maybe it's the way they do the work.

5. "It could be all of these reasons, couldn't it? We'll just have to check to find out which one of these reasons explains why coffee is so important in Brazil, and why so many people are dependent upon it to make a living. More than one reason may be correct. As we discover reasons, we will write them on the board."

DEVELOPMENT

1. "Let's see how much we can find out from our maps.

2. In what part of Brazil will we find the greatest amount of coffee grown?" Refer to the world map on which the teacher has circled coffee-producing countries.

3. "Now let's look at a larger map of this region. What do you notice about the surface of this region? Notice the Serra do Mar Mountains along the sea."

4. The teacher needs to explain the term *escarpment*. There may be a picture in the textbook to verify the conclusion drawn by the children. "Notice the red line which crosses the escarpment. What is the meaning of the red line? *Railroad*. What would you think about a railroad crossing the escarpment at this place? We are going to find out some very interesting things about this railroad.

5. What type of elevation is found here? *Plateau*. How high is it? Coffee grows very well on plateaus 3,000 to 6,000 feet high. Would this plateau be flat, rolling or mountainous? *Rolling*." Teacher writes on the board: 1. Rolling land. "Notice the rivers which cut up the surface into hills. Why would this be an advantage? *Air and water drainage*." These terms would need to be explained.

6. "Now look at these rainfall maps. How much rainfall does Brazil receive in this region?" Teacher writes on the board: 2. 60 inches rainfall. "Is this an even distribution, or is it seasonal? When is the drier season? We'll have to find out if that is good for the coffee industry. *Brazil harvests its coffee crop between March and September, when rainfall is at a minimum.*

7. Look at this climatic graph of Sao Paulo. The line tells the temperature and the columns show the amount of rainfall. Can anyone tell me what growing season means? *It is the time from the last frost in the spring to the first frost in the fall, or the interval of time in which plants can grow.* If the temperature would not go below 32°, there would not be any frost, would there? This graph shows average temperature for each month of the year. That means that the temperature may be higher or lower than this average. But plant growth will not take place unless the temperature is 57° F., or above. How many months is the temperature above 57° F.? Yes, this is a frost-free climate and the area has a year long growing season." Teacher writes on the board: 3. Frost-free climate and year-long growing season. (Length of growing season thus can be determined from an examination of temperature graphs.) "About how much rain does Sao Paulo receive annually?

8. Now, let's look at the population map. What can you tell about the distribution of people in this region? *The population is quite dense in this region.* Many people have probably come here for work." Teacher writes on

SAO PAULO, BRAZIL: TEMPERATURE AND RAINFALL GRAPHS

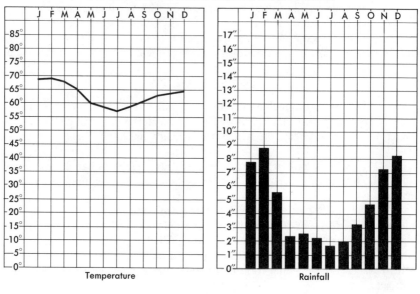

Temperature   Rainfall

Figure 1

board: 4. Plentiful labor. "I wonder from what country these people came originally? That's something else we will want to find out. It will be interesting to learn what their lives are like on the coffee *fazenda*. Do you suppose that they will live as we do? Will they have television sets, transistor radios, horses to ride, telephones, electricity? Usually the owner of the *fazenda* is a wealthy man. He has money to invest in the industries of Sao Paulo. Sao Paulo is the fastest growing city in the world partly because the wealthy *fazenda* owners have money to invest there.

9. We have found and listed four reasons why coffee is such an important crop, but there are many of the answers we want which our maps will not tell us. For instance, we will want to know about workers on the *fazendas*, what it would be like to live on one, and what work has to be done to raise and prepare coffee for market. In your textbooks you will find some very interesting information about how coffee is grown, and about *fazendas*. On this paper I have several challenging questions for you to answer. You will need to think about what you have read to answer them." These questions have been prepared previously. They will require application of the information given in the textbook and will involve situations of interest to the child.

a. What would your home be like if you were the child of a worker on a *fazenda*? What kind of work would you do to help?
b. Give reasons for your opinion about the following question: Would there

be compulsory education on a *fazenda?* Of what value would education be to these children?

c. During what months would you have school on the *fazenda,* if there were a school? When would you have vacation? (Remember the difference in seasons in the hemispheres, and the time of the harvest season for coffee.)

d. What other crops would your parents help to harvest? Do you think it would be better to cultivate coffee over the entire *fazenda* than to raise some other crops? Why?

e. What would be your main foods?

f. How would a heavy frost during the blossoming season affect you and your family, if such a thing occurred?

g. Check the graph and name the months when an extremely heavy rainfall would cause the greatest damage.

h. What do you think the people on a coffee *fazenda* are doing today?[a]

[a] This will test understanding of the difference in seasons between the northern and southern hemispheres.

After allowing the children twenty-five to thirty minutes to read and apply the information to the questions, discuss the answers. If the textbook in use does not give a description of life on the *fazenda,* the teacher should read one to the children in order to help build the concept of how people live on one. An excellent book which may be used is *Jorge's Journey* by Alice Curtis Desmond.

SUMMARY

At the close of the lesson, the teacher summarizes the work by having the pupils write the relationship in an arrow statement:

The importance of the ⟶ 1. _____ .
coffee industry in Brazil   2. _____ .
                               3. _____ .
                               4. _____ .
                               5. _____ .

APPLICATION

a. Make a plan of a coffee *fazenda* showing where the owners' and managers' houses would be, the group of workers' homes, the coffee trees, the wooded areas and the fields of other crops, the drying floor, the storage sheds, and so forth.

b. Make a sketch showing some step in the raising of coffee and the preparation of the coffee for market. (Sketches need not be works of art. Stick figures may be used to represent people and animals. In geography we picture ideas rather than show art ability. Stick figures are just as valuable for illustrating people and animals as are elaborate drawings. In order to make a sketch, a child has to have a mental picture. When the sketches are completed, commend and discuss those which best portray the relationships, regardless of their artistic merit.)

EVALUATION

Have the pupils evaluate the quality of their work and make suggestions as to how their work might be improved.

The teacher evaluates his own work by noting improved pupil interest and response. He should view his work critically with the intention of improving his teaching techniques the next time he teaches the material.

The value of summarizing a lesson with a relationship or arrow statement is shown in the foregoing lesson. It brings the important points of the lesson together. The pupil can see what he has learned during the period. Using a relationship matching exercise as application work at the close of the lesson or unit is an excellent way to discover whether the pupil really understands the relationship. Every lesson should be summarized and opportunity provided for the pupils to apply what has been learned.

In an application relationship-matching exercise, the first parts of several arrow statements are placed in the left-hand column. In the right-hand column groups of factors which explain the first parts of the relationships are arranged. No group of factors should be opposite the correct answer, of course. In this type of exercise, it is wise to have more items in one column than in the other in order to help eliminate guessing. An example of such an application test follows.

Application Work

These are relationship (arrow) questions which have been divided. Select the number of the group of statements in the right-hand column which best completes each of the statements in the left-hand column. Place the number selected in the blank space to the left of each statement in the left-hand column.

_____A.	The importance of the coffee industry in Brazil	1. a. decline of the rubber trade. b. climatic conditions.

_____B.	The sparse settlement of the rainforest in Amazonia	2. a. climatic conditions of a small area.
		    b. river trade.
		    c. good harbor.

_____C.	Lack of good means of transportation	3. a. elevation of land in East Central Brazil.
		    b. rolling land which gives air and water drainage.
		    c. frost-free season.
		    d. sixty inches of annual rainfall.

4. a. escarpment along the east coast.
   b. cost of building railroads over mountains.
   c. sparse settlement of inland regions.
   d. undeveloped lands do not need railroads.
5. a. high, year-round temperatures.
   b. heavy rainfall: 60–100 inches.
   c. soils of low fertility.
   d. difficulty of building roads and railroads.
   e. difficulty of carrying on agriculture.
   f. shifting agriculture.
   g. no large stands of one particular kind of tree.

ANSWERS: A—3; B—5; C—4.

An additional method to use in testing with relationship study is shown below.

Relationship Activity

HUMAN OR CULTURAL ITEMS	NATURAL ITEMS
1.	A. 1. mountains and slopes. 2. forest covering mountains and slopes. 3. cool, moist climate.
B. Many people spend their vacations in the Pacific states.	2.
3.	C. 1. warm winters. 2. winter rains. 3. irrigation water. 4. warm air from the ocean.

Directions: 1. Fill space number 1 with a sketch of the industry which would result where the natural items listed in space A occur.
2. Fill space number 2 with a sketch showing where the people spoken of in space B might like to go.
3. Fill space number 3 with a drawing of fruits which depend upon the natural conditions listed in space C.

Arrow statements make excellent test questions, as the foregoing illustrations indicate. When children are asked to write out complete, essay-type explanations, be sure to insist on definite, meaningful answers. Words such as "good," "enough," and "sufficient," when used to describe markets, climate, rainfall, and soil, may not mean anything. "Enough" rainfall for bananas is too much for wheat. "Good" climate for sugar beets would not be good for sugar cane.

Adults often give the same answer to two different questions which may be asked of them, expecting the listener to make the correct interpretation. Children are prone to do the same thing in responding to questions. We must help them to understand that geography is a science. If they are to understand it as a science, then we must insist upon definite answers. We must not accept watered-down, parrot-like repetition of memorized fragments. To do so deprives the pupils of the education to which they are entitled.

How to Develop Relationships Sequentially

In the primary sequences there are many opportunities for making the children aware of the relationships between man's activities and his environment. Many of the children are having their first contacts with things beyond their homes. They are curious and eager to learn the reasons for things being what they are, and they are capable of learning a great deal. However, when one teaches relationship geography, it is wise to remember to teach less, but teach it well since every relationship has so many facets; hence, only four main topics are considered in the primary sequences.

The four topics covered in the primary geography readiness program are direction, weather, sun position, and seasonal change. There are innumerable relationships included in these topics which need to be explained to the children and repeated in a variety of ways as they build concepts. For example:

⬥ We have night when the earth turns away from the sun.
⬥ Plants need sunshine and rain in order to grow.
⬥ The weather influences man's work and play.
⬥ Our shadows point north at noon because the sun is always in the southern sky in our hemisphere.
⬥ When the sun is low in the sky at noon, it is winter.

Basic readers contain many stories and poems which are full of implied relationships. They are there if you look for them. In a third grade reader, the poem "Skycrapers"[1] is found:

[1] Reprinted by permission of the publisher from *Pointed People* by Rachel Field. Copyright 1924, 1930 by The Macmillan Company.

> Do skyscrapers ever grow tired
> Of holding themselves up high?
> Do they ever shiver on frosty nights
> With their tops against the sky?
> Do they feel lonely sometimes
> Because they have grown so tall?
> Do they ever wish they could lie right down
> And never get up at all?
>
> —RACHEL FIELD

What geographic relationships can be found in this poem? The teacher asks:

- "What are skyscrapers?
- Why are skyscrapers built? *The skyscrapers are related to the need for space.*
- Why cannot some cities spread out as they grow? *They are limited by rivers, islands, valleys, and mountains.*
- Why might the tall buildings shiver against the sky? *Temperature is related to elevation.*
- Sometimes people live in skyscraper apartment buildings. Would it be fun to live in one or would you rather live where you do? Why?
- How would skyscrapers affect nearby buildings? *They cut off sunlight and cast shadows, thereby affecting plant life on the streets or in windows.*
- Which side of the skyscraper in the northern hemisphere would have more sunlight?
- Which side would get little sunlight? *Sunlight is related to the position of the sun in the southern sky.*"

Encourage primary children to look for the reasons why things are as they are. We want them to have inquiring minds. We want them never to cease wondering about the world around them. Let us capitalize on their natural curiosity to promote the study of relationships in the primary grades.

In the fourth sequence, the first formal study of geography is begun. It is most important that these pupils be given a good foundation on which to build a real understanding of important geographic principles. This foundation depends in part on their ability to understand simple, direct, one-step relationships between certain human activities and contrasting types of natural and cultural environments. Usually the first work in geography begins with a study of regions near the equator where man has been greatly influenced by his environment, and where the effect of such factors as sun position, length of day, and seasonal change can be easily understood by the children. This work will provide the teacher with many opportunities to develop relationships.

In the primary grades the pupils may have discussed relationships orally with their teacher. Now they should be able to discover relationships for themselves and to record them in arrow statements. But how are relationships developed?

Let us assume that the teacher has built the concept of conditions in a rain forest so clearly through pictures, descriptions, and stories that the pupils can feel the heat and humidity as it builds up into a daily storm and can see the forest gloom, pierced here and there with shafts of sunlight where the sun's rays break through the dense mass of trees. The problem for the class to consider in this lesson is, what kind of house is practical for these forest dwellers? This topic is then discussed and the pictures are re-examined. Several models of the houses might be made from corrugated paper, letting the ridges of the paper run vertically. Raffia pasted between the ridges would simulate the appearance of forest materials.

In the summary of the lesson on rain forest homes, the teacher might ask: "Why do the houses of these people have such slanting roofs?" He then writes the relationship on the board in sentence form:

The slanting roofs $\xrightarrow{\text{(are related to)}}$ heavy rainfall.

"Of what are the houses built?"

The materials for houses $\longrightarrow$ the trees and vines found in the forest.

"Why are the roofs thatched?"

The thatched roofs $\longrightarrow$ daily rains, hot sun, and materials at hand.

"Why are some of the houses built on poles?"

The building of the houses on poles $\longrightarrow$ the heavy rainfall, the floods, and the soft, wet ground.

These four simple relationships will summarize the lesson on rain forest homes quickly, clearly, and easily.

Children are often confused by the mass of material to which we subject them. They are unable to select the important information from the mass of information, to separate the significant from the insignificant. By summarizing with relationships, our pupils are made conscious of the significant facts and the reasons why the facts are true. The children will soon be able to complete relationships for which they have been given only the first part if their introduction to the concept of relationships has been carefully conceived and executed. Eventually, they will be able to discover simple relationships in their reading and to write them in arrow statement form. When pupils of the fourth sequence can do this, they have begun to think logically.

In the fifth and sixth sequences, the study of relationships should be part of each day's work. The pupils should form the habit of looking for reasons behind the facts. As they increase their ability to reason, and to analyze material, they are adding depth to their geographic understandings. They will be able to discover relationships and to complete many partially hidden relationships suggested by pictures, textbooks, and reference material. Not all the pupils will develop the same degree of ability to "see" relationships, but it is reassuring to find that even the slower pupils can work out simple relationships, thereby increasing their ability to think.

Relationships may be expressed in paragraph form, but there are advantages in using the arrow-statement. It is much more easily checked and it promotes logical thinking on the part of the pupil. Speak of the arrow statement form as geographical shorthand when you talk to your pupils. Presented in this way, the idea appeals to them.

In the fifth and sixth sequences, one- and two-step relationships will be used. If your pupils have not had relationship study, develop it as you would with pupils in a fourth sequence. An example of a one-step relationship follows.

The growing of cotton in ⟶ 1. level to rolling land.
the South

2. two-hundred-day growing season.
3. twenty-five to forty-five inches of annual rainfall.
4. dry harvest season.
5. need for cotton by industry.
6. demand for cotton clothing.
7. need for cotton by other countries.

Another way to express this relationship would be to put the natural items in one column and the cultural items in another:

	NATURAL ITEMS	CULTURAL ITEMS
The growing of cotton in ⟶ the South	1. level to rolling land.	1. need for cotton seed in industry.
	2. two-hundred-day growing season.	2. demand for cotton clothing.
	3. twenty-five to forty-five inches of annual rainfall.	3. need for cotton by other countries.
	4. dry harvest season.	

The simple, one-step relationship might be extended to a two-step relationship as follows:

The manufacture ⟶ 1. the growing of ⟶ 1. two-hundred-day growing season.
of cotton cloth in   cotton in the
the South   vicinity of the
    mills

2. twenty-five to forty-five inches of rainfall.
3. dry harvest season.
4. level to rolling land.

2. market for cot- ⟶ 1. climatic   conditions
   ton goods, do-   which favor the wearing
   mestic and   of cotton clothing.
   foreign   2. climatic conditions in
                          many lands which pre-
                          vent the growing of cot-
                          ton.

In the sixth sequence, relationships will be more complex because the pupils are studying regions or countries outside of the United States. The natural environmental items are only one factor to which human activities are related; hence, in the sixth sequence the characteristics and culture of the people should be included in the analysis of the relationships.

In the seventh and eighth sequences, relationships will need to be worked out on a world-wide basis. They will be numerous, varied, and very complex. In some instances, three-step relationships will be needed to unlock meaning. For other understandings, one- and two-step relationships will suffice.

By this time the student should understand thoroughly that a relationship serves as an excellent framework upon which facts may be placed in logical order. He should also be aware that they help him to retain knowledge while increasing his general understanding. Teaching your pupils to see relationships is one of the most valuable things you will ever do for them. Relationship study is more than a method to be used in teaching geography. It is a way to increase the ability of pupils to think. It is, above all, a means whereby geography can be taught and learned with understanding.

Become world minded by using the globe

To see the world in a grain of sand,
 And a heaven in a wild flower;
Hold infinity in the palm of your hand
 And eternity in an hour.

—WILLIAM BLAKE, *Auguries of Innocence*

Our pupils are fortunate to live in a century when it is possible for them to
see photographs of large sections of the earth's surface regularly in newspapers and popular magazines. These photographs have been taken by
cameras mounted in satellites which circle our earth, or by our astronauts
as they travel through space. Geographers make use of these photographs
to confirm or deny the accuracy of their efforts to map and understand our
planet, the earth. Generally speaking, our cartographers have been quite accurate in plotting the land and water masses on the earth. However, high
altitude photographs occasionally reveal an error that has been made in
mapping. One such error was discovered as a result of pictures taken by
the National Aeronautics and Space Administration's weather satellite,

Nimbus I. The satellite, which took photographs covering one million square miles of earth surface in a single picture until it stopped operating in September, 1964, helped members of the United States Geological Survey discover that a mountain group thought to be part of the Kohler Range area in Antarctica actually did not exist. Similar photographs helped them to reposition Mount Siple, a 10,000-foot high peak, forty-five miles further west than it had been mapped.

Aerial photographs are valuable because they show the curvature of the earth and the actual positional relationships existing among land and water masses, but they also distort areas which appear near the edges of the photographs. The same thing is true of the flat maps we find in our atlases and geography texts: distortion is inevitably present. There is really only one true representation of the surface of the earth and that is a globe. Study of the globe and the development of concepts related to it provides us and our pupils with the background necessary to eventually "see the world in a grain of sand . . . [and] hold infinity in the palm of [our] hand," as William Blake expressed it in the verses quoted at the beginning of this chapter.

How well acquainted are you with globes? It would seem logical that if we expect to teach our pupils something about our earth and its representation, the globe, we ought to know something about it ourselves. Without looking at a globe, test yourself on these questions:

- ✓ Which city is farther west, New York or Santiago, Chile?
- ✓ Which state of the United States is nearest to Africa?
- ✓ Which direction would you fly from San Francisco if you were taking the shortest route to Tokyo?
- ✓ Which city is nearer the North Pole, Anchorage, Alaska or Moscow, U.S.S.R.?

Now examine a globe. Were your answers correct? Did you guess at the answers because you have learned that globe facts are frequently the opposite of what you assumed to be true, and because you felt that the questions asked were "trick" questions? "Trick" questions are only "tricks" because of our misconceptions about the earth, and these misconceptions are due to our lack of knowledge about the globe. Recent events in international affairs, as well as the interest in the achievements of the astronauts and photographs of our earth taken from outer space have emphasized the genuine need for the correct interpretation of globes and maps. We need to become acquainted with our globe to learn how it functions and how it affects our ways of living. We also need to think about the people and the conditions on every part of the earth since everything that affects other people eventually affects us, also.

The globe is the best representation of the earth that we have; consequently, it is valuable in geographic instruction. On it, meridians and parallels are in correct relation to each other, the scale of distance is the same in all directions, and land areas are represented correctly in relation to one another. When the globe is used to observe the distance and direction of any region from the equator, the approximate length of days and length and time of seasons may be inferred. Pupils must be taught not only how to use the globe, but also the kinds of information which they can read from the globe.

Many teachers have failed to recognize the globe as an essential tool of instruction. Globe and map skills are simply not taught once and for all, but are developed as the need arises for certain information which only globes can supply. Globe concepts and skills must be developed carefully and gradually, and must be strengthened every time there is an opportunity to use them.

Globe Concepts for the Primary Sequences

Globes should be available informally for children to handle even in the first sequence. The preferred type of globe for use in the primary sequences is a twelve-inch cradle globe which is a simple but realistic representation of the earth in two colors, showing land and water forms. As children handle the globe, they will realize that the earth is round like a ball and that there is no top or bottom to the earth. Large project globes are excellent for the primary sequences, too, because they can be used in so many ways. They are so much larger that the land and water bodies can easily be seen by all pupils in the class, and chalk marks can be made upon them.

Although there is little formal globe study in the primary sequences, the children will learn many things about the globe in their discussions about day and night, seasonal change, sun position, direction, interesting current topics about space travel, and in the questions which they ask their teacher about these topics. Children will show interest in the size and shape of land bodies and where they live on the globe. By tracing the outlines of the continents and talking about the oceans and seas, they will become familiar with the land and water bodies. In the first sequence, children can be told that the globe is the shape of the earth, that we live on the earth, and that we can find the location of our homes on the globe. Later on, through observation, the children will notice the differences in the size and shape of land bodies. With little difficulty they will be able to name them, as well as the oceans, as a result of a little incidental instruction on our part.

In connection with the incidental study of the globe in the primary grades, concepts must be developed pertaining to sun position. The sun is the most influential factor in the determination of many of man's activities. Sun position, or sun behavior, must be understood in order to interpret this influence. It must be remembered that a teacher cannot give children concepts. Concepts are based upon the experience of the individual child. Not all of the children will interpret the experiences planned and executed by the teacher in the same manner due to differences in background, mental ability, and maturation. Consequently, these concepts concerning sun position must be built gradually and purposefully. They must be used regularly and added to as the need for new understandings concerning sun position arises.

In the first sequence the children learn through discussion and observation where the sun rises, where it sets, and that the sun is always in the southern sky in our part of the world. (See Map Readiness in the Primary Sequences, page 123.) Have the children observe the path of the sun in the sky at different intervals during the year and record their observations. Discuss the effect of the "shorter" day and of seasonal change upon man's activities.

> To observe the changing position of the sun during the seasons, if the schoolroom faces east, west, or south, select a point or place where the sunlight strikes a desk, the floor, or the wall at a certain time during the day, for instance at 9:30 A.M. Note and mark the place early in September. Discuss this in connection with direction and sun position. The teacher and children watch how this spot moves from week to week, or at longer intervals, marking it each time with the date observed. This sun spot will change until December 22, then, it will begin a return journey. Thus, through their own observation and with the discussion directed by the teacher, the children learn that the changing position of the sun is related to seasonal changes and length of day.[1]

When the sun is lowest in the sky in the Northern Hemisphere (December 22), the mark showing the position of the sun's rays will be highest on the wall. The children will conclude that when the sun is low in the sky at noon, if the measurement is taken at noon, the days are shorter and we have colder weather.

In the second sequence, concept building experiences concerning sun position should be planned in new and different situations. Children will vary in the degree to which they understand concepts and in the time at which concepts become meaningful to them. Plan to make the relationship between sun position and length of day and change of season more mean-

---

[1] Zoe A. Thralls, *The Teaching of Geography* (New York, Appleton-Century-Crofts, 1958), p. 279.

ingful by observing and recording the changes in a different way from that used in the first sequence.

A shadow stick may be used to show the seasonal path of the sun. A shadow stick can be made by fastening a stick the size of a pencil or a long nail to a flat piece of wood about six inches square. Place the shadow stick on a desk or table near a window where the sun will shine on it during the day. Under the board place a large piece of paper on which the class can mark the length of the shadow and the date. The observation must take place at the same time of day each time the record is made. September 22 is a good date to begin recording the length and position of the shadow. Thereafter, make monthly observations and records. Summarize the observations made so that the children will understand the significance of what they are observing. Observation of the shadow made by the "class tree" (a tree "adopted" by the class as theirs to observe throughout the year) will verify the conclusions made with a shadow stick in the classroom. Be sure to notice the change in the direction of shadows at different times of day, too.

Pupils in the second sequence should know the cardinal directions. Take the children out of doors at noon to observe the direction in which their shadows point. Have them stand with their backs to the sun. They know that the sun is in the southern sky. They will see that their shadows point north. Check this with a compass. At that time, have them note the length of their shadows. A few of the shadows might be measured with a yardstick or tape and the record kept for comparison later in the year.

During the third sequence, review what the children have learned about shadows. Read poems and stories about shadows. Particularly appealing to children is Robert Louis Stevenson's "My Shadow." Others are "Influence" by Anna E. Hamilton, "For a Sundial" by Hilaire Belloc, and "Evening at the Farm" by John Townsend Trowbridge. Notice shadows in pictures to discover direction and time of day. Check all of the children during the year to see if they associate the length of the noonday shadow with the season of the year and the length of day (number of daylight hours).

Have the children trace several of their classmates' shadows on wrapping paper at noon on September 22. Keep the shadow pictures and in a month or two repeat the activity. Trace the shadow of the same pupils in order to note the change in the size of the shadow. Record the date on the top of the shadow head. Ask the children to interpret the difference in the size of the shadows. (The sun is lower in the sky at noon than it was a month ago and so the shadow is longer. Your district is on daylight saving time on September 22. Therefore, make the observation at 1 P.M. All areas return to sun time, or standard time, on the last Sunday in October, so observations subsequent to that date can be made at noon.) At the same time you ask the children to interpret the difference in the size of the

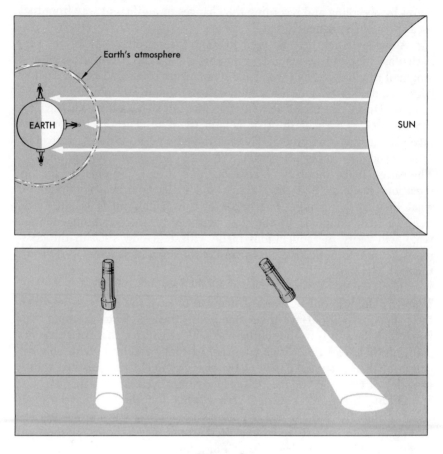

Figure 2

shadows, consider temperature differences and help the children infer that when the sun is lower in the sky it is cooler because the rays of the sun, although still vertical, meet the curvature of the earth at a more acute angle. As a result, the vertical rays of the sun must travel through a thicker layer of the earth's atmosphere to reach the surface of the earth. (See Figure 2.) The concentrated warmth of the sun's rays is dispersed, also, much as the circle of light from a flashlight beam is dispersed when the angle of light projection is changed from a right angle to an oblique angle.

Apply sun position understandings as often as the opportunity arises. Ask questions such as these:

⌁ "On which side of your home do you have awnings? Why?
⌁ How many of you have lawns which face south? On which lawn does the

snow melt more quickly, on yours or on your neighbor's across the street? On which side of the street can you find the coolest spot to play in during a hot summer day?"

Rotation, the Cause of Day and Night

Discuss the activities which take place during the day and the night. Encourage the children to watch the sun rise and set. Make it clear that the sun is a sphere many, many times larger than the earth, but that it looks small because it is so far away. Be certain, also, to make it clear that the sun does not move across the sky but that it merely appears to do so. Using the globe, show how the earth rotates from west to east. (NOTE: At any time the globe is used, *always* rotate it from west to east. This should become a matter of habit on your part and it should always be pointed out to the children. *Do not* simply spin the globe in either direction.)

The earth travels very fast in its rotation from west to east but it takes twenty-four hours for it to make one complete turn. To illustrate this, darken the room, and using a lighted flashlight or electric light bulb in a small base to represent the sun, hold the light a few feet from the globe. The children will see that one-half of the globe is lighted at one time. As the earth rotates, one-half of it is always having night. With tape, attach a large headed pin or a bit of pipe cleaner to the globe to represent a child and show how the child travels through night and day. Rotate the globe slowly. As the "figure" comes from the dark side of the globe toward the light, explain that in this position this part of the earth is just becoming lighted, that daylight is just arriving. Then, as the earth turns, the child would see the sun on the horizon. The earth continues to turn and the sun appears to be higher in the sky. (Be careful not to move the position of the light representing the sun.) Explain that the sun's position in our skies is highest at noon. Then the place that we have marked as our home turns away from the sun, which is now in our western sky, and we have afternoon, and finally evening. Now the people on the other side of the globe are having day and we are having night.

This demonstration will have to be made several times in each of the sequences so that all of the children will understand the concept. The most difficult concept for them to grasp is that the sun does not move, but that the earth does. Talk about the appearance of motion. Call attention to the children's experience when riding in a car or bus. They may have noticed that telephone poles or fence posts seem to be moving. Then mention that they may have noticed that when a car passed the car in which they were riding, their own car appeared to be standing still, or moving very slowly.

A chart made of cardboard will illustrate this concept in another

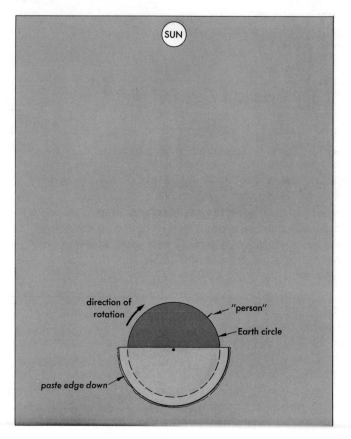

Figure 3

medium. Cut out a large circle of cardboard to represent the earth. Some outlines may be drawn on the circle to suggest continents. Attach the circle of cardboard to a large cardboard square with a paper fastener so that the circle will turn. Now, cut a half-circle of colored paper one inch larger in diameter than the circle representing the earth. Paste this colored half-circle over the lower half of the earth-circle, attaching only the outer edges of it to the square cardboard backing. The earth-circle must be free to rotate beneath this colored half-circle, since the colored half-circle represents night. Fasten a small strip of black paper about one-half inch long to the edge of the earth-circle to represent a person on the globe. Above the earth-circle, place a small yellow circle to represent the sun. Now, move the circle slowly, clockwise (west to east), to simulate the rotation of the earth. The explanation given can be much the same as that given for rotation when using the globe and a flashlight. The device just described will also help strengthen the concept that the earth moves and the sun does not. (See Figure 3.)

Suggestions for Teaching Some of the Globe Concepts for the Primary Sequences

SUN CHART   Often the times of sunrise and sunset are given in television, radio, and newspaper weather reports. This information can be used to make an interesting sun chart. Make three columns on the chart and head them DATE, TIME OF SUNRISE, and TIME OF SUNSET. A weekly record can be made which will show the increase or decrease in the number of daylight hours, depending upon the season of the year.

THE GLOBE IS A MODEL OF THE EARTH   It is difficult for a small child to think of the globe as a model of the earth because he can see so little of the earth at one time. To develop the concept of the globe as a model of the earth, the teacher might make use of a toy automobile. He might ask:

"Do all of you know what this is? What does it represent? Can you show me about how long your farther's car is? This car is very small when it is compared with the length of a real car, isn't it? Yet it is like a real car. This miniature car is a model of an automobile. The globe is a tiny model of our earth."

AXIS   When the teacher introduces the concept of rotation, he will need to explain and demonstrate the word *axis*. He can demonstrate the meaning of the word by piercing a rubber ball with a long knitting needle or strong wire. He can then show how the ball can be made to spin on its axis. Next, he will explain that a real or imaginary line passing through the center of any object that spins is called an axis. It may also be pointed out that the word "axle" comes from the same Latin root word as *axis*. At one end of the make-believe line, or axis, passing through the earth is the North Pole, and at the other end is the South Pole.

EQUATOR   The teacher writes the word *equal* on the board and asks the meaning of the word. He might cut an apple in equal parts to demonstrate. He then explains that man has drawn an imaginary or make-believe line around the earth which divides it into two equal parts. Man calls this imaginary line the equator. The teacher then puts a tape or string around the globe at the equator, and writes *equator* on the board beneath the word *equal*, calling attention to the similarity in the spelling of the two words.

HEMISPHERE   Have two clay or rubber balls ready with the equator and poles marked with red or white tempera paint. The teacher now speaks to the children.

"We have called our earth a sphere. What does that mean? I'm going to cut this sphere, which represents the earth, in half. Notice where the markings are to show the North and South Poles. If I cut this ball of clay at the equator,

I shall have two halves, or half-spheres, or hemispheres." The teacher writes *hemi-sphere* on the board, and then writes *half-sphere* beneath it. "One of the hemispheres is the northern half of the earth and one is the southern half. What do you notice about the position of the North Pole in the northern hemisphere? What do you notice about the position of the South Pole in the southern hemisphere? Now, let's look at the globe. I will hold this string at the equator. What continents are in the northern hemisphere? In the southern hemisphere? What continent is in both?

We can divide our earth into two equal parts another way. How shall we cut this ball to do this? We can cut it from the North Pole to the South Pole. Now we have an eastern and a western part; an eastern hemisphere and a western hemisphere." Hold a string or tape at about 20° west longitude and 160° east longitude. "This string will show about where the dividing line comes. What continents do we see in the western hemisphere? Which do we see in the eastern hemisphere? What continent is in both? Which hemisphere has more land? Which has more water?"

TEACHING "UP" AND "DOWN"   Ask the pupils to point up. "What do you see when you look up in the classroom? What would you see if you were outside looking up? How would you be pointing in relation to the earth? *Away from the earth.* Now point down. What do you see in the classroom when you point down? What would you see if you looked down when you were outside? You would be pointing toward the center of the earth, wouldn't you?"

Fasten stick figures made of pipe cleaners to the globe with a little clay. A cradle globe is more convenient for this work, although it can be done with a globe having a steel meridian if the globe can be moved within the base fastening. Place one of the stick figures at the North Pole and one at the South Pole. Have a child show which way the figure will point if it points up at the North Pole. Invert the globe and have another child show which way is "up" to the figure attached at the South Pole. Then have the children select two other places on the globe where they wish the stick figures to be placed. Have each figure pointing away from the earth, regardless of where it might be placed. Repeat the procedure to demonstrate the meaning of "down." (Stick figures made of pipe cleaners will, of course, have "arms" made of pipe cleaners, too. The stick figures should have one "arm" pointing toward the sky—away from the earth—when the concept of "up" is taught. Point the "arm" toward the earth when teaching the concept of "down.")

Check to see that all pupils have the concept that "up" means away from the earth, and that "down" means toward the center of the earth. This concept can be broadened in future sequences by checking children on their understanding of "up" and "down" when they use the words in conversation or find them in stories. Statements such as these might be used to illustrate correct meaning:

1. They went up hundreds of feet in the airplane.

2. The boat moved down the river toward the sea.

3. The men climbed up the mountain to the little village.

Careful development of the concepts of "up" and "down" will help our pupils avoid making the incorrect assumption that north is "up" and south is "down." "Toward the north" should never be confused with the correct meaning of "up," nor should "toward the south" be confused with the correct meaning of "down."

By the end of the primary sequences, the children will have the following concepts concerning the globe:

◇ The globe is a model of the earth.
◇ The earth is a huge sphere.
◇ There is more water than land surface on our earth.
◇ The place farthest north is the North Pole. The North Pole is on water.
◇ The place farthest south is the South Pole. The South Pole is on land.
◇ The *equator* is midway between the poles.
◇ Half a sphere is a *hemisphere*.
◇ There are four hemispheres which may be considered in globe study, depending upon whether the earth is divided at the equator, or from pole to pole.
◇ The sun is many times larger than the earth and is a great distance away from it.
◇ The earth is lighted by the sun.
◇ The sun gives the earth heat. The amount of heat varies with the time of day and the time of year.
◇ The earth rotates from west to east every twenty-four hours. When the earth turns away from the sun, that portion of the earth has night.
◇ The *axis* is a make-believe line running through the center of the earth from the North Pole to the South Pole.
◇ "Up" is away from the earth; "down" is toward the center of the earth.
◇ When the sun is low in the sky at noon, the days are shorter (fewer hours of daylight) and it is colder.
◇ When the sun is high in the sky at noon, the days are longer (more hours of daylight) and it is warmer.

Globe Study for the Fourth Sequence

The pupils are now ready to begin their first formal work in geography. They need to be taught to use a globe just as they are taught to use a textbook. By the time the pupils have reached the fourth sequence they will have developed some skill in using the globe to help them answer their questions concerning geographic problems and to satisfy any curiosity that has been aroused by current events. But now they need to build definite globe concepts, gradually and cumulatively, through experiences planned by you. Basic globe concepts should be carefully selected. Their development should be planned sequentially and so skillfully that geographic principles will evolve.

A certain amount of equipment is essential for this work. The twenty-two inch slated project globe showing continents and water bodies is an almost indispensable tool for this work because information can be placed on it with colored chalk or with clay. It is big enough to be seen by all the pupils in the room, an extremely important consideration since so many incorrect concepts and misinterpretations are the result of pupils' inability to see clearly what you are trying to demonstrate. A twelve-inch beginner's globe, showing land and water bodies in two colors and with a few place names significant at this level, will be of value and interest to your pupils. A small, slated globe, six inches in diameter, will help in teaching many geographic understandings, especially those concerning revolution.

Your curriculum will probably recommend teaching a series of fairly contiguous regions from the equator to the North Pole and from the equator to the South Pole as a means of helping the pupil acquire an initial globe concept. There are some curriculums which suggest beginning with the polar regions and working north or south toward the equator. The former plan is preferred because geographic concepts, such as length of day, sun position, and seasonal change at the equator, are less difficult for the pupil to understand than are those same concepts at the poles. The climate of both Alaska and Norway is influenced by ocean currents and winds, concepts which are too complicated for the first formal unit of geography. At the equator, in Amazonia or the Congo region, the relationships between the simple cultures of the people and the environment are more easily understood by beginning geographers than is the environment of Antarctica or Alaska where the length of day and seasonal change are widely different from any the pupils may have experienced.

In the study of successive regions in the fourth sequence, the pupil will discover how lands in the same latitudinal belt are alike and different. You then need to help him to see how man's use of the land may differ in the two hemispheres, even though climatic conditions may be similar. This fundamental work is needed so that he can build basic world concepts and understand relationships. What globe concepts need to be developed in the fourth sequence? It is necessary to check to see that all pupils understand the globe concepts recommended for the primary sequence. Many of these concepts need to be expanded in the fourth sequence and others need to be introduced. Listed below are concepts concerning the globe which interest children of this age and which will prepare them for the work they will study, together with suggestions for teaching the concept.

1. The shape of the earth. Many people have been a little disturbed to learn from the orbiting Vanguard satellite that the earth is not a round sphere slightly flattened at the poles, but that it is somewhat pear-shaped. This is true, but it should not be disturbing because the variation in shape is so slight. The earth "bulges" about fifty feet at the North Pole and is depressed about fifty feet at the South Pole, making the earth an imperfect, or slightly pear-shaped, sphere. The two variations of fifty feet are hardly noticeable when one considers that the north-south diameter of the earth is about 7,900 miles.

2. The appearance of flatness on the curved surface of the earth. Why does the earth seem to be so flat, if its surface is curved? This is a question asked by many children. You can show why the earth seems to be so flat by drawing three circles of different sizes on the board. Then mark off a short distance (about three inches) on the circumference of each circle. Your pupils will see that three inches on the circumference of the largest circle is almost a straight line; on the other hand, the same distance, three inches, on the circumference of the smaller circles is clearly a curved line. Comparing these circles with the size of the earth will bring a realization that the earth appears flat to us because we see such a small part of it.

3. The "tilt" or inclination of the earth. When working with the globe, always have the axis pointing toward the north, just as when you rotate the globe, always turn it from west to east. Explain to your pupils the meanings of the word "tilt" and "inclination" and then apply this information to the position of the earth in our solar system. If the earth's axis were not tilted, we would have equally long days and nights throughout the year everywhere on the earth. Tilting and *rotation* of the earth are responsible for different amounts of daylight in different latitudes. Tilting and *revolution* are responsible for seasonal change in all latitudes.

4. Knowledge of the globe. Pupils of the fourth sequence should be able to answer the following questions about the globe:

✓ Count the large masses of land on the globe. What are the names of these continents?
✓ Which continent is the largest? The smallest? Name the continents in order of size.
✓ Notice the shapes of the continents. (Most of them are roughly triangular, except Australia and Antarctica.)
✓ On which continent do we live?
✓ Is there more land or water on the globe?
✓ Does the northern or southern hemisphere have the greater amount of water?
✓ Name the oceans. Which ocean is the largest? (The Pacific Ocean covers nearly one-half of the world.)
✓ What is the shape of the Pacific Ocean? (Generally oval.)
✓ What continents does the Pacific Ocean touch?

✓ The Atlantic Ocean is roughly the shape of a figure eight. At the narrowest part it is only about 1,850 miles across. (When talking about the oceans, tell exciting stories about people crossing the oceans in sailing ships as Columbus did; or by raft, as told in *Kontiki*; by small boat as Robert Manry did; or by air, as Lindbergh did. Compare and contrast these adventurous undertakings with present-day flights, ocean voyages, and the journeys of our astronauts.)

✓ Name two continents through which the equator passes. Name two continents south of the equator.

✓ Name the continents which touch the Indian Ocean.

✓ Look down on the North Pole. What is the shape of the Arctic Ocean? What continents nearly surround the Arctic Ocean?

5. Activities.

a. Let's fly around the earth. "How many of you have ever been in an airplane? Do you recall what you saw as you looked down? How did the clouds appear? Did the forests look different from the farmlands? Could you see the roads? Suppose we take a trip in this miniature airplane. Tell me what you might see by naming the continents and bodies of water as we journey around the world. Jim will be the pilot and the rest of us will be passengers in the plane, looking out of the windows." Jim takes the little airplane and slowly moves it around the globe, above the continents and the large bodies of water. Several pupils are given the opportunity to name the bodies of water and the continents over which the class is flying.

b. Another device to use in visualizing the appearance of the globe is for the pupils to pretend to be members of the Explorers' Club. Children love to explore and they have the imagination to make such situations seem real.

"We've all heard about explorers, people who are curious about little-known areas on the earth, or unexplored regions of study, such as science and medicine. Our astronauts are really explorers, aren't they? They have been exploring outer space. Right now our scientists are working on space ships. What do you know about space ships? Let's pretend that we belong to an explorers' club and plan to take a trip in a space ship. We will pretend that we are beginning our orbit over the east coast of North America. Let us look down on our rotating globe and see if we recognize anything. You watch as I turn the globe and tell what you would see from the space ship." Pupils tell what would pass under the space ship, such as water bodies, continents, large lakes, large islands, high mountains—if shown on the globe, ships, airplanes, cities, and so on. "Let us orbit in another direction, traveling from north to south around the globe. Now what would you see?"

6. The effect of sun position. Give as much explanation of seasonal changes as the pupils can comprehend. Some classes may be able to understand only the two motions of the earth, revolution and rotation, and how the sun lines (Tropics of Capricorn and Cancer, the equator, and the Arctic and Antarctic Circles) were determined. Other classes may be able

to enlarge this concept into length of day and seasonal understandings. Revolution is a difficult concept for children to understand. It will need to be retaught and expanded in future sequences.

A description of how to teach revolution will be given in its entirety. This concept should be presented gradually, making sure that each step is understood by all the children before the next is presented. Ideally, the first lesson should be taught when sun position is making news: September 22, the Autumnal Equinox; December 22, the Winter Solstice and shortest day of the year (smallest number of daylight hours); March 21, the Vernal Equinox and beginning of spring in the northern hemisphere; and June 21, the Summer Solstice and the longest day of the year (greatest number of daylight hours).

There are several ways to demonstrate the revolution of the earth. Some teachers are successful with the following method.

Place a light on a table to represent the sun. Move a globe with the North Pole pointing to the north, around the light in a large circle, the large circle representing the orbit of the earth around the sun, to show the different earth positions at various times during the year. (The orbit of the earth is not a perfect circle, but an elliptic or oval.) The globe should be rotated as it makes its journey around the sun—from west to east.

This method has certain disadvantages because it is difficult to focus the light on the globe so that the pupils can see how the sun lines are determined. Sometimes it is impossible to darken the room sufficiently to illuminate only one side of the globe. If the room is completely darkened, it is difficult for all of the pupils to see the demonstration.

Another way to introduce this concept is as follows:

If you have a sixteen-inch globe mounted on a floor stand and equipped with a movable meridian, place it in the center of a large circle drawn on the floor with chalk. The large circle represents the orbit of the earth. Cover the globe so that it loses its identity as a world globe and represents, instead, the sun. This can be accomplished by wrapping a piece of yellow cloth or crepe paper around the globe and under the movable meridian. (A hemmed piece of yellow cloth, twenty-seven inches by fifty-one inches, with drawstrings in the top and bottom, will make a cover which is easily put over the floor globe and which can be used again and again.) As an eight-inch globe (a slated one is preferable) is carried around the "sun" to illustrate the earth's movement, be sure that the axis of the globe representing the earth is always in the same position, pointing north.

To show how the tropics, Cancer and Capricorn, were determined, have the globe held or placed in the position where the earth would be in relation to the sun on December 22. Fasten a tape to the metal meridian on the "sun" at the center of its north-south distance. This tape will represent the direction of the vertical rays of the sun. Fasten a piece of chalk to the other end of the tape. Have a pupil slowly rotate the slated globe which represents the earth. As he does so, hold the chalk at the end of the tightly drawn tape against the globe. He will see a circle drawn on the globe. This circle is the Tropic of Capricorn. This imaginary line made by the sun's vertical rays is the southernmost point where the rays of the sun touch the earth at a right angle, and also the southernmost point where anyone can see the sun directly overhead. In the northern hemisphere this is the "shortest" day and the first day of winter. It is called the Winter Solstice. (*Solstice* is a Latin-derivative word meaning the standing still of the sun.) Now the hours of daylight in the northern hemisphere will begin to increase.

Have the pupil walk around the circle with the slated globe to the place in the orbit which the earth reaches on March 21, being careful as he rotates the globe not to raise or lower it. If the metal meridian on the "sun" is one which will swing, keep the tape taut to show that the sun's rays maintain the same vertical direction at all times. The pupils will see that the sun's rays meet the earth at a right angle and will make an imaginary line where they strike the equator. At the equator, on about March 21, the sun is seen directly overhead at noon. Day and night are of equal length everywhere on the earth. This event occurs twice a year, March 21 and September 22. These days are called equinoxes, which means "equal nights"; the spring, or Vernal Equinox, is March 21, and the fall, or Autumnal Equinox, is September 22.

Have the pupil continue around the circle, or orbit, to the place where the earth will be on June 21, the Summer Solstice. Draw the Tropic of Cancer on the small, slated globe in the same manner in which the Tropic of Capricorn was drawn. The Tropic of Cancer marks the northernmost point that the rays of the sun touch the earth at right angles. Also, this is the northernmost point where anyone can see the sun at noon directly overhead. This is the day having the greatest number of daylight hours in the northern hemisphere. It is our first day of summer. Now the days will grow "shorter."

On September 22, the vertical rays of the sun are at the equator. Again, the number of hours of daylight and darkness are equal all over the world. September 22 is the Fall Equinox and is the first day of fall north of the Tropic of Cancer. The hours of daylight continue to decrease. During the year, every place on earth receives the same amount of daylight, but the distribution varies with the time of year.

The placing of the Arctic and Antarctic Circles must be demonstrated. Place a large globe on a table or desk with the North Pole tilted away from the light. Use a flashlight or light bulb to show day and night on the globe. Point out the circle of illumination, the circle where light ends and darkness begins. Have a child trace the circle of illumination around the globe with his finger. Call attention to the fact that, as the earth rotates, the location of the circle of illumination changes. This is the point between day and night. Have a pupil hold a piece of chalk at the highest point on the globe on the circle of illumination. Rotate the globe slowly. A circle will be drawn on the globe. Notice that all the area from the circle to the pole is in shadow, or is having night. In winter, the people living on the Arctic Circle experience one whole twenty-four hour period when they do not see the sun. At the North Pole at this time of the year there is night for six months. As the earth proceeds in its orbit after December 22, the sun will appear above the horizon at the Arctic Circle for increasingly longer periods of time.

Notice that the area from the Antarctic Circle to the South Pole and from the Arctic Circle to the North Pole will, at different seasons of the year, be in the sunlight continuously from one day at the Circles to approximately six months at the Poles. These areas are often referred to as "lands of the midnight sun" because the sun can be seen above the horizon continuously during at least one full twenty-four hour period. As we move the globe on the orbit of the earth about our stationary "sun," we can see that people living on the Antarctic Circle or the Arctic Circle will lose sight of the sun for a short time each day (depending upon the position of our earth in its path around the sun), with the length of time increasing—or diminishing—slightly as the earth continues in its orbit around the sun. (See Figure 4.)

June 21

December 22

Figure 4

Duplicate a diagram of the earth in the correct position on December 22 and June 21 for each child. (See Figure 5.) Have the pupils shade in the part of the globe away from the sun's rays with pencil, and parts toward the sun in yellow. Now ask them to draw in the Arctic and Antarctic Circles on both the December 22 and June 21 positions.

The Arctic Circle is drawn from the circle of illumination to a point

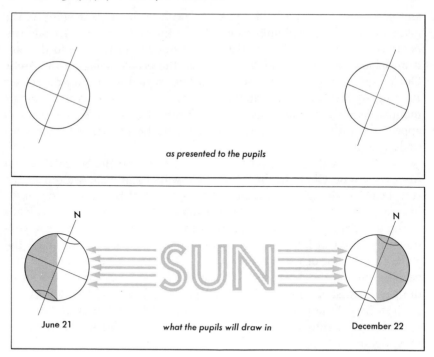

as presented to the pupils

June 21   *what the pupils will draw in*   December 22

Figure 5

the same distance from the North Pole on the other side of the globe. This shows the northern polar region. It is drawn on the June 21 position. The Antarctic Circle is similarly drawn on the December 22 position. On December 22 is the land of the midnight sun at the North or South Pole? On June 21, which polar area is able to see the midnight sun?

As an additional exercise, ask the pupils to draw five lines on a sheet of paper. On each line they should be able to write the name of one of the five sunlines, from north to south, beginning with the first line on their papers.

6. Some parts of the earth are warmer than others. We know that if the rays of the sun reach the earth at right angles, there will be greater heat than if the rays strike the earth obliquely. The curve of the earth toward the poles causes the rays of the sun to hit the earth at an oblique angle. Thus, the sun's rays must pass through more atmosphere before reaching the earth, and are greatly cooled.

This understanding can be made clear to pupils by demonstrating with a flashlight. Hold the flashlight so that the light from it strikes the floor directly at a 90° angle. The light forms a strong, clear, round spot of light. Slant the flashlight so that the light forms an oval spot on the floor. The light will appear much fainter. Ask the pupils to think about what part of the earth receives the rays of the sun directly, i.e., at right angles. What effect will these rays of the sun have upon the land? (Effect of insolation.) Vertical rays of the sun generally produce higher temperatures than "slanting" rays. This should help them understand why some parts of the earth have warmer climates than others. (Insolation refers to the amount of solar radiation any place on the earth's surface receives as a result of its latitude. The atmosphere of the earth is responsible for the weakening of the rays received from the sun. In addition, dust, clouds, and so forth, in the atmosphere also contribute to the amount of solar radiation received by the surface of the earth. If the sky is cloudless, as much as one-half of the solar radiation received from the sun is lost to the surrounding atmosphere. If clouds are present, they tend to "trap" solar radiation and retain it at the surface of the earth for longer periods of time.)

7. "Climatic zones" is a misnomer. Some people consider four of the sun lines to be the boundaries of the "climatic zones." If you think about it, you will realize how inaccurate it is to believe that all places within the boundaries of the Tropics of Cancer and Capricorn have a tropical climate. It is true that lowlands in these latitudes, where the sun is overhead at noon, are very warm; but snow can be seen throughout the year on many of the mountains. It would be more accurate to call the parts of the world where the sun is directly overhead at some time during the year the low latitudes. This would set the boundaries of the low latitudes at the Tropics of Cancer and Capricorn, but would give no misinformation regarding climate.

In high latitudes not all places have a very cold climate. Other factors beside latitude, such as mountain barriers, ocean currents, and prevailing winds, affect climate. Consequently, there is much warm weather in summer in some of the lands north of the Arctic Circle.

> In Arctic Alaska, the coldest weather is, so far as we know, in the Yukon basin; in Canada it is in Yukon Territory; and in Siberia it is in the province of Yakutsk. All these places have been inhabited for a quarter of a century or more by Europeans who are not known to have been materially discouraged in their work by the mere disagreeableness of the climate, although they have been handicapped by the frozen ground and in other things that result directly from the cold . . . . There is probably no spot on a lowland in the continental Arctic, whether in Asia or America, that does not occasionally have a summer temperature warmer than 80° F. in the shade. Or, if there is such a place, it must be on a peninsula, or on a narrow coastal strip between ice-covered mountains and the sea. Many places in the continental Arctic have occasional temperatures above 85° in

the shade, and at least one Arctic weather bureau station, that of the U. S. Government at Ft. Yukon, Alaska, has a record of 100° in the shade. The slowness of the public to realize that there is such great summer heat in the Arctic is due partly to the prevalence of the ancient view that all the Arctic is always cold, and partly to the reports of travellers whose entire Arctic experience has been on the ocean or on a sea-coast.[2]

Instead of the two polar regions being climactic zones, they are regions affected by several factors, one of which is sun position. These polar regions, from the Arctic and Antarctic Circles to the Poles, can correctly be called the high latitudes.

"Temperate" does not correctly describe climatic conditions between the tropics and the polar circles. Some geographers give the following classification: 0°–30°, low latitudes; 30°–60°, middle lattitudes; 60°–90°, high latitudes. Conditions found in southern Florida differ a great deal from the conditions found in the region around Great Bear Lake, Canada. Several geographic factors cause wide variations in the climate in this area. Between the Tropic of Cancer and the Arctic Circle, the sun at noon is never directly overhead, and is always seen in the southern sky. Between the Tropic of Capricorn and the Antarctic Circle, the sun is never overhead and is always seen in the northern sky. These regions are called, correctly, the middle latitudes because they lie between the two extremes of sun position in the low and high latitudes.

Activities

A CUMULATIVE GLOBAL CHART   Make a large circle on a piece of cardboard. Put in the five sun lines. Cut out pictures of animals which live in different parts of the world, such as a giraffe, an elephant, a lion, a wolf, a polar bear, and a seal. Discuss how each animal is suited for life in its environment and paste the picture on the cardboard representation of the globe in the approximate location of the animal's natural habitat. This can be a cumulative project, adding to it throughout the year as different animals are studied. This idea can be adapted to all grades, using types of homes, dress of the people, and crops. This chart work can be of great value because it shows how environment affects people as well as animals. Generalizations can be made after a comparative study is done.

The preceding work should familiarize the pupils of the fourth sequence with the globe in general. Globe concepts should be reviewed and broadened with the study of each part of the world. Locate the region or country being studied on the project globe by means of colored chalk or colored paper. Call the attention of the pupils to the size of the region and

2 Encyclopædia Britannica, Vol. 2, 14th ed. (1937), p. 304.

its position in relation to the world as a whole. Then discuss the location of it in reference to the equator. Is this spot near the equator? Far from the equator? What will that mean with regard to climate?

The teacher of the fourth sequence lays the foundation for the work on latitude in the fifth sequence.

Geographic Globe Skills and Abilities for the Fourth Sequence

At the end of the fourth sequence, the pupils should have developed the following abilities through the mastery of globe skills.

◈ To identify the continents, the oceans, and larger seas by name.
◈ To understand the significance of the location of the equator, the Tropics of Cancer and Capricorn, and the Arctic and Antarctic Circles.
   a. The equator marks all places halfway between the North Pole and the South Pole.
   b. The sun is always nearly overhead at noon for lands at the equator or near the equator. On *lowlands* near the equator there is summer weather all year. Days and nights are nearly always equal in length at the equator.
   c. For lands between the Tropic of Cancer and the Arctic Circle, the sun at noon is always in the southern sky and the sun is lower in the sky than it is in lands near the equator; there is a winter and a summer season; the summer comes in June, July, and August.
   d. For lands between the Tropic of Capricorn and the Antarctic Circle, the sun is always in the northern sky at noon; the sun is lower in the sky than it is in lands near the equator; there is a winter and a summer season; and the summer season comes in December, January, and February.
   e. For lands north of the Arctic Circle the sun is always low in the southern sky. There is a time during the summer season when the sun can be seen continuously for more than twenty-four hours, and during the winter season a time when the sun is not seen for more than twenty-four hours.
   f. For lands south of the Antarctic Circle, the sun is always low in the northern sky. There is a time during the summer season (December, January, February) when the sun can be seen continuously for more than twenty-four hours, and during the winter season when the sun is not seen for more than twenty-four hours.
   g. As one goes farther north from the equator, one finds cooler regions.
   h. As one goes farther south from the equator, one finds cooler regions.
◈ To read directions on the globe.

◈ To read comparative distance in respect to the equator, to either of the tropics, and to the circles and the poles.

◈ To read the same symbols on the globe which they have learned to read on maps.

◈ To make certain inferences, such as:

    a. The approximate length of day.

    b. The sun's position and the noonday shadow at any given place.

    c. The natural conditions and human activities associated with distance from the equator in such terms as "near the equator," or "near the poles."

4

Become world minded by using the globe, continued

Globe Study in the Fifth and Sixth Sequences

All new work should begin with globe study. The continent to be studied in the fifth sequence is usually North America. In some curriculums only the United States is studied. The size and shape of North America should be noted and compared with other continents. The location of North America in relation to other continents, to the Equator, the Tropic of Cancer, the Arctic Circle, and to large surrounding water bodies, should be observed. Distances should be measured on the globe with a string or a narrow strip of paper. (On a sixteen-inch globe, one inch represents 500 miles; on a twelve-inch globe, one inch represents 666 miles; and on an eight-inch globe, one inch equals 1000 miles.) Inferences can be drawn by the pupils about climate, differences in seasons, and length of day from a study of location. As the class in the fifth sequence studies the various regions of the United States, Canada, and Mexico, the globe should be used in each introductory discussion.

Pupils of the fifth and sixth sequences need diverse experiences to expand the globe concepts previously introduced. Do not take for granted that the pupils understand the concept because they have been exposed to it during the preceding year. As has been noted, pupils will vary in the degree to which they understand concepts, and in the time at which the concept has meaning for them.

Begin with what you find the pupils already know concerning globe concepts. If they only understand that there are two motions of the earth, enlarge their sun behavior understandings to include seasonal change and length of day concepts as the need arises for these facets of revolution. (See Globe Study for Fourth Sequence, page 43.) These concepts take on new meanings as they are applied to new situations and used in the daily solution of problems. Have the pupils explain relationships in terms of sun behavior, such as:

1. Grapes are more often planted in north-south rows than in east-west rows.
2. Spring wheat ripens quicker in Canada than in northern United States.
3. In winter the children of Anchorage, Alaska wear white arm bands as a safety precaution when going to school, because they go to and from school in the dark.
4. Oranges grown in the southern part of the Valley of California ripen about two weeks later than those grown in the northern part of the valley.
5. Poultry houses in the United States generally face south.
6. Summer tourists can do more sightseeing in Norway than in Spain.
7. In Buenos Aires, north-facing rooms in an apartment house are more desirable, particularly on cool days.

The concept of great circle routes can be used many times in these sequences in determining the routes taken by ships and airplanes and in finding the shortest distances between points. Ships have made limited use of Great Circle Routes for a long time, but airplanes can make much more extensive use of them because they can fly above many of the obstructions which handicap ships following a Great Circle Route. But airplanes cannot always follow Great Circle Routes, either. They have stops to make which may not be on the Great Circle. Parts of the route may not have refuelling stations. Airplanes require air rights to fly over certain foreign countries. So it is not always possible for the airplane to take the shortest route.

A Great Circle Route is the shortest and most direct route between two points on a sphere. The Great Circle divides the surface of the earth into two equal parts and can be drawn in any direction. The equator and each pair of opposite meridians are great circles.

A Great Circle Route can be shown by taking a piece of string and stretching it tightly around the globe, dividing it into two equal parts. Another way is to cut two cardboard crescents, each of which will fit halfway around the classroom globe. For a sixteen-inch globe, make the two crescents from a circle having an eight-inch radius. By placing the crescents opposite each other, the teacher can show Great Circle Routes in any direction. Inch marks can be placed on the inside of the curve of the crescents to aid in determining distance. (See Figure 6.)

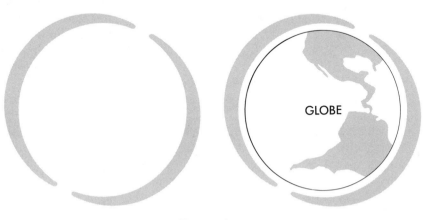

GLOBE

Figure 6

Questions such as those which follow will stimulate interest in Great Circle Routes:

- On a Great Circle Route from New York to Paris, you would fly over three countries. What are they?
- Flying a Great Circle Route from Chicago to Calcutta, over which of the following countries will you fly? Spain, Iran, Sweden, Ireland, England, Russia, Mexico.
- The shortest air route from Montevideo, Uruguay, to Melbourne, Australia, would take you over what continent?
- Over what famous island would you fly on a direct route from Tokyo to Tanarive, Malagasy?
- Flying directly south from Detroit, over which foreign country would you have to fly first?
- What group of islands would you skirt on your way from San Francisco to Tokyo by a Great Circle Route?
- How much greater is the distance westward from Chicago to Tokyo than by a Great Circle Route?
- On a Great Circle vacation of your dreams, you might see a fashion show in __(Paris)__ , swim in __(the Mediterranean)__ , ski in __(Switzerland)__ , and ride a camel in __(Arabia)__ .

Latitude

The study of latitude is introduced in the fifth sequence. The concept of latitude is difficult to acquire because it is abstract and is dependent upon a background of experience with globe concepts. In the fourth sequence, the teacher has constantly spoken of locations as near the equator, far from the equator, and near or far from the poles. The pupils have begun to associate length of day, sun position, and climatic conditions in terms of distance from the equator. For example: At the equator the sun is nearly always overhead and consequently the climate is hot. Day and night are of about equal length at the equator. As you go farther from the equator, the climate is cooler and the amount of daylight and dark varies.

In the fifth sequence, the pupils learn about latitude not only as distance from the equator and as a means for locating places, but also as a geographic factor which affects climate and man's food, clothing, shelter, and activities. It is the importance attached to these learnings, through constant application, which makes latitude meaningful. Pictures and slated globes are valuable aids in building these concepts.

In several textbooks we read statements which indicate that latitude is shown by east-west lines which are used to measure distances north and south of the equator. Of course, this is confusing to a pupil who has had little opportunity to think through such a statement. It is important to know how to present this concept clearly and concisely.

How to Teach Latitude

MOTIVATION

"During our work in the fourth sequence we were studying places that were sometimes near to the equator. At other times we studied places far from the equator. Is Pittsburgh (or any other large city you wish to name) near the equator or far from it? Find the equator on the globe. Now find about where Pittsburgh is. It looks as though it is about halfway to the North Pole from Pittsburgh, and halfway to the equator, doesn't it? I wonder how many miles Pittsburgh is from the equator?"

DEVELOPMENT

"Suppose your mother wishes to measure something that is round. What does she use? *Tape measure.* Suppose we put a tape measure around the globe to see if we can measure distance from the equator this way." Draw a chalk mark at each inch mark and extend the lines a little so that they can be seen. This will be easiest to do on a slated globe. "What do you notice about these chalk lines which I have drawn on the globe? *They are the same distance apart.* What do we say about lines that are the same distance apart? *They are parallel if they are the same distance apart for their whole length.* Now suppose we extend these lines the whole way around the globe, keeping them the same distance apart. Would they be parallel? Yes, and that is exactly what these lines which measure distance north from the equator and south from the equator are called: parallels. But we don't measure this distance in inches. That would be rather difficult to do because the world is so large. We measure this distance in *degrees*. There are 360 degrees in a circle." *Degree* (°) comes from the Latin word, *de gradus*, which means "step." "How many degrees would there be in half of a circle? From the equator to the North Pole would be what part of a circle? *One-fourth*. How many degrees would we have in one-fourth of a circle? Then we have 90° from the equator to the North Pole, and 90° from the equator to the South Pole." Show this to the class with the globe. "Open your textbooks to a large map of the United States.

Find New Orleans on your map of the United States. Do you notice a parallel passing very near to New Orleans? Now, follow that line to the margin of the map. The figure there tells you how many degrees north of the equator New Orleans is. How many degrees north of the equator is New Orleans?" Next try a large city near where the pupils live. "Denver is very close to a parallel shown on your map. How many degrees north of the equator is Denver? Pittsburgh? Now we don't have to say 'near to the equator' or 'far from the equator' any more. Those are very indefinite terms, aren't they? We can now say that a place is a certain number of *degrees* from the equator, can't we? The number of degrees represents distance.

We call distance north or south of the equator, *latitude*." Teacher writes "latitude" on the board. "What is the latitude of Chattanooga, Tennessee? Houston, Texas? Now, let us find approximately how many miles some of these cities are from the equator. Each degree of latitude is approximately seventy miles. How many miles from the equator is Pittsburgh? *Forty degrees times seventy miles for each degree*. How far is New Orleans from the equator in miles? Your own city? And how far is New Orleans from Pittsburgh, approximately? Approximately how far is Memphis from New Orleans?"

SUMMARY

"What is distance north and south from the equator called? What are the lines which measure latitude called? How many miles are represented by one degree of latitude? What two kinds of latitude are there?"

APPLICATION

Have the pupils find the latitude of several large cities.

Applying the Concept of Latitude

The only way that the concept of latitude can be made meaningful is with continued application. It is altogether possible for pupils to use latitude efficiently in locating places and not be aware of its effect upon man and his activities. After the location of the region or country to be studied is established, have the pupils note the number of degrees of latitude through which the region or country extends. From their knowledge of the effects of latitude the pupils should be able to formulate hypotheses concerning the climate the region or country may have, the crops which can be raised, and the way people in the region live. Obviously, the next step would be to check these hypotheses for validity.

A study of the Pacific States is a good one to illustrate the effect of latitude through comparison and contrast. The following lesson can be entitled "The Effect of Latitude as Shown in a Study of Two Pacific States: Alaska and California."

SPECIFIC OBJECTIVE

To make the pupils aware of the effect of latitude on the people living in the Pacific states of Alaska and California through comparison and contrast.

MOTIVATION

"We have been locating places by means of latitude and we have said that latitude affects man in many ways. Today we are going to take two of our Pacific states, California and Alaska, and see in how many ways latitude has affected the people there. We shall also discover that climatic conditions within each latitude contribute to the many problems of living which must be solved. Let us make a list of the ways that latitude affects people, as we go along."

DEVELOPMENT

1. "Let us see how many people live in these states. Find the population of Alaska and of California.

2. What is the approximate latitude of Southern California? 32°. Northern Alaska? 71°. How many degrees of latitude are they apart? How many miles would this be if each degree of latitude represents, roughly, seventy miles? 2,730 *miles*. There will be many ways in which this great difference in latitude will affect the lives of the people living in these two states.

3. One of these differences will be in the number of daylight hours during the different seasons. On June 21, San Diego, California, 32° 44′ north latitude,[1] has 14.3 hours of daylight. Fairbanks, Alaska, 64° 44′ north latitude, is about 115 miles south of the Arctic Circle. On June 21, the sun rises at about one o'clock A.M. at Fairbanks, and does not set until eleven o'clock P.M., or about twenty-one hours of daylight.

Point Barrows, 71° 20′ north latitude, the northernmost city in Alaska, has continuous daylight from May 12 to July 31, a period of eighty days. On December 22, San Diego has 10.15 hours of daylight and Fairbanks has four hours of daylight, but Point Barrows has not seen the sun since November 22. It will not see the sun again until January 21, a period of sixty days. Atmospheric refraction is a factor in causing the 'long night' to be shorter than the 'long day.'

Although the number of hours of daylight varies with the latitude and season, every place in the world receives the same number of daylight hours in the course of a year. The difference lies in the uneven distribution of the hours of daylight." Explain with a globe why there is such a difference in the number of hours of daylight in California and Alaska on the same day of the year. "In

---

[1] A degree is composed of 60 minutes (′).

what ways would the uneven distribution of daylight hours affect the people of Alaska?" Under the heading LATITUDE AFFECTS on the blackboard, the teacher lists "Length of day" as the first item.

4. "In what other way will latitude affect these states? *Climate.* What type of climate does most of California have? *Mediterranean climate, with dry, warm summers and mild, rainy winters.* In what way would this climate be an advantage? A disadvantage?"

5. Describe the climate of Alaska. Several factors in addition to latitude affect the climate of Alaska. Some of these are mountain barriers, ocean currents, and prevailing winds. Account for the variation in climate in the different parts of Alaska. Teacher writes "Climate" under the heading LATITUDE AFFECTS.

6. "What will be the length of the growing season in Alaska? What will compensate for the short growing season? *Number of daylight hours.* What is the length of the growing season in California? Why is the length of the growing season important? *It determines what can be grown.*" Teacher adds "Length of growing season" to the list on the board.

7. "The amount of precipitation is influenced by latitude since prevailing winds at certain latitudes bring moisture to the land. The Westerlies bring heavy precipitation to the coastal areas of Alaska. Much of it fails to reach the interior due to mountain barriers.

8. Now, let's make lists of crops grown in these two states. In what way does latitude determine the kinds of crops grown?

9. Latitude affects man's work. Account for the great difference in the amount of manufacturing done in these two states. How does latitude affect other industries in Alaska and California? *Lumbering, fishing, trapping, canning, truck gardening.*"

10. Explain how food, homes, clothing, travel, and sports in California are affected by latitude. Add these to your list of things which latitude affects.

11. "In Alaska there are different groups of people to consider: the white man, the Indian and the Eskimos who have adopted some of the white man's ways, and the few Eskimos who live as their ancestors lived." Explain how latitude affects the food, clothing, homes, and travel of each group.

12. "Latitude creates problems of living which have to be solved. In the high latitudes there are problems such as street lighting, pure water, sewage disposal, road construction and maintenance, and the construction of houses. In Fairbanks, Alaska, for instance, antifreeze must be used in fire hydrants. In some places in Alaska, water mains cannot be laid deep enough to be below the frost line because of permafrost. Pipes have to be made of wooden staves bound with wire. The water must be heated before it is pumped into the houses in some areas; the water must be kept moving because it will freeze if it stands in pipes. When people build houses in Alaska, they must take into account the freezing and thawing of surface layers. The movement caused by these changes makes it impossible to have plaster walls in some areas. Most of the houses are made of wood. Double windows are a must to keep out the cold. Residents of Sitka, Alaska, where the winters are long and rainy, say, 'If you've lived through one of our summers, you won't mind the other 364 days.'[2]

California has problems of living, also. One of the most vital is the problem

2 Ernest Gruening, "Alaska Proudly Joins the Union," *National Geographic Magazine,* Vol. CXVI, No. 1 (July, 1959), p. 62.

of obtaining enough water for irrigation and for human use. The harvesting of the many crops in California causes a need for seasonal workers who also create many problems, as has the rapid population and industrial growth in Southern California. Los Angeles suffers from smog, caused by temperature inversion which "traps" city air over the Los Angeles basin. Can you name other problems California might have?"

SUMMARY

List the ways in which Alaska and California are affected by latitude.

APPLICATION

Tell how latitude affects Washington and Hawaii, two other Pacific states, by filling in the chart:

Latitude Does Make a Difference!		
	WASHINGTON	HAWAII
Climate		
Growing season		
Food, homes, clothing		
Crops		

Activities to Strengthen the Concept of Latitude

A MATCHING EXERCISE   On a strip of brown wrapping pa-
per at least six feet long, draw horizontal lines to represent the following
parallels: 0, 20, 40, and 60 north latitudes; 20, 40, and 55 south latitudes.
Prepare a series of pictures which illustrate conditions found at each of
these latitudes. Descriptive paragraphs of each region, written by the pupils
and mounted on construction paper, can also be used. Have the pupils
match the pictures or written paragraphs with the correct latitude. A variation of this activity would be to have at hand a series of uncaptioned pictures showing landscapes of different latitudes of North America. Have the
pupils try to place these pictures on the wall map in their correct location.
They might also make a series of their own sketches showing the landscape
one might see at 0°, 20°, 40°, and 60° north or south latitude.

A SEARCHING PARTY   In the column to the left you have six
specific parallels of latitude listed. Search for a large city in the European
country named and also for a large city in the United States which would
be located very near the parallel given in the column at the left. (You can
have more fun if you divide the class into two groups and have a contest.
Have one group try to find the European cities and the other group search
for the American cities. Set a liberal time limit.)

LATITUDE	EUROPE	UNITED STATES
40° N.	——————— , Spain	———————
45° N.	——————— , Italy	———————
50° N.	——————— , Germany	———————
55° N.	——————— , England	———————
60° N.	——————— , U.S.S.R.	———————
70° N.	——————— , Norway	———————

Longitude

The concept of longitude is usually introduced in the sixth sequence
but it should not be taught until latitude is thoroughly understood.

MOTIVATION

"Have you ever played hide-and-seek? That is what we are going to play on
maps this morning. Turn to your map of South America. I am going to hide
in some city and we shall see if you can find me. Find the equator. Trace it with
your finger. I am in a city just about on the equator. Where am I? *Quito,*

Belem, Manaus. Find the Tropic of Capricorn. Suppose I said that I was hiding in a city near the Tropic of Capricorn. In which city might I be? If I said that I was in Brazil on the Tropic of Capricorn, in which city might I be? If I were in a city farther west, in which city might I be? It is rather difficult to know just where I might be unless I tell you the country, isn't it? Now, let's see if you have any better luck finding me if I am north of the equator. Turn to a map of the United States. Trace the 30th parallel across the map. Suppose I said that I was in a city that was very close to the 30th parallel. In which city might I be? *New Orleans, Houston, Austin.* Find the 35th parallel north. Find some of the cities near the 35th parallel. *Memphis, Chattanooga, Albuquerque.* Now, suppose I said that I was 40 degrees north. In which city would I be? I might be in any one of the cities which were near this parallel across the United States. Why have you had such a time guessing in which city I might be hiding? Yes. There was nothing to tell you definitely where I might be. If an aviator radioed from his plane that he needed help and that he was over the 40th parallel north, where might he be?" Have a pupil trace the 40th parallel across the world map. Radar might help locate the pilot, but it would not extend the whole way across the continent. "If I told you that I lived on Hickory Street, would you have trouble finding me? Of course you would. You would have to stop to inquire at every house. Ships and planes would have trouble, too, if all we had was a way to measure distance north and south from the equator."[3]

DEVELOPMENT

"We, in the United States, during the early days of our country, decided that we could measure east and west of Washington, D.C. Would it have helped you to find the place you were looking for if I had told you how far west of Washington I was? That would have helped, wouldn't it?

At that time, people in England measured distance east and west from London. People in Italy were measuring distance east and west from Rome. The French measured distance and time east and west from Paris. How do you think this would work out? Of course, there would be confusion with ships crossing the ocean so near to many of these countries. The sea captains just had to have the same point from which to measure. A meeting of important men from all countries was held in Washington, D.C. in 1884. It was called the Washington Meridian Conference. Great Britain was the most powerful nation represented at the conference and it also had the largest fleet of ships. The Conference decided that the town of Greenwich, England would be the starting point from which to measure distances east and west because Greenwich had a world-famous astronomical observatory. On the globe, they drew a line through Greenwich from the North Pole to the South Pole. All places on this line would have noon at the same time, wouldn't they? It would be a midday line, or a meridian. The line which passed through Greenwich was the Prime (first) Meridian.

Greenwich was a little district that is now part of London. Today, the

---

[3] Early navigators were able to cope with the lack of lines of longitude through the use of the Latitude Stick. See "Navigating with the Kamal," *Journal of Geography* (Vol. 60, September, 1961), 268–273. This article by Ronald L. Ives is both informative and interesting.

Royal Greenwich Observatory has been moved to Herstmonceux Castle, 58 miles southeast of London, but the Prime Meridian still is drawn through Greenwich. So, to make it easier to remember, I'm going to talk about distance east and west of London, since Greenwich is completely surrounded by metropolitan London.

We usually think of a yardstick or tape measure when we want to measure anything. Let us see if we can measure distance east of London or west of London with a tape measure." The teacher takes a tape measure and holds it around the globe near the 50th parallel to give the idea of measuring distance from London. "If this distance east and west of London were measured in inches we could extend the inch marks toward the poles. Then these lines, or meridians, would measure the distance for us. But the earth is so large that we cannot measure it in inches. How do we measure latitude? *In degrees.* How many degrees are there in a circle? How many degrees are there in half a circle? If we measure east of London 180°, and west of London 180°, we would meet on the other side of the globe, wouldn't we? Degrees are numbered at the Equator on a globe. How many degrees apart are the meridians on this globe? On globes, meridians are fifteen degrees apart. Meridians measure the distance in degrees east and west of London. John and Don, will you help me to show the class something else about meridians? Find where a meridian crosses the equator on this globe. Have you each found one? Now, move your finger along the meridian as you trace it northward. What did you find that the meridians did? *They met at the North Pole.* Now, trace the meridian southward toward the South Pole. What happened? What have you found out about meridians? *They meet at the poles.*

Open your book to a map of the United States. Trace a meridian north toward the top of the page. What do you find in the margin there? What does that figure tell you? *How many degrees west of London any place on this meridian is.* Some of these large cities which I will name for you will not be exactly on the meridian, but tell me what meridian is nearest to each. We shall then know how many degrees *west of London* each is.

Philadelphia. *75° west.*
New Orleans. *90° west.*
Denver. *105° west.*
Now, let's find some cities *east of London.*
Amsterdam, Netherlands. *5° east.*
Hamburg, Germany. *10° east.*
Catania, Sicily. *15° east.*

We call distance east and west of LONdon, LONgitude." The Teacher places these words on the board, one under the other, then underlines LON in both words to help the pupils associate longitude with distance east and west of London. Longitude should always be spoken of as *distance* east and west of London.

"We need both latitude and longitude to tell exactly where places are. I am going to pretend that I am in an airplane and that I radio my location to you. See if you can find the country over which I am flying. Turn to the map of Europe. We shall work one out together first to see how it is done. Where are the degrees of latitude on this map? Trace with your left hand the 40th,

45th, and 50th parallels of north latitude across the map. Where are the figures showing the degrees of longitude? Find the Prime Meridian. That would be 0 degrees. Now, find the meridian marked five degrees east and trace it from north to south on your map with your right hand. Find the country over which I would be flying if I were at 50° north latitude by tracing the 50th parallel with your left hand, and with your right hand trace the meridian which is numbered 10° east longitude. Move your hands until your fingers meet over a country as the lines you are tracing intersect or cross. What country is it? Now, let's see how many of these countries you can find.

40° N. lat.	5° W. long.	*Spain.*
60° N. lat.	15° E. long.	*Sweden.*
45° N. lat.	10° E. long.	*Italy."*

SUMMARY

* "What is distance east and west of London called?
* What are lines which measure this distance called?
* What does meridian mean?
* When we trace meridians north or south, what do we find that they do?
* What is the greatest number of degrees a place can have in east or west longitude?"

APPLICATION

Give the pupils the latitude and longitude of five large cities and expect them to find them within a reasonable length of time.

Globe Study for Junior High School

The study of the globe is never completed. New and exciting interpretations can be discovered in every day's use of the globe. Junior high school pupils ought to have an understanding of the significance of the location of a region on the earth with respect to climate and accessibility to other regions, and how such factors will affect man's activities.

By the time pupils reach junior high school, they should have mastered most of the sun behavior and globe concepts introduced in earlier sequences. All of the concepts can be expanded and made more meaningful by exploring them in depth and applying them in situations conducive to more mature thought.

Many articles in current magazines and achievements in the field of science can be more easily understood if the pupils have a thorough understanding of all geographic concepts. The orbiting of astronauts in space, with their rapidly paced periods of day and night, can be better understood when sun behavior has been explored. Some understanding of the two methods for measuring the number of orbits around the earth of a space vehicle can be grasped with an understanding of rotation and revolution. (The Russians measure orbits in terms of passing a fixed point on the earth's surface. The United States measures orbits in terms of passing a fixed point in space, regardless of the rotation of the earth on its axis while the flight is in progress.) The significance of the Aswan High Dam in Egypt can be better understood if relationships between water and crop production have been developed. The importance of the ten billion kilowatt-hours of electricity to be produced by the dam can be grasped if relationships between natural and cultural factors have been adequately taught in sequences preceding the junior high school. The mere noting of facts is not enough in the study of geography. Facts, gleaned from past and present learning and experiences, must be used and evaluated critically. Most important, however, they must be applied, almost automatically, as pupils encounter reports of man's activities in their reading, and as they meet problems in their lives.

Most junior high school pupils would be interested in obtaining information about such projects as the DEW Line (Defense Early Warning System) which provides defense command centers in the United States and Canada with advance warning of the approach of airplanes and missiles over the Arctic regions. They would be interested in being able to place it on the project globe and in understanding the relationships involved.

Almost all of the pupils are interested in travel. Have them plan trips on Great Circle Routes telling why they would want to make certain stops. Route maps of the airlines might be available to study. It would be interesting to find how many of their flights are planned along Great Circle Routes.

Interesting world patterns to study which would involve the use of the physical-political and project globes are climate, wind systems, population, production of crops, transportation, and trade. Each topic is made more interesting with the use of globes.

Have the students make a collection of puzzling statements concerning the globe, which they will try to explain. For example:

1. At the Panama Canal the sun rises in the east over the Pacific Ocean and sets in the west over the Atlantic Ocean.
2. Cape Farewell, Greenland, is the nearest point in North America to the continent of Africa.

The answers to the following questions will disclose which concepts need to be corrected, reviewed, or retaught:

- What is the relation between rotation and time?
- What changes would take place on the earth if it became perpendicular to its orbit?
- What would happen if the earth ceased to rotate?
- Of what importance is latitude in human affairs?

Time Belts

Prior to 1883 the railroads of the United States and Canada used fifty-three different time systems. Every town and city followed sun time, and before the advent of rapid transportation by rail, the arrangement caused very little confusion. With the increase in the number of railroads and the wide use of the facilities they afforded for rapid communication, it soon became evident that some system of standardizing time over large areas would be necessary in order to plan train schedules and timetables. In 1883 the railroads of the United States and Canada were provided with the means for uniform timetables when their owners agreed to set up a series of five time belts for Canada and four for the United States.[4] Each time belt has boundaries traced irregularly along lines of longitude. Since the earth rotates three hundred sixty degrees in every twenty-four hour period, it travels 360° ÷ 24, or fifteen degrees in one hour. The time belts are, therefore, approximately fifteen degrees wide and have as their midpoints the 60th, 75th, 90th, 105th, and 120th meridians. All places within the belts or time zones use the time of the central meridian of the belt. The Eastern Time Belt uses the 60° west meridian, the Central Time Belt uses the 90° west meridian, the Mountain Time Belt the 105° west meridian, and the Pacific Time Belt the 120° west meridian. Alaska has two time belts, the Alaskan Time Belt, which uses the 150° west meridian as its center, and the Bering Standard Time Belt, centered on the 165° west meridian. The state of Hawaii also makes use of the 150° west meridian as the center of its time belt.

How can we make this concept of time meaningful to our pupils? The following plan shows how to introduce and develop the concept of time belts.

SPECIFIC OBJECTIVE

To introduce and develop an understanding of time belts.

MOTIVATION

"How many of you are interested in baseball? At what time do we hear the broadcast of the night games? Sometimes we hear the broadcasts at eleven o'clock at night and sometimes at nine o'clock. Night ball games usually start at about eight o'clock when they are played at home. How can we explain this?

How many of you saw the Rose Bowl football game? It began late in the afternoon on New Year's Day for some of us. It may have been dark in your part of the country when you watched it on television, but at what time was it being played in California?

[4] Since the admission of Alaska and Hawaii, the United States extends through three additional time belts.

Have any of you visited as far west as Chicago? Denver? Los Angeles? Or as far east as New York? Pittsburgh? In which time belt do you live? In the city which you visited, how did the time differ from that of your home town? In which time belt is each of the cities which we have mentioned? Why do you suppose time belts are necessary? Let's find out how these time belts were established and whether some of the occupations of people are affected by them."

DEVELOPMENT

"Before 1883 there were no time belts in our country. How do you think the different towns and cities determined the correct time? How do you tell when it is noon if you have no clock to look at? Why would the method used by these early towns and cities to determine time cause confusion? What effect would the development and use of railroads have upon this problem? The railroads of the United States and Canada had to do something about it." See explanatory material at the beginning of this section.

"Let us examine this map of the time belts in our forty-eight mainland states." Teacher uses an opaque projector or overhead projector to show map, or calls attention to a map in the textbook which shows time belts. "Trace the 75° west meridian. Do you see that it is roughly in the center of the Eastern Standard Time Belt? What meridian do you find in the middle of the Central Standard Time Belt? In the Mountain Standard Time Belt? The Pacific Coast Time Belt? How many degrees of longitude apart are these central meridians of each time belt? 15°. What is the difference in time between each time belt? Then how many degrees of longitude make a difference in time of one hour? There is another way we can figure this out. How many degrees are there in a circle? 360°. An imaginary line drawn around the earth would be nearly a perfect circle. If the earth rotates once in every twenty-four hour period, it rotates 360°, or a complete circle. In one hour it would rotate one twenty-fourth of 360°, or 15°. Thus, the earth turns 15° in one hour. Have you noticed that the time belts have very irregular borders? Let us list some reasons which would account for this irregularity.

Now we can tell what time it is in different parts of the United States when we know what time it is in our own time belt." Draw seven vertical lines, equally spaced, to represent the central meridian for each of the time belts. "Label each meridian with its correct degree designation and write the name of a well-known city found in each time belt."

"In what direction does the earth rotate? Which of these cities will see the sun first in the morning? Suppose it is noon in Denver. Will it be before noon or after noon in Los Angeles? In Philadelphia? If it is noon in Philadelphia, what time will it be in Chicago? In Denver? In Los Angeles? In Anchorage,

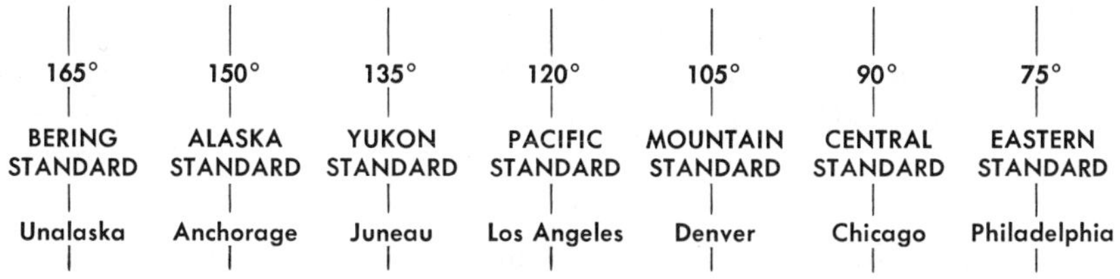

165°	150°	135°	120°	105°	90°	75°
BERING STANDARD	ALASKA STANDARD	YUKON STANDARD	PACIFIC STANDARD	MOUNTAIN STANDARD	CENTRAL STANDARD	EASTERN STANDARD
Unalaska	Anchorage	Juneau	Los Angeles	Denver	Chicago	Philadelphia

Figure 7

Alaska? If Philadelphia is approximately 75° *west* of London, how many hours difference in time are there between the two cities? *Five hours.* If Early Bird Satellite were beaming a London program to us and we received it at eight o'clock in the evening, at what time would it be given, live, in London? When it is noon in London, will it be before noon or after noon in Philadelphia? In Berlin?" Berlin is approximately 15° *east* of London. "In Moscow?" Moscow is approximately 30° *east* of London. "What time would it be in each of these cities if it were noon in London?" Teacher adds 15°, 30°, and 45° east meridians to the diagram, Figure 7, and places fictitious names of towns on the meridians shown, and continues to question in order to strengthen the concept of differences in time.

SUMMARY

"Name the seven time belts of the United States. Upon what are the time belts based? How many degrees of longitude does the earth rotate in one hour?"

APPLICATION

"Now, let us see if we can use what we have learned. Suppose that we leave Kennedy Airport in New York by jet at 8 o'clock on Monday night. If it takes us eight hours to fly to Berlin (15° E.), at what time, according to our watches, will we arrive in Berlin? *Four p.m., if we have not adjusted our watches as we crossed each time belt.* What time will it be according to Berlin time?" (*Ten p.m., Monday night.*)

A newscast beamed from London at 8 p.m. today would be heard here (your city) at what time? In Denver? In Berlin?

Passengers who travel by jet airliner find that they have to make several physical adjustments to the difference in time. When it is 10:30 p.m. in New York, a person who has just arrived by jet from San Francisco will not feel particularly sleepy, because it is only 7:30 p.m. by his customary time. He would be much more interested in having a late dinner than in preparing to retire for the night.

When we are having breakfast at 7 o'clock, what will the people of London be doing? The people of India?

A jet airliner leaves on a flight to Los Angeles from New York. Through how many time zones will it fly? On the return trip to New York, will the passengers set their watches ahead or back?"

The International Date Line

When you are certain that the pupils understand time belts, they are ready for the development of the concept of the International Date Line.

TEACHER PREPARATION

Draw twenty-five vertical lines spaced equidistant across the blackboard to represent the central meridian of each of the time belts. Number them by 15's from 0° to 180° east longitude, and from 0° to 180° west longitude. (See Figure 8.) In addition, prepare a strip of paper about three inches wide and long enough to encircle your room globe. If you have a sixteen inch globe, the paper will need to be about fifty and one-quarter inches long. Place lines on this paper similar to those shown in Figure 8,

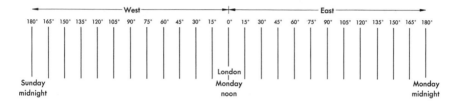

Figure 8

which you have placed on the board. This paper band will be used to show that it is one day on one side of the International Date Line and a different day on the other side of it.

SPECIFIC OBJECTIVE

To teach the pupils why there is an International Date Line and to explain why one loses a day when he crosses the line going west and gains a day when he crosses it in traveling east.

MOTIVATION

"Jim was on a troop ship going to Vietnam. His birthday would be on the next day, Tuesday, March 15. He thought of the celebration he might have enjoyed if he had been at home.

As Jim prepared for bed on Monday night, March 14th, he wondered what his birthday would be like tomorrow, and if it would be a memorable one. Imagine his surprise when he awakened the next morning to find that it was Wednesday, March 16th. He was puzzled. What had happened to his birthday? Somehow, he had lost it!

Where do you think the ship was on Monday night? What had happened during the night? *The ship had crossed the International Date Line.* Let us see if we can find out why Jim lost a day in travelling westward over the line. Do you think that he will ever be able to regain this day?"

DEVELOPMENT

"Let's pretend that it is noon on Monday in London. London is located on the Prime Meridian. What time is it in each of the time belts to the east? At fifteen degrees east, it is one o'clock. At 30° east, it is two o'clock. At 45° east, it is three o'clock in the afternoon on Monday." Continue giving the time of each time belt until the 180th meridian is reached. "At the 180th meridian east it is Monday midnight." Be sure to mention that the time given for each

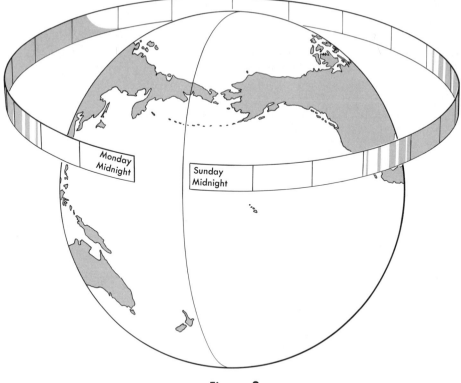

Figure 9

time belt as you move eastward is the time at its central meridian. Write
MONDAY MIDNIGHT on the 180th east meridian.

"Now, give the time prevailing in each of the time belts as we travel west,
remembering that it is noon on Monday in London. What time will it be at
15° west? *Eleven o'clock.* At 30° west? *Ten o'clock.* At 45° west? At 60° west?
Now we are near New York at 75° west. What time will it be in New York
when it is noon in London?" Continue with similar questions until you reach
the 180th meridian. "Here it is midnight on Sunday night." Write SUNDAY
MIDNIGHT on the 180th meridian west. Take the strip of paper which you
have previously prepared. Hold it under the meridians drawn on the board to
show the pupils that it is a copy of the diagram on the blackboard. Place the
paper strip around the globe so that the ends meet at the International Date
Line.

"On the east side of the line, the paper strip indicates that it is Sunday
Midnight, and on the west side of the line it reads 'Monday Midnight.' Can
you now explain what happened to Jim's birthday?"

Questions such as the following, which require the use of facts learned
in connection with the International Date Line should be given to
strengthen the time concept.

"Trace the International Date Line on a globe or wall map. Do you notice that the International Date Line does not follow the meridian exactly? What do you think is the reason for this? At what places on the globe would the International Date Line cause confusion if it followed the 180th meridian exactly? In crossing the International Date Line from west to east, would you lose or gain a day? Which direction would you sail, east to west, or west to east, if you wished to be able to celebrate two Christmas days? What is the difference in degrees between Manila (120° east) and Honolulu (150° west)? How many hours of time does this equal? On a flight from Los Angeles, California to Tokyo, Japan, do the passengers add twenty-four hours or subtract twenty-four hours when they cross the International Date Line? Do they gain a day or lose one? *They add twenty-four hours when they cross the date line, thus they lose a day as they fly to Japan. When they return to the United States, they subtract twenty-four hours and regain the day that they lost.*"

SUMMARY

Summarize the facts learned about the International Date Line. The questions included in the development of the lesson indicate the course which the summary should take.

APPLICATION

Have each pupil make up problems or puzzling statements concerning the time belts and the International Date Line. Have a committee choose the best of these problems to test the class's understanding of these concepts.

The Analemma

"Have you noticed the device on your globe, in the east central Pacific Ocean, which resembles a figure 8? It is called the analemma, a word which means sundial. It shows the precise latitude at which the sun will be directly overhead at noon on a specific date. It also shows 'equation of time,' the difference between sun time and clock time.

Notice that the analemma (Figure 10) extends from the Tropic of Cancer to the Tropic of Capricorn, a distance of 47°. Probably you have incorrectly called this area between the two tropics a climatic zone (Torrid Zone). It is a light zone on which the rays of the sun shine vertically at noon on succeeding days of the year. The sun shines directly overhead at each spot on two days each year. Can you give the two dates when the noon sun can be seen directly overhead at the Equator? Study the analemma and, as you do, notice the names of the months and the dates around the figure 8.

If you want to know on what days the sun shines directly on a particular place, follow its parallel to the analemma. The point at which the parallel touches the analemma gives the dates when the noon sun will be directly overhead. As has already been noted, there will be two days when the noon sun will be directly overhead at places in the area between the Tropic of Capricorn and

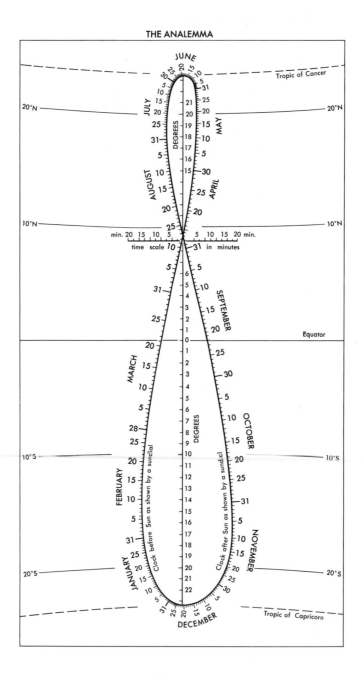

Figure 10

the Tropic of Cancer. Let us try to find the days when the noon sun will be directly overhead at Caracas, Venezuela. What is the latitude of Caracas? *10° N. lat.* Trace the 10th parallel to the analemma. At what dates does the parallel touch the analemma? *April 16 and August 25.*

Where the lines of the analemma cross, you will notice another scale showing the difference between sun time and clock time. The time from sun-noon to sun-noon is a solar day. The length of time from sun-noon of one day to sun-noon of the next day varies during the year. If solar time were commonly used by us, rather than clock time, the length of the day would vary. The average length of time from sun-noon to sun-noon is called the mean solar day. This is the length of time which we call a day and which we have divided into twenty-four parts which we call hours. If an accurate clock is set with the sun at noon on December 25, you will find that it will agree with sun-time on only four days of the year: December 25, April 13, September 1, and June 15. On these days the time from sun-noon to sun-noon is 'average' or 'accurate-clock' length. The sun is neither fast nor slow on these days, but is 'on time.' On March 21 when the clock indicates noon, the sun is not at noon position until the clock indicates 12:08.

To find the difference between clock time and solar time for any given day, find the day on the analemma and with a slip of paper measure its distance from the meridian or axis running through the center. Mark these points. Lay them on the Time Scale in Minutes (indicated on the analemma), and count the minutes between the two points. The result gives the number of minutes the solar time is fast or slow compared to clock time. If the date falls to the right, the clock is slow. If it falls to the left, the clock is fast."

5

Make maps indispensable

Maps have a remarkably comprehensive story to tell to anyone who has learned to read them well. It is careful reading of maps which enables us to glean full meaning from them. Maps not only show the physical features of the world reduced to the size of man, making them more comprehensible, but they also provide us with a summary of the accumulated geographic knowledge of generations. They can literally widen our horizons and reveal to us a whole new world of interesting and valuable information that may be significant to us in gaining understanding about places and relationships. Everyone needs maps to be able to give full meaning to the news of the day. They can increase our enjoyment of leisure time reading and television viewing, facilitate our travel, and help us to understand the economics of daily life. They are indispensable to modern society. To be unable to read them and use them handicaps modern man, whatever his station in life may be.

It must be remembered, however, that maps are not perfect. Every flat map of a large area is inherently wrong because it is impossible to picture the curved surface of the earth on a flat piece of paper. Yet the amount of information which can be obtained from good maps is amazing, and the variety of relationships which can be discovered is almost unbelievable. Geography is largely a story of distribution—the distribution of surface features, rainfall, natural resources, crops, people, trade routes, and many other things—all of which can be shown on maps. A physical-political map, for instance, shows the exact location of a country or continent, and its relative size in relation to other countries or continents. Distances can be determined by using the scale of miles. The coastline may indicate the presence or absence of harbors, and the depth of the waters, indicated by various shades of color, or lines which connect all places of similar depth, may suggest a continental shelf with the possibility of fishing. The elevation of the many kinds of surface is shown by color bands or contour lines and the legend. Several factors affect climate, but latitude and elevation, as shown on the physical-political map, give important clues as to the probable climate. The location of the cities and the railroad network gives information pertaining to the distribution of population. It is true, also, that inferences can be drawn from the physical-political map about the work activities of the people. If the land is level and the length of the growing season and amount of precipitation permit, agriculture will undoubtedly be carried on. If the land is hilly and the rainfall is light, the land will probably be used for grazing.

The Reading and Interpretation of Maps

The reading and interpretation of maps is the basis of all geography work, yet there is no part of the work less thoroughly done. As teachers of geography it is our job to teach the reading of maps so thoroughly that the pupils will be able to "look through" the map to the reality behind it. Map reading is what we do when we look at a map to find where a place is, the direction in which a river flows, or any other geographical fact. It is done to obtain information, but never as an end in itself. Map interpretation, however, is much more. Map interpretation is the process of making inferences and drawing conclusions about conditions because of facts shown on the map. Interpretation is "reading between the lines" to discover what meaning lies behind the symbols shown on the map.

When you read the map of Norway you may notice the high latitude, the irregular coastline with its chain of islands, the mountainous terrain, the few areas of lowland, and the scattered cities. A hasty interpretation of what you have read on the map might lead you to expect an uninviting frozen land. But after noting the course of the warm, North Atlantic Drift as it is shown on the same map, and having informed yourself about the latitude and direction of the westerly winds, you would be able to draw a conclusion regarding the possibility of farming in Norway. Since you know that latitude affects many things—the length of day, seasons, travel, clothing, food, the type of house that can be built—you are able to draw further conclusions about the activities of Norwegians. The irregular coast-line, the group of islands surrounded by a low continental shelf, and the meeting of a warm and a cold ocean current all indicate the presence of a good fishing ground. Fishing would add to the income of a Norwegian farmer who has difficulty earning a living on the small patches of level land available at the heads of the fiords. Constantly making and checking in-ferences and conclusions such as these leads to interesting, motivated study and research as the country is studied.

What should our objectives be for map reading and interpretation? How shall we reach them? We want our pupils (1) to be able to clearly visualize the landscape which any map and its symbols portray; (2) to be able to make inferences and draw conclusions on the basis of what they see on a map; (3) to be able to read relationships from a map; (4) to form the habit of consulting maps for information; and (5) to be able to place information obtained from statistics, field trips, and reference materials, on outline maps. These objectives are not easily reached, nor are they achieved automatically. They are the result of carefully planned and guided ex-periences, and the thorough teaching that we must carry on, day after day.

Maps are not self-revealing. We, as teachers, have much work to do to build the concepts which underlie each of the symbols on a map. We must remember that what is very simple or obvious to the experienced adult mind may present problems to a child who is learning to read a map. A child who has lived all of his life in Kansas will have difficulty picturing a seacoast unless he has been to the shore, and a child who has never been outside of Florida may not "see" mountains when he looks at the color bands on a map. The teacher must realize that map reading, like word reading, is not grasped during a single lesson or in a week or a year. It takes sustained effort on his part and constant reteaching for the mastery of this skill. Maps can only be interpreted by the child in relation to his past experiences. Consequently, we must plan experiences which will make the concept of each map symbol clear.

In teaching map symbols there are several points which should be remembered. Every symbol should be visualized by the pupils before it is used on a map. Visualization can be accomplished in several ways. These include taking field trips, studying pictures, making sketches, describing scenes, and constructing models in a sand pan. A large loaf-cake tin, ap-proximately nine inches by fifteen inches in size, will serve as a miniature sand table in which to model tributaries, capes, peninsulas, or other geographic features in sand or clay prior to introducing the map symbols. Remember that the pupils often do not learn what the teacher teaches. One device will help develop the concept for some, while other devices will be more effective with others.

After the concept has been introduced, preferably in more than one way, place the symbol (without a caption) on the outline map which is being used. If a caption is written near the symbol, the child is more likely to read the word than he is to "see" the landscape feature for which the symbol stands. In any event, be certain that the pupil has a mental image or concept of the geographic feature before he uses it on a map. This principle is applicable to pupils in all grades when we introduce new map concepts.

Semipictorial symbols should be presented before nonpictorial symbols. Semipictorial symbols are easier for children to visualize because they bear some resemblance to the landscape feature which they represent, such as an irregularly outlined spot for a lake, or a crooked line indicating a seacoast. Nonpictorial symbols are more difficult to read because they do not resemble what they represent. Color bands, the various shadings used in precipitation or crop distribution maps, and dots and other abstract symbols are nonpictorial.

Introduce map symbols only when they are needed. It is a waste of time and energy to do otherwise. Unless the symbol is associated with something definite, the meaning is soon forgotten and there is no learning. Learning takes place only when there is a need for the material to be learned. The map symbols introduced to the child should be those needed in developing a unit or some geographic concept. They should never be introduced in isolation from meaningful material.

The children should know the cardinal directions when they begin to read maps. The teaching of direction is done in the primary grades in connection with sun position, but there needs to be reteaching and practice of this skill in almost every grade.

Teaching Map Symbols

We take too much for granted when we teach children. We assume that they understand everything completely, long before they actually do. Consequently, we do not think that it is necessary to develop concepts step by step as we should. We often "tell" children rather than teach them, because "telling" takes less time, and we lack the ability to draw from the child the correct response through skillful questioning. However, all of the time spent in the thorough development of a concept will eventually pay dividends in the increased understanding gained by children and the skill with which they will be able to transfer their conceptual understanding to completely new situations, or to situations slightly similar to the original. This is especially true in the teaching of map symbols. How does one develop a concept for a map symbol? For instance, how does one develop the concept that a dot is used to represent a city on a map? Should one take for granted that every child knows that a dot represents a city, or should some time be spent to be sure that the symbol "makes sense?"

Certainly, the time required to develop the concept is well spent. It could be developed in the manner described below.

"In our story today we read that Tom lived in a city. We all know what a city is, don't we? We are familiar with houses, streets, automobiles, and stores. What do you see in this picture of a city, something we haven't mentioned?" Teacher shows several pictures which show factories, taxis, buses, and nighttime views of the city. "The city looks very different at night, doesn't it? What other differences can you point out among these pictures? *Some of the pictures were taken at street level and some from tall buildings.* From where do you think this picture was taken?" Teacher shows an aerial photograph. "How does this view of the city differ from the others? *You can see more of the city. The houses and buildings are much smaller. Some of the parks and other open spaces may be seen, and streets look like lines.*

The pilot of the airplane could see the whole city, couldn't he? How would an astronaut's view of the city be different from this one? It would appear much smaller and would seem to be just a spot, wouldn't it? The spot might not be exactly round. All cities differ in shape to some extent. Our map makers decided that the symbol would be a round spot because that is how a city would look from a great height. The city symbol on a map is, therefore, a dot or circle. Some of our maps try to show the population of the city by making the spots in a variety of shapes, but you and I will just make a dot as nearly round as we can when we locate a city on our outline maps."

Map concepts like these, and the discovery of many relationships, should be a part of every lesson until pupils form the habit of searching the maps for facts and relationships to answer their questions and to solve problems.

Teaching the Scale of Miles

Sometimes it is necessary to take more than one class period to prepare the pupil's mind for the concept you wish to introduce. This is true when the concept of the scale of miles is developed. One way to introduce the concept is described below.

"Let's draw a plan of our classroom today. John, measure the length of our room with the yardstick, and Don, please measure the width. What did you find the length to be, John? *Thirty feet.* And Don, what was the width? *Twenty-four feet.*

Of course, I don't have a place large enough where I could draw a plan of our room using the actual dimensions, do I? If I wanted to draw the plan on the board, how could I manage to reduce its size and still be sure that I would draw it in the right proportions?" Discuss the various possibilities. "Yes, we could use a smaller unit of measure to represent each large unit of measure. We stated the dimensions of the room in feet, didn't we? Now, suppose that we let one inch represent each foot of length and width. Fred, how long will the line have to be to represent the length of the room if we do let one inch represent each foot of actual length? *Thirty inches.* Our scale, or representation of measurement, then, is one inch to one foot. We can write this scale in this manner: one inch to one foot. How wide will our plan or drawing have to be if one inch is used to represent each of the twenty-four feet that the room is wide? *Twenty-four inches.* Fred, will you make a drawing of our room thirty inches by twenty-four inches? Put the scale, 1 inch to 1 foot, under the drawing. This label helps us to remember how we have gone about reducing the actual size of our room to a smaller size.

Suppose that I want to draw a plan of our room on an ordinary piece of drawing paper instead of on the board. I would have to make it still smaller, wouldn't I? How could I change the scale? *Let one-half inch represent one foot.* How many half inches would I need to show the thirty foot length of our room? *Thirty half-inches.* And how many inches would that make since it takes two half-inches to make one inch? *Fifteen inches.* How many half inches would I need to show the width?" *Twenty-four half-inches.* "How many inches would that be? Now, let's draw this smaller plan. We'll be sure to put the scale of our plan under the drawing. What will it be? ½ *inch to 1 foot.*

Let's measure the tops of our desks and draw rectangles to represent them. Be sure to put the scale underneath the drawing." Have the children measure the tops of several things, such as tables, benches, boxes, and books, and draw them to scale.

The next day have two outline maps of different sizes, representing your state, on the board. The larger map should be larger than a route or road map. The second one should be much smaller. On each map place a dot to represent the location of the city in or near which they live.

"How many of you have visited _____ (a familiar city at least fifty miles away)? How far away is it?" Have the pupils give the approximate mileage distance in round numbers.

The teacher places the dot showing the location of the city. With a tape or string, he measures the distance between the home city and the distant city. Then he shows the pupils the measurement on the tape.

"The distance between our city and _____ is fifty miles. This much of the tape represents fifty miles. Let's draw a line under the map to represent this distance. We will make it the same length as the portion of the tape we have used to reach from city to city. Because this line represents miles, we shall call this line under our map the 'scale of miles.' Draw a line as long as needed to show the fifty miles. Under it label the line, SCALE OF MILES.

"Now, let's see what our scale of miles will be on this smaller map." Place the dots on the smaller map in the same manner in which they were placed on the larger map. While the pupils watch, measure the distance between the two cities with the tape or string. With the tape still in his hands, the teacher shows how much of the tape represents the distance between the two cities on the smaller map. Then the scale of miles is placed below the map and labelled. If the line is too long to be practical, use half of it to represent half the distance.

"Every good map has a scale of miles. Why are the scales of miles different on the two maps? The scales of miles will vary because our maps are of different sizes."

When measuring distances on a wall map or on a map in a textbook, instruct the children to use a strip of paper or the edge of a sheet of paper. Mark the location of the two places on the paper with pencil and then take the paper to the scale of miles to find the distance. It is difficult to measure the distances with a pencil or ruler because the roll made by the binding of the book at the inner margin will cause inaccuracies. This skill should be practiced as often as the opportunity arises in the intermediate grades.

Kinds of Maps

There are hundreds of different maps available in a variety of projections. Not all of these are suitable for use with the pupils of the elementary school. The maps most commonly found in the elementary classrooms are the political, the physical-political, and various types of distribution maps. Purely political maps which show the locations of cities and political divisions in a variety of colors are of little value in the teaching of geography. The ideal geographical map for the classroom is one which shows related cultural and environmental features, the physical-political map. This is the type which teaches. The relationships are there if the reader of the map has the ability to discover them.

DISTRIBUTION MAPS   Some classroom wall maps are distribution maps. These maps are also found in the pupils' textbooks. They are of two principal kinds, those that are shaded in various intensities of one or more colors, and the "dot" maps. The rainfall, growing season, land use, and some crop maps fall under the first classification. These maps are difficult for pupils to make because the lines of demarcation are not always definite. In any case, having pupils make such a map would be a matter of copying, which is of little value unless the map is to be used for a definite purpose and the copying is not an end in itself. However, through careful development of the concepts related to these maps, the pupils can easily acquire the ability to interpret the shaded distribution.

Pupils in the fifth sequence will come across dot maps in their textbooks. Their meaning should be carefully explained, and later on dot maps can be made by the children. Dot maps are very informative, and teaching pupils how to make them places another important geographic tool in their hands. With statistics or reference material they can make maps which illustrate a point they wish to make in their problem solving.

The concept of the dot distribution map is one which requires thorough, step-by-step development. Remember to hang new knowledge on old pegs of learning and experience. The development of the dot distribution map concept might proceed in the following manner:

"Let's make a floor plan of a school." Use the children's own school as a model, if the floor plan of it lends itself to this purpose easily. "On our plan, let's show the number of children in each room."

The teacher draws a plan showing the several school rooms. He then tries to put the required number of stick figures in each room—one to represent each child—and shows how impossible it is to do this. Then he draws a similar plan of the school and says:

"Perhaps if I just draw a tiny circle to represent the head of each child I might be able to put the right number of people in each room."

He then draws another plan with the same arrangement of rooms and similar in size to one which could be placed on an ordinary sheet of drawing paper.

"What could we do if we found that the right number of circles could not be placed in this small plan? Has anyone an idea? *A dot, rather than a circle, might be used to represent each person.* Now, that really works, doesn't it? How many dots would I have to place in this room if I let one dot represent two people? If we let the dot represent more than one person, we want to be sure to explain what we have done in a key. Keys unlock doors, don't they? This key will unlock the meaning of the map by telling us the meaning of a dot. We shall place a key under the plan."

For the next lesson, draw several hypothetical counties on the board (see Figure 11) and place numbers in them to represent the number of inhabitants. All of the numbers should be divisible by ten. Ask the pupils to tell you how many dots would be needed in each county to represent the population if each dot represented one hundred people.

Next, change the numbers to provide further drill, using rounded

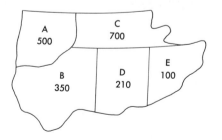

Figure 11

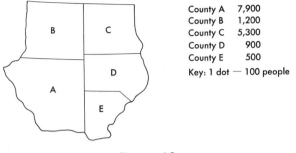

County A   7,900
County B   1,200
County C   5,300
County D   900
County E   500
Key: 1 dot — 100 people

Figure 12

numbers and arranging them in columns. Ask the pupils to estimate the number of dots needed if each dot represents 100 people. (See Figure 12.)

Be certain to arrange the rounded numbers in order of size, since it will make estimating the number of dots required much easier and help to show the pupils the logic in our number system.

Additional drill may be provided by using population figures for the New England States, changing the key, as indicated in the example listed below:

Population of New England States in Rounded Numbers[1]

Massachusetts	5,300,000
Connecticut	2,500,000
Maine	1,000,000
Rhode Island	900,000
New Hampshire	600,000
Vermont	400,000

Key: 1 dot represents 100,000 people

[1] Population figures are from the 1960 census, rounded from the actual figures given in the 1966 edition of *The World Almanac* (New York, The New York World-Telegram and Sun).

Vermont is shown as having a population, in round numbers, of 400,000 people. Ask the pupils, "If one dot represents 100,000 people, how many dots will be needed to show the population of Vermont? New Hampshire? Rhode Island?" Give plenty of drill to make sure that every child is able to do the simple arithmetic necessary to determine the number of dots for the distribution map. The children will now be ready to make distribution maps of the New England States. Before they begin to work, point out to them the following criteria for making a good distribution map.

1. The map must have a meaningful title.
2. Show only one thing on the map, that which is mentioned in the title.
3. The shape and size of the country, state, or region, should be accurate.
4. The dots should all be made the same size and color.
5. The dots should be scattered evenly in the area, unless exact areas of concentration in the distribution are known.
6. The map must have a scale of miles and a key.
7. Two parallels must be indicated inside the margin, in the case of fifth sequence work. The distance between the two parallels will determine the scale of miles. Each degree of latitude is approximately seventy miles. If the distance between the parallels represents five degrees, then a line as long as that distance will represent 5 × 70 miles, or 350 miles. If the map is being made by a pupil in the sixth sequence, then meridians should also be indicated.
8. The source of the data used to make the map should be neatly printed at the bottom of the map near the margin.
9. If two separate dot distribution maps are used to compare the production of two different crops in a country or region, be sure that the key is the same on both maps.

It is altogether possible for pupils to make maps and not know the meaning of what they have shown on them unless the teacher insists upon having an interpretation written under the map. In this statement the pupils point out existing conditions portrayed and account for them. The interpretation requires additional study of the map and often sends the pupils to other maps to find reasons for the distribution made on their maps.

THE OUTLINE MAP   The outline map is probably the most frequently used and abused of all maps. Making maps can certainly be a waste of time if no worthwhile purpose is served. We should, therefore, never give a pupil map work unless he will profit from it. Having a pupil simply copy an existing map has very little teaching or learning value. Instead, give the pupil statistics or other data and allow him to picture the information or relationship on a map.

It is far better to use a prepared outline map than to spend time trying to draw one which will give inaccurate concepts because of its imperfections. Outline maps are time savers and can be used in all parts of the lesson to show geographic facts and relationships, or to apply learned facts. Prepared outline maps are inexpensive when they are purchased in quantity from commercial map companies. If budget limitations make it impractical to purchase commercially prepared outline maps, they can also be carefully traced from an atlas by the teacher and duplicated for class use.

A map should never be overloaded with detail. The simpler and more direct it is, the better does it serve its purpose. It should be remembered that each map is made for the specific purpose which appears in its title and that only information which pertains to that title should be shown.

The value of the map is increased immeasurably if an interpretation is added. Teachers should always remember that no useful purpose is ever served by accepting poorly done work in map making. The quality of work we get from the pupils is directly related to the standards which we set as teachers. Accepting less than the best work that the child is capable of doing is poor educational practice, indeed.

Several reliable sources for statistical material which may be used for maps are listed below.

Commodity Yearbook, Commodity Research Bureau, Inc., 82 Beaver Street, New York 5, New York.
Statistical Yearbook, New York, United Nations Publishing Service.
The Statesman's Year-Book, London, Macmillan & Co. Ltd.
Yearbook of Agriculture, Washington, U.S. Government Printing Office.
Agricultural Statistics, Washington, U.S. Government Printing Office.
Statistical Abstract of the United States, Washingon, Supt. of Documents.
The World Almanac and Book of Facts, New York, The New York World-Telegram and Sun.
Richard M. Highsmith, Jr., and J. Granville Jensen, *Geography of Commodity Production,* Philadelphia, J. B. Lippincott Company, 1963.
Foreign Agriculture Circular (monthly), Washington, U.S. Government Printing Office.

The reference section of any reasonably good library will provide sources of statistics. The most up-to-date statistics will be for a year or two preceding the current year. This is understandable because of the difficulty in securing accurate information, and the time it takes to collect the data. *The Statesman's Year-Book for 1966–67,* for instance, contains statistics for 1964–65, and many of them are of necessity estimated. Census figures, if they are accurate and not based upon estimate, are usually for the year marking a change of decade (1950, 1960, 1970). Census figures for the intervening years must be estimated in most cases. It is wise, in recording statistics for the use of your pupils, to make certain that you have recorded the world total for the crop or product, as is done in the tables found at the end of this text.

SKETCH MAPS   Sketch maps are free-hand maps drawn quickly on the chalk board to present geographic ideas, facts, and relationships clearly and forcefully without striving for accuracy. They are of value because they help the pupil understand what the teacher is trying to explain to him. The value of illustrating the topic being discussed is great. A few lines sketched on the board will often clarify a point more quickly than a long, oral description. The sketch map helps the child to visualize the geographic pattern and the relationships associated with it. The presentation of the sketch map is rapid and holds the attention of the pupils.

Why are such maps not used more often? Perhaps the outstanding reason is that the teacher feels that drawing ability is needed, or that he will not be able to sketch the map with great accuracy. This fact should not disturb him because the pupils are more interested in the point he is trying to illustrate than in the accuracy of the sketch map he is drawing. The map can be quickly erased after the explanation is over, and there is little likelihood that inaccurate concepts of shape will be retained.

PICTORIAL MAPS   Pictorial maps are decorative, but often accuracy is sacrificed, and many misconceptions on the part of the pupils result. Many times, the size of the symbol is out of proportion to the importance of the product. Often the symbol covers too great an area and creates the impression that this particular product is the only one grown in the area where the symbol is placed. Teachers should not take for granted the accuracy of every printed map. They should carefully check for inaccuracies in any pictorial maps which the pupils are likely to find in their textbooks or reference books. If some inaccuracies do occur, have the pupils try to find them. This will test their power of observation as well as their knowledge of the subject.

ROUTE OR ROAD MAPS   Road maps can perform a great service in the study of geography. Many adults have difficulty in reading them and so it is obvious that road maps, with their multiplicity of symbols, cannot be thrust upon young pupils without explanation.

The first step toward understanding them can be taken in the primary sequence when the pupils make their first basic maps in the map readiness program. (See page 123.) By the time the pupils reach the sixth sequence, many of them will be able to read the symbols on the road map and understand their meaning.

One of the interesting ways to study the home state is to travel vicariously along the most important routes crossing the state, stopping to "see" interesting places along the way. Study the reasons for the importance of large cities on the routes as you come to them, and learn about the leading industries in them. When an important agricultural center is reached, take time to discuss why an agricultural center is necessary, the type of agriculture in the region and how it compares with other agricultural regions in the state. There will be plenty of interest in this type of study because it is a life situation and because the children will often be talking about places which they have visited or with which they are otherwise familiar.

Introducing the Concept of Elevation

The concept of elevation is introduced in the third or fourth sequence. It should be developed before the first physical-political wall map is used to any extent. Units on any of the mountainous countries can be used as vehicles for teaching an understanding of the different kinds of surface and developing the concept of how elevation affects the activities of man. The study of Switzerland will provide many opportunities to develop and enlarge this concept.

Introductory Lesson on Elevation

To make meaningful the word "surface" as it relates to geography, take the pupils on a short trip near the school building to observe the kinds of surface in the immediate area, or make use of carefully selected pictures.

MOTIVATION

"How many of you live where the land is flat? Do any of you live on hilly land? There are several kinds of land (surface) in this world of ours." The words "surface" and "land" should be used interchangeably. "We have named two kinds, hilly and flat. Let's go on an exploring trip (in the neighborhood of the school or by means of pictures) to see how many kinds of surface we can see. Perhaps we shall discover how people use these kinds of surface." Talk about the various uses made of the land.

DEVELOPMENT

After returning to the classroom (or concluding the examination of the pictures), discuss what you have observed. The discussion which follows is based upon a field trip near the school.

"On what kind of surface is our school built? What kind of surface could we see in the distance? On which kind of surface did we see more houses? When would it be an advantage to live on hilly land? When would it be a disadvantage? On which kind of surface would it be easier to build roads? Why? How does where you live affect what you do? *If you live on hilly ground in an area where there is snow in the winter, you can sled, and so on.* During which season of the year is this more noticeable? Several of you live on flat land. What are the advantages and disadvantages of living there? How do people use the land around your home? How do people in the cities use flat land? How would flat land in the country be used? How many of you have seen mountains?"

Show the class several pictures of mountains. "How do mountains differ from hills? *They are higher and they have steeper slopes.*

We have talked about two kinds of surface, the flat land or plains, and mountains."

The teacher then draws a sea-level line and above it sketches plains and mountains, placing the appropriate label above each. (See Figure 13.)

Figure 13

"There is another kind of surface which is higher than the plains but not so high as the mountains. This kind of surface is called a "plateau." Plateaus can be rather flat on top, but often they are worn down by rain, wind, and rivers into hills. Look at this picture and see how the land or surface differs from mountains or plains. Now, let's fill in our sketch so that we can show the three chief kinds of surface." (See Figure 14.)

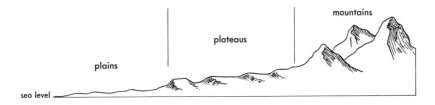

Figure 14

"Let us see if we can model these three kinds of surface in a sand table or sand pan." Sand or clay can be used. "See if you can match the pictures of the different kinds of surface with the model we have made." If no sand table or sand pan is available, have the children match the pictures with the type of surface shown in the simple profile sketched on the chalk board.

SUMMARY

Ask short questions about the work covered. "What three kinds of surface have we talked about? How do people use plains in the country? In the city? Would our lives be different if we lived on mountains (plains)? Would they be different if we lived in a city with (no) hills? How many of you have seen or visited land similar to the land shown in these pictures?" Show three or four pictures of the types of surface discussed.

APPLICATION

Have the children turn to a few pictures in the textbook which have been selected by the teacher, asking them to identify by name the type of surface shown.

Developing the Concept of How Elevation Affects People

TEACHER PREPARATION

With an opaque or overhead projector make an outline map of Switzerland on the board or on wrapping paper. Put in a few lines to suggest the steep slopes of the Alps with brown chalk. Color the Swiss Plateau with a few strokes of orange chalk. (See Figure 15.) We want the pupils to associate the type of surface with the color which they will later see on the physical-political map.

Make a simple profile of Switzerland on wrapping paper or on the board, as long as the outline map of Switzerland is wide. The purpose of the profile is to give the pupils a general idea as to the relative heights and the proportion of the natural regions in Switzerland, and to help them identify these regions in pictures which the teacher will show them. (See The Making of Profiles, page 93.)

On a cookie tin, model the Alps, the Swiss Plateau and the Jura Mountains out of clay. More than half of the model should show high mountains (three-fifths, to be exact). These mountains would be about two and one-half inches high if made to the scale ¼ inch represents 1,000 feet in elevation. The plateau should be rolling land, and the Juras rounded hills. Spray a few of the peaks with a commercial spray cleaner, such as Bon Ami, or white paint to give reality to the model. Between some of the "snow" covered peaks place crushed tissue paper to represent glaciers. Here is an opportunity to show the pupils one way in which rivers originate.

Another simple device for showing the surface of Switzerland is to crumple heavy brown wrapping paper into the different natural regions and attach it with paste to a cardboard base so that the wrinkled mountain forms will not spread apart.

MOTIVATION

"Yesterday we talked about the different kinds of land which can be found on the surface of the earth. What were they? We also talked about how the surface affected the people living on it. Do you remember when we studied

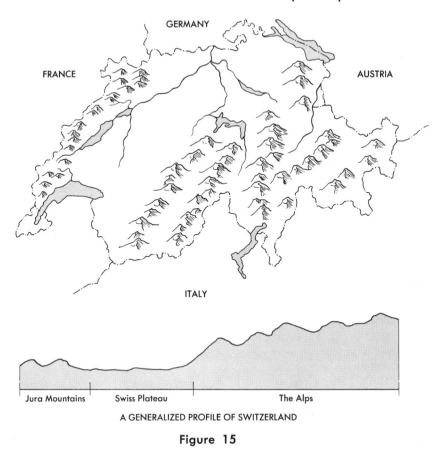

A GENERALIZED PROFILE OF SWITZERLAND

Figure 15

about the people who lived in the rain forest? We learned that water did not drain off flat land very easily. Consequently, the people who lived in the rain forest built their homes very differently from ours. Why were some houses built on posts? The rivers were rather lazy rivers, too. They moved slowly and in wide curves. After the land was cleared the flat land wasn't very difficult to work. I'm sure that you remember the stories about how people lived on the flat land near the equator.

Today you and I are going to take a make-believe journey to a mountainous country to see how people live there. We shall take a jet and fly over the ocean to a little country called Switzerland."

Teacher points out the location of Switzerland on the globe and marks it with chalk or clay. Mark the approximate location of the home town, also. Simulate the journey by means of holding a tiny airplane and moving it slowly toward Europe, asking the children what you might see as you fly over the ocean, and so on.

"Have any of you heard anything about Switzerland? *It has mountains, winter sports, and lakes. They make watches and many beautiful carved articles, and so forth.* I wonder how the mountainous surface has affected the lives of the people." This could be the problem set up for the entire unit.

DEVELOPMENT

"Let's pretend that we are flying over these very high mountains and are looking down out of the plane." Show the children the previously prepared clay model made on the cookie sheet or in a large cake tin. "This is the way the land would look to us. These are the very high mountains called the *Alps*. Here is a picture of the Alps. Notice how pointed some of these peaks are. Some of them have snow on them even in the summer time. Why doesn't the snow melt? Yes, the higher you climb, the colder the air is. Notice this river of ice between the mountains. This is a glacier. Sometimes the heavy snows of winter pack in the valleys between the mountains and become ice, and a glacier is formed. Notice this land at the foot of the Alps." Show the model again. "This is the Swiss Plateau. It is not so high as the mountains and it is fairly level. How would you think this land might be used? Which of these two pictures do you think was taken on the Swiss Plateau?" Show pictures of the Jura Mountains and the Swiss Plateau. "Now, we have one more surface region in Switzerland. If we were flying northwest over the Swiss Plateau we would soon see the Jura Mountains. Look at this picture again. These mountains seem very low and rounded after seeing the Alps. Now, let's see if we can see these three regions in our model.

Look, also, at this sketch of the three natural regions of Switzerland." Show the simple generalized profile, Figure 15. "What is the high land called? Place this picture on this sketch where it belongs. What are these rounded hills called? Place the picture of the Swiss Plateau where it belongs." Allow several children to place pictures on the sketch.

Applying the Concept of Elevation to the Map

"This is a large map of Switzerland. On the globe we saw that Switzerland is a small country surrounded by larger countries. Notice the countries which are close neighbors: France, Italy, Austria, Germany, and a tiny one called Liechtenstein." Teacher traces boundary, a broken line — .. — .. —, between countries. "Show us in what part of Switzerland we might find the Alps. Place the picture of the Alps where you think the picture might have been taken." If possible, the simple profile should be large enough to be placed below the map so that there will be a clearer concept of elevation. "On our sketch of the surface we see the Swiss Plateau between the Alps and Jura Mountains. Let's find these regions on our map. The mountainous regions are colored lightly with brown. This does not mean, however, that all places in that region are the same height. There are wide valleys in some places. The plateau is colored lightly with orange chalk. This land is rolling land in some places, and rather flat in other places. The colors are there to give us a general idea of the surface of the region. Now, see if you can match each picture with the surface region on the map.

We have been in our jet for some time while we were getting acquainted with the surface of Switzerland. Let's land and get to know some of the people and find out how they live in these different parts of Switzerland. Listen to this interesting story and see if you can tell just where these people live, what their work is, and how they have fun."

Two excellent books which describe life in the highland pastures, lower mountain valleys, and the plateau are *An Ear for Uncle Emil*, by Eva (Roe) Gaggin and *Heidi*, by Johanna Spyri. As you read these, or other stories, try to emphasize the beauty of the region, how the work of the people is related to the temperature, the amount of rain and snow, the crops grown, and the type of homes which are built. All of these are related to elevation.

SUMMARY

Through a review of the story and the regions on the map and the sketch of the surface regions, check to see if all of the children have the correct concept of surface and its effect upon people.

The foregoing lesson has introduced the concept of elevation and has shown the pupils that elevation does affect the lives of people who live in Switzerland. Further study of Switzerland's transportation, agriculture, dairying, hydroelectric power, tourism, and the development of a high degree of technical skill among the Swiss people, will strengthen and expand the concept. Be certain to further enlarge upon it whenever the opportunity arises in the study of other regions and countries.

The Making of Profiles

Landscapes on maps can be more easily visualized and the relationship of human activity to elevation can be more readily understood if the pupil can draw profiles and interpret them. Usually, the making of profiles is taught in the sixth sequence, but teachers of the fourth and fifth sequences need to become proficient in sketching profiles easily and quickly so that they may be used when they wish to illustrate elevation or explain the relationship between man's activities and elevation. The sketching of profiles is another way to present the concept of elevation. It often has more meaning for the pupil than the colors on the relief map.

One great difficulty in drawing accurate profiles is the necessity for using two scales, a horizontal one for the base, and a vertical one for elevation. Obviously, a young pupil would not be able to do this. However, this difficulty need not deter the teacher from using this valuable aid in developing the concept of elevation and the ability to read and interpret maps. Any pupil who can transpose what he reads on the physical-political map to the graphic form of a profile can really read and "see" landscapes on the map.

As we all know, children have to be taught step by step when we are developing a new concept with them. Consequently, in the development of the profile we have to sacrifice some degree of accuracy until the skill is acquired. With the first profiles the children draw, the lines of the vertical scale will need to be far apart and represent fairly large ranges of elevation. As the skill of the pupils increases, however, the vertical scale of the profile can be greatly reduced.

Teaching the Drawing of a Profile

PREPARATION

On a cookie sheet mold some mountains, plateaus, and plains with clay. Slice through this model with a knife so that a "side view" is obtained containing all three types of surface. Press the model together again lightly so that it will be ready to pull apart when you wish to use it to demonstrate the meaning of a geographic profile. (See Figure 16.)

SKETCH OF CLAY MODEL

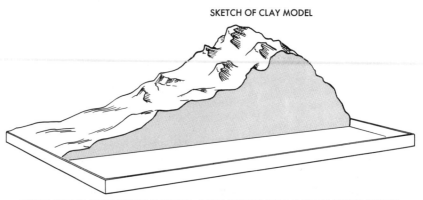

SHOWING PART OF THE MODEL REMOVED AFTER CUTTING WITH KNIFE TO REVEAL PROFILE

Figure 16

MOTIVATION

Discuss the meaning of the word "profile." Usually the pupils will think of a side view photograph or a silhouette. If so, mention that in a profile photograph of a person, the shape of the nose, lips, forehead, and chin seem to stand out. Point out that we also have profiles in geography.

Take the clay model and point out the three different kinds of surface. Cut it and explain that a profile will look like the flat or sliced side of these mountains, plateaus, and plains.

DEVELOPMENT

Call attention to the fact that a geographic profile shows the elevation or height of land. Ask: "If we wanted to draw a profile of the land, where would we be able to find what the different elevations of the land were?" *Atlases, physical-political, and physical maps.*

Ask the pupils to turn to a physical-political map in their textbooks. Ask them how they are able to tell what the elevation of the land is. Be sure to point out the size of the color steps which show elevation. The color steps may represent 0 feet to 500 feet, 500 to 1,000 feet, 1,000 to 2,000 feet, or 2,000 to 5,000 feet, all on the same map. The steps in a profile, like those on the physical-political map, must all be the same width, but the space between the lines on the profile may represent 500, 1,000, or 2,000 feet. Emphasize this point because the profile will not be an accurate representation of elevation if one space represents 500 feet and the one above it represents 1,000 feet. The pupils will need help at first in reading the elevation on the map. They must be made aware of the fact that not all of the land shown in the same color is the same height throughout, something which they may already have learned in their study of elevation.

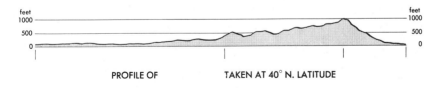

PROFILE OF   TAKEN AT 40° N. LATITUDE

Figure 17

For the first profile, which the teacher will draw on the board so that the pupils will understand the procedure, select a region which has only two steps in elevation, sea level to 500 feet, and 500 feet to 1,000 feet. Profiles may be taken from any direction on the physical-political map. Decide upon the place where the profile is to be taken. If possible, take the profile along a parallel shown on the map. It is so much easier for the children to follow. Have the pupils trace the surface along the parallel of latitude with their fingers and then read the surface in feet above sea level as they trace the parallel again. Pupils will need practice in reading elevation. The initial practice should be under the close supervision of the teacher. Decide on how many lines will be needed to show the surface elevation of this country. (One line at sea level; one at 500 feet, and one at 1,000 feet.) Draw the sea-level line and two others. Be sure that they are the same distance apart. On the first profile made, let one-eighth inch represent 500 feet in elevation. Later on, one-eighth inch can represent 1,000 feet, and, finally, 2,000 feet as skill is gained. Number the lines at both ends with the appropriate elevation figures. (See Figure 17.)

Now you are ready for the "pegging-down" points. Remind the children that a tent is pegged down to hold it in place. Pegging-down points in the profile help to keep it in the correct proportion. The pegging-down points may mark a change in the type of surface, a city, a river, or some other landmark. Say, "This river may cross the parallel about one-third of the distance across the profile. We place a dot on the sea level line one-third of the distance along it toward the west. When we reach the dot, we should be at the river as we draw." The pupils will need help in deciding what to use for pegging-down points for several of the early profiles which they draw. They will not all choose the same things for these points, but accept them as long as they are consistent. There should be several pegging-down points on the sea level line.

Now sketch in the line to show the surface. Trace the surface with your left forefinger on the map as you draw so that you will not lose your place. In drawing plains, suggest to the pupils that they make the land profile gently rolling, sloping gradually to the next elevation shown by a different color. There are very few plains in the world where the land is really flat. Fill in the profile with chalk so that the pupils can see how the land looks in a profile or side view. Beneath the profile write the latitude at which it was taken and place an appropriate title above it.

You are now ready to go through the same procedure with the pupils as they draw a profile. Choose a country or region which has just two types of surface for the first of these pupil-drawn profiles, and carefully follow these steps:

1. Read the elevation on the map.
2. Decide on the number of lines needed in the profile.
3. Draw the sea level line and the lines needed to show the elevation.
4. Place the appropriate elevation figures at both ends of the lines.
5. Decide upon pegging-down points.
6. Draw the line which represents the surface, following along the physical-political map with your finger so that you do not lose your place.
7. Fill in the profile with color or lightly shaded pencil.
8. Beneath the profile print the latitude at which the profile was taken. Above it, print an appropriate title.

After the profile is finished, use it in some way. Above it, at the correct locations, you might ask the pupils to list the products produced in the different parts of the country, or the industries carried on along the latitude at which the profile is taken. Some of the pupils will have enough artistic ability to enable them to draw sketches of portions of the country represented at different points along the profile. These can be mounted at the correct places above the profile to show what the country looks like, or the activities of the people living there.

6

Make maps indispensable, continued

The Use of Maps

Someone has said that maps are the most important shorthand picture of man's accumulated geographic knowledge. If this is true, we want to provide our pupils access to that knowledge by using maps whenever the opportunity arises, remembering that "accumulated geographic knowledge" includes both the cultural and the physical landscapes. Maps can be used effectively in each part of the lesson or unit. In fact, the complete development of a unit of subject matter can be based upon maps. Maps may be used in the motivation, development, summary, application, and testing steps of the unit.

MOTIVATION

It is a good plan to use maps in the motivation portion of the unit to help orient the pupils to the region which they are to study. Pupils cannot ask questions about a portion of the world with which they are unacquainted and about which they know nothing. A short map study, planned as a part of the motivation, will often present natural and cultural facts and relationships which will not only help acquaint the pupils with the region to be studied, but may also arouse their curiosity.

Often during the motivation, problems may be raised as a result of reading unusual or surprising facts from a map. For instance, with the population explosion a reality, how can sparsely settled lands be made habitable? To answer this question, pupils would need to study and synchronize the population map with the physical-political, rainfall, and length of growing season maps. They would then be encouraged to draw inferences as to how man might be able to adapt the physical conditions of the sparsely settled lands being studied to his needs. Remember that our pupils cannot learn to think unless we require it. Ask questions about maps which require interpretive use of the facts shown. Help them to recall geographic concepts previously learned so that they can apply them to the problem being discussed. Each time they are led, step by step, by the teacher to reach a conclusion they are becoming more familiar with the thinking process.

Another motivating question which might result from a study of maps, or which might be used to lead the pupils to study maps could be, "Why is the water supply a problem in almost every part of the world? Man often has too much or too little water, depending upon where he lives. How can he maintain, control, or improve his water resources?" Pupils of the fifth through eighth sequences, in studying about water problems in their own areas, would need to answer the following questions:

- Where do we obtain our water supply? *Rivers, springs, wells, lakes, reservoirs, rain, melting snow.*
- What factors determine the amount of rainfall in our region? *Latitude, elevation, mountain barriers, winds, condensation, and evaporation rates.*
- How does the topography of the land influence the source and amount of available water? *Topography determines the rate of flow of rivers and streams, and whether or not it is possible to build dams and reservoirs on them. It also determines whether flood control will be necessary.* Would flood control dams interfere with commercial navigation, if production in the surrounding area makes water transportation necessary?

A study of many different kinds of maps will help the pupils answer these and related questions.

The use of maps would be necessary in answering a motivating question such as this: Of what value is our fourth seacoast, the Great Lakes and St. Lawrence Seaway? To thoroughly study this timely question pupils would be required to study not only the physical conditions indicated by the physical-political, rainfall, land use, and population distribution maps, but they would also have to consider man's cultural environment in the area,—his port facilities and their limitations, the cultural and ethnic differences of the people along the seaway on both the Canadian and American sides, and the effect of the short growing season and short shipping season on the mines, farms, and factories in the hinterlands. Maps of these hinterlands along the Fourth Seacoast would have to be studied as well as maps of the land immediately adjacent to the seaway.

In the motivation for the study of Norway, the teacher might say:

"Over seventy per cent of Norway is wasteland; that is, it is not used in production of any kind. How do the three and one-half million inhabitants of the country make a living? Let us turn to our physical-political map and see if we can find a partial answer to our question. Note the areas of lowland scattered along the coast and in the southern part of Norway. For what might these lowlands be used? *Farming.* In order to answer this question we will have to consult other kinds of maps. We will look at rainfall maps, land use maps, and population distribution maps.

On our physical-political map, notice the mountainous land, the rugged coastline, the fiords, the skerry-guard, and the continental shelf which surrounds the Lofoten Islands."

Have the pupils draw inferences as to what industries these physical features and conditions would encourage. One such inference should be about the fishing industry. Another should deal with the canning of fish. These inferences should be listed on the board as the pupils give them. Even though some of the inferences drawn by the pupils are not logical, they should remain on the board with the others until the pupils are able to rule them out as possibilities.

"What would you expect the climate of a country in this latitude would be like? *Cold, forbidding.* What can you see on this rainfall map which might make you question the statement made about climatic conditions in Norway? *The map should show the distribution of rainfall and the direction of ocean currents.* What are the prevailing winds in this part of the world? If these winds blow over a warm current of water (North Atlantic Drift), what effect will they have on the coast of Norway? *They will cause heavy rainfall on the west side of the mountains. Warmth brought by westerly winds will keep many harbors ice-free.* What kind of work would people do in the port cities of Tromso, Narvik, and Hammerfest? Draw inferences from the location of these cities on the physical-political map. With the mountainous terrain and heavy rainfall, what natural resource will Norway have? *Potential hydro-electric power.* What use will the people make of it?"

The pupils will discover many puzzling relationships on physical-political, length of growing season, rainfall, mineral, and land use maps to further motivate their work. The development of the unit will be to check the inferences made from the maps with other geographic sources, such as textbooks, pictures, encyclopedias, and other reference books and stories.

Another interesting way to motivate and develop a unit through maps is by planning a trip of considerable length, transcontinental in the fifth sequence, an air trip to Latin America or extended vacation trip through Europe for other sequences. In the fifth sequence, each child would have his own outline map of the United States on which to plot his trip each day. Use a large wall map of the United States for class work. Have the children plan the route over which they would travel. Ask them to decide which cities they would like to visit, and suggest interesting places en route which they might see, but be careful not to over-emphasize the unusual, such as National Parks. Make the trip as real as possible by planning and making preparations as though it were an actual trip.

In the fifth sequence have the class decide upon a coastal city from which to begin the trip. Throughout the trip place emphasis on the character of the country through which the pupils will "travel." Discuss the use of the land, the industries which could be seen in cities, and interesting places en route. This requires a detailed study of physical-political, precipitation, length of growing season, population, and highway maps. Try to have pictures of the different areas traversed which can be placed on the wall map so that the children will have mental images of them. The children will enjoy this vicarious experience, not only because it is an exciting life situation, but because they will be discovering things for themselves. We know that the ability of pupils to obtain information from maps will increase with practice. A unit such as this one provides the daily application which the children must have in order to improve their map interpretation skills.

DEVELOPMENT

During this part of the unit, maps should be in constant use. In the search for information, it will often be necessary to synchronize the study of several maps in order to solve problems. The motivating problem or question in the study of Africa might be, "How can the new nations of Africa deal with the geographic factors which have helped or hindered their march toward modernization?" Let us consider how the development of a unit having this motivating question might proceed through the synchronized study of maps.

"Let us study the physical-political map to discover which geographic factors have helped and which have hindered the developing new nations of Africa. What is the nature of the coast line of Africa? *Regular, with few good, natural harbors.* Compare Africa's coastline with that of Europe." *Use world map.* "How would this lack of good, natural harbors affect those new African countries which have coastlines? *Several of these countries would need to build deep harbors in order to encourage trade with countries who might desire to purchase their products.* Most of Africa has what kind of surface? Notice the narrow coastal plains. Most of the surface of Africa ranges from 2,000 to 4,000 feet in elevation. How will this type of surface affect Africa? *The land will be hilly and a little cooler because of elevation.* Where are the areas of highest land? How high are the Ruwenzori Mountains? *The highest rise to 16,795 feet. The snow line begins at 14,500 feet and there are many glaciers, although at the base of the mountains there are hot, equatorial forests.*" Even though these mountains are only 53' north of the equator, the pupils should understand that it is possible to have cooler climatic conditions there, due to changes in elevation. "In how many ways will the various surface conditions of Africa affect the development of the new nations?

Of what value will the large rivers be? Trace the following rivers from source to mouth: Nile, Niger, Zambezi, Orange, and Congo. Notice the mouths of these rivers. Which of them have deltas? If the river has a delta at its mouth, what does that tell you about the river? *It is a slow-moving river.* Would a delta be a good location for a seaport? What is true of most of these rivers, a few miles inland, where the plateau meets the coastal plain? In what way would the falls be a help to a country? A hindrance? Find falls in the Zambezi, Congo, and Nile Rivers." Trace carefully the contour lines on the physical-political map which show the differences in elevation along the courses of the rivers named.

"Find the chain of lakes east of the Congo Basin. They are located in and near the Great Rift Valley which extends in an almost unbroken line from Ethiopia to Mozambique." This valley was formed thousands of years ago by a series of earthquakes where, in 1961, were found the remains of a prehistoric juvenile believed to have lived over 1,750,000 years ago. "Why are these lakes of little value? Compare their present value with the value of our own Great Lakes.

The climate will affect the progress of these new countries to a great extent." A physical-political map and seasonal precipitation maps are necessary to build the concept of Africa's climate. A natural vegetation map of Africa will indicate the effect of differences in climate if a map of climatic regions is not available.[1] "Through what degrees of latitude north and south of the equator does Africa extend? What does this indicate about the temperatures of Africa? Upon what factors do climatic regions depend? *Latitude, winds, sun position, elevation, mountain barriers, nearness to large bodies of water, position in large land masses and others.* Trace the equator across Africa. Through what part of Africa does it pass? What can you tell about the temperature and rainfall of countries near the equator? *Hot, humid, heavy rainfall, with the sun nearly always directly overhead.* "Would this type of climate be a help or a hindrance to such countries as the Republic of the Congo, southern Nigeria, and southern Ghana? How can these countries combat the effects of this type of climate? How has the climate limited the type of crop which can be raised, the methods of transportation, the kinds of buildings, the industries which would be most likely to develop, and the ways the people live?

Which part of Africa receives the greatest amount of rainfall during our North American summer? During our winter? *During our summer, the region of heavy rainfall moves north with the vertical rays of the sun. During our winter, the region of heaviest rainfall is farther south.* The region near the equator has two seasons, the season of heavy rainfall and the season of little or light rainfall. Notice on the rainfall and vegetation maps that as one travels north or south from the equator there are diminishing amounts of rainfall. How does this affect the vegetation of these regions? How can countries in these areas overcome the handicap of climate? What human activities will be carried on in spite of environmental conditions?"

After studying the several maps mentioned in the lesson above, as well as mineral resource maps, special products maps, and maps showing various

---

[1] A serviceable atlas for the elementary teacher is *Goode's World Atlas*, 11th ed. (Chicago, Rand McNally & Company, 1960).

kinds of transportation facilities to acquaint the pupils with the natural and cultural conditions of Africa as a whole, each of the new countries of Africa needs to be studied individually since geographic factors vary from region to region, as do cultural backgrounds and technological advances. To understand each country and its prospects for modernization, it will be necessary to synchronize the study of all the maps we can obtain, in order to discover the natural resources of each country and how the country is presently using them. As the pupils interpret the maps and see relationships, they will begin to understand the problems which each of these countries must face as an emerging nation.

Every teacher of geography should understand that in order to develop any lesson in geography, constant reference must be made to maps of all kinds. The pupils should acquire the habit of consulting many different kinds of maps, and of synchronizing the information obtained from them in order to draw inferences and see relationships regarding the natural and cultural landscape of the region being studied.

SUMMARY

The purpose of the summary is to draw together the worthwhile learnings of the unit. The making of maps in the summary is of great value in group and individual work. To summarize the work on Africa just described, have committees work out land use on enlarged maps for each of the several African countries studied. On them show where the cultivated land is, the areas where the most important crops are grown, where mineral deposits are located, and where the grazing lands and forests lie.

If your pupils are studying the United States, the work which they have done may be summarized by having each pupil in the class show information about the United States on an outline map which he contributes to a book of maps made by the class. Such a book might be given the title, *The Story of the United States through Maps.* Using commercially available outline maps, (those which are 10½″ by 15″ are easiest to work with), each pupil makes a map based upon information which he may gather from various sources. *The Statistical Abstract of the United States* is an excellent source of statistics for dot distribution maps, and is available in most libraries. The various almanacs also are excellent sources of statistics for the United States. Using statistics which they gather, there is no limit to the number and kinds of maps which the pupils can make. They can make maps which show surface conditions, distribution of rainfall, the length of growing seasons, population distribution, crop, mineral and animal production, and land use. (Dots for the distribution maps can be kept the same size by using a hole punched in a piece of cardboard as a pattern for the dots, each of which is filled in with colored pencil. See criteria for a good distribution map, page 85.) Each map should have a written interpretation of what is shown on it. For example, if the map is the population map of the United States, in his written interpretation the pupil should account for the areas of dense population as well as those of sparse population. When maps and interpretations are completed, mount them on sheets of oak tag or colored art paper and bind them all into book form.

APPLICATION

We can never be certain that our pupils have learned what they have been taught until they are able to apply their learnings in new situations.

An application exercise for the conclusion of a unit might be to have the pupils use outline maps on which to plot air trips over the country studied, and then describe what they would see on their trips.

Another application exercise might consist of arranging pictures or news items relating to the country studied around a large outline map of it. Connect each picture or item to its location in the country or region with a colored string. In order to associate appropriate pictures and news items with the areas studied, the pupil will have to recall much of what he has learned in class.

An association test, similar to the one which follows, may also be used to test application ability.

On the outline map of the United States, numbers are placed in regions which answer the questions below it. Select the number which you believe to be the correct location for each scene described.

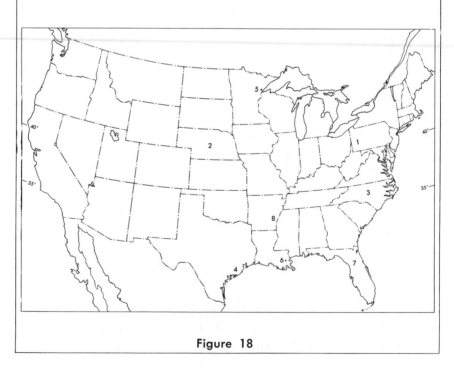

Figure 18

(3)	Where in the United States would one see men working in a peanut field?
(8)	Where could one see rice being harvested?
(1)	Where might steel mills be seen?
(7)	Where could one see grapefruit and oranges growing?
(2)	Where could one see winter wheat growing?
(4)	Where could one see oil derricks?
(5)	Where would boats be taking on loads of iron ore?
(6)	Where would boats be unloading bananas?

The Use of Maps in Testing

Locational skills, landscape imagery, and map interpretation can be tested with maps. Testing with maps is a valuable technique for both teacher and pupil alike in discovering inaccurate geographic concepts which the pupil may have acquired. The most common use of maps in testing is in checking knowledge of locational geography. Students are asked to identify cities, rivers, lakes, and countries shown by symbols or numbers on an outline map. However, there are other concepts which can be tested with maps.

In constructing and administering the test which tests map reading skills, there are several points which should be considered. Provide a range in subject matter great enough to detect weaknesses in the most elementary learnings and difficult enough to challenge the best pupils in the grade. Include at least three questions requiring the same skill. The results of a test which samples widely are more reliable. Plan the test so that brief, preferably one word, answers will suffice. The spelling of proper names is especially difficult for the pupils. If they are expected to supply words in the test, give them a list of words which cause difficulty, and which might be needed in the test. Such a list should be alphabetically arranged and should include more words than will be needed to take the test.

The sample test which follows may be helpful in planning geography tests for your own classes.

TESTING MAP SKILLS

Open your books to the map of Europe found on page _____, to answer the following questions.

1. Can you tell direction?
   a. _____ What direction is London from Oslo?
   b. _____ What direction is Hannover, Germany, from Hamburg?
   c. _____ What direction is Uppsala, Sweden, from Oslo, Norway?

2. Can you use the scale of miles?
   a. —————— How many air miles would you fly in going from London to Paris?
   b. —————— What is the approximate length of the canal from Bordeaux to the Mediterranean Sea?
   c. —————— Estimate the time it would take to fly from Milan to Rome at a speed of ——— miles per hour.

3. Can you read the physical features on a map?
   a. —————— Which are the highest mountains of Europe?
   b. —————— What kind of surface does Spain have?
   c. —————— Name a country which has a large area of plains.

4. Maps answer many kinds of questions for us. Use the skills you have learned and answer these questions.
   a. —————— In what direction does the Thames River flow?
   b. —————— In going from Paris to the coast do boats go up or down stream?
   c. —————— What two kinds of boundaries are shown on the map? —————— Give examples of each.
   d. —————— Arrange these cities in order of size: Edinburgh, Glasgow, —————— Manchester.
   ——————
   e. —————— In which sea is the water deeper, Black or Caspian?
   f. —————— Name two cities in England connected by canal.
   g. —————— Does a railroad follow the Rhone River to the Mediterranean Sea?
   h. —————— Does Belgium have a dense or sparse population?
   i. ——— Which country would be likely to have the cooler climate, southern Norway, or northern France?
   —————— Western France, or Switzerland?

5. Find three reasons on your map for London being a large seaport.

TESTING LANDSCAPE IMAGERY   Maps can be used to test the ability of the pupil to associate the landscape with the place. Nine numbers are placed on a map of South America, for instance. Nine descriptions are given and the pupils are asked to identify each description with the number of the country.

—————— The farm buildings of the *estancias* and the clusters of trees which surround them break the endless stretch of the plains. Here cattle are raised and wheat is grown. (Ans. Argentina)
—————— A thick forest grows here, the result of the extreme heat and heavy rainfall. A modern capital city is near its center. (Ans. Brazil)
—————— This country has a long, narrow valley between two mountain ranges. The valley is irrigated and produces citrus fruits, wheat, and grapes. (Ans. Chile)

Figure 19

_____ Here we would see rows of coffee trees in fields surrounding the *fazenda*. Near the large home of the owner we would see the smaller homes of the workers. (Ans. Brazil)

_____ We see oil derricks on "stilts" over a lake, and more oil derricks along the shores of the lake. In the mountains we would see iron being mined. Oil and iron ore are the two largest exports. (Ans. Venezuela)

_____ Many railroads converge on a city in the southern part of this country which has thousands of acres of fine grazing lands where cattle and sheep are raised. (Ans. Uruguay)

_____ 90% of the people of this country are Indian and mestizo. Two of its exports are quebracho extract and yerba maté. (Ans. Paraguay)

—————————— Plantations of cacao grow on a low coastal plain which has abundant rainfall. Cacao is its chief export. (Ans. Ecuador)

—————————— From west to east this country has irrigated valleys where cotton and sugar cane are grown; then, higher lands where barley, potatoes, and quinoa are grown; then, a tropical lowland. (Ans. Peru)

TESTING MAP READING SKILLS WITH A HYPOTHETICAL MAP   The ability to read and interpret facts shown on maps can be tested by using a hypothetical map with accompanying reference questions. The test which follows illustrates this testing technique.

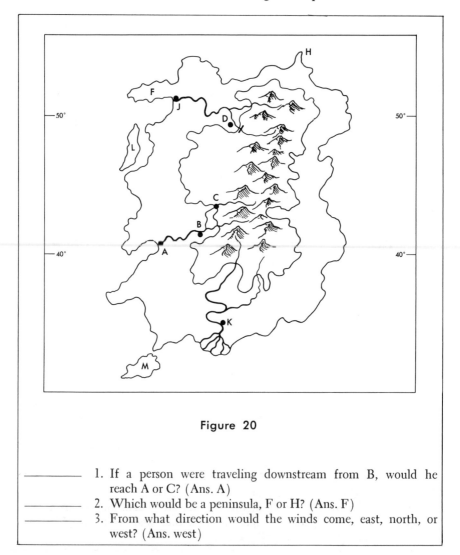

Figure 20

—————————— 1. If a person were traveling downstream from B, would he reach A or C? (Ans. A)

—————————— 2. Which would be a peninsula, F or H? (Ans. F)

—————————— 3. From what direction would the winds come, east, north, or west? (Ans. west)

_____ 4. Which island would most likely be a sand bar, L or M? (Ans. L)

_____ 5. Which side of the island would be the drier, west or east? (Ans. east)

_____ 6. Write the word "strait" where you find one. (Ans. South of the large island, separating the large and small islands)

_____ 7. What direction would you travel in flying from A to C? (Ans. northeast)

_____ 8. How many miles is it from the 40° to the 50° parallels? (Ans. 700 miles)

_____ 9. Which city is located near the falls, D or B? (Ans. D)

_____ 10. Which city is on a river having a delta, A or K? (Ans. K)

Recording Map Skills

On a wall chart record the names of the pupils and in columns across the chart, list the various map skills which they should acquire. The columns may be headed: KNOWS DIRECTIONS; CAN USE THE SCALE OF MILES; CAN USE LATITUDE; CAN USE LONGITUDE; KNOWS MAP SYMBOLS; and so on. After testing, have the pupils check off each skill they have mastered. This chart will show you where remedial work is needed. Pupils are interested in seeing their own progress as it is recorded and will take pride in their achievement.

Enlarging Maps

The ability to enlarge maps is a skill which will be very valuable to pupils. It will give them a feeling of achievement and independence to think that they can now make maps of any size they wish. Do not make this skill an end in itself. Always have pupils enlarge maps for a purpose; for example, to show the number of sheep raised in each of the states and territory of Australia.

Have the pupils make a half-inch grid on tracing paper. Place the grid over the map to be enlarged. Trace the map on the grid, being careful to trace the boundaries and coastline exactly. Put in at least two parallels and the scale of miles. Pupils of the sixth sequence may put in meridians, also. Number the vertical rows of squares with figures, and the horizontal rows with letters. Numbering the rows helps the pupil to keep the place as he enlarges the map. Then draw a grid on a large sheet of paper or cardboard, making one, one and a half, or two inch squares, depending upon the size of the map desired. Draw the lines of the grid very lightly because they will have to be erased later. Number the rows of squares as those on the half inch grid are numbered. The outline of the map may be started at any point. Mark the sides of each square where the outline of the map crosses

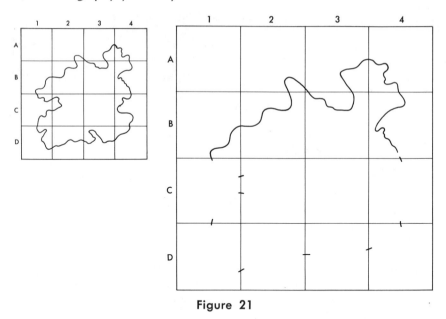

Figure 21

them. This keeps the proportion accurate. Then sketch the map, square by square. As the final step, once the map has been completely sketched, erase the grid and strengthen the outline of the map.

Pupil-Made Maps

Creative map making is an important way for children to apply geographic concepts which they have learned. This activity has "built-in" motivation because it capitalizes on several innate drives of the pupils, such as the drives to be active, to be creative, and to satisfy curiosity. Pupils derive satisfaction from activities which have meaning for them and which give them some understanding of the world about them. They also have a feeling of accomplishment when they have completed a map which contributes to the understanding of the problem the class is studying.

"Creative map-making requires the translation of facts from one form of expression usually in the language of words to an altogether different form of expression, that of the language of lines, shapes, color and other symbols which in certain combinations we call a map."[2] It is this reorganization of information into a graphic sort of "shorthand" which creates a

[2] Mapes, Carl H., "Creative Map-Making of Historical-Geographical Units," *Journal of Geography*, Vol. 39 (April, 1940), p. 156.

learning situation for the pupil. Making maps is excellent for developing both map reading ability and increasing the pupils' power to interpret data on maps. The pupils need to have a reason for making a particular map. Map activities should never descend to the level of busy work.

Map making can be a waste of time. It is a waste of the pupil's time to make maps unless he grows in knowledge and understanding of the subject as he makes them. There is little value in map making if the pupil merely copies data from another map. Maps in textbooks and reference books need to be checked carefully by the teacher before the pupils use them as a source of information. Even fifth grade pupils can make simple distribution maps if they are given the statistics with which to work. (See lists of books of statistics, page 86.)

Map making can be a waste of time if the pupils are not taught to interpret what they are showing on the map. They should read more from the map than the obvious facts. In making a distribution map of the production of corn in the United States, the pupil should explain why corn is not grown more extensively to the north and to the west and give the reason why corn is grown to such a great extent in the corn belt.

Map making can be a waste of time if it does not have educational value commensurate with the time spent in making it. Too much time is spent in trying to achieve perfection in drawing freehand maps. No particular value is derived from this time-consuming activity. Pupils should be able to make fairly accurate maps by enlarging them or by using prepared outline maps. The value of map making is in the clear portrayal of certain geographic facts and relationships which will contribute to a major understanding.

Map making can be a waste of time if the map does not pass the test of accuracy. Be critical of the way rivers are drawn and the direction mountains extend, and the location of cities, especially those located on rivers. There may be a very good reason why a city is located on one or the other side of a river. It should be located correctly on the map and the relationships leading to its situation and development should be noted. Every map must have a scale of miles. Fifth sequence pupils should indicate the latitude, and sixth sequence pupils should show both latitude and longitude at the margin of the map. Boundaries, too, must be correctly drawn. (For additional criteria for maps, see page 85.)

SUGGESTIONS WHICH WILL PROMOTE QUALITY WORK IN MAPS

WHEN PUPILS are doing map work, insist on light colors shaded in one direction. Vivid colors detract from the quality of the map. Coloring for physical maps should be the standard international map colors. Use green for lowlands, yellow and orange for plateaus, and brown for mountains.

WHEREVER POSSIBLE, the printing should be horizontal. It is more easily read this way. Draw pencil lines very lightly when printing so that the words are straight and the letters all of the same size. The pupils will need to be advised as to the size of the letters in the title and on the map. See that the letters are not out of proportion for the size of the map. Never allow the letters to touch the margin of the map or the edge of the paper on which the map is drawn.

FINISH the map by going over the irregular coastline with India ink, if the pupil is old enough to handle it. Younger pupils can trace the coastline with a well-sharpened lead pencil or a black ballpoint pen.

DISCUSS with the class the importance of the general appearance of a map and on the chalkboard list suggestions which will improve the appearance of their maps. Erasing construction lines used for printing and removing soiled spots will be high on their list of suggestions. Remember, you will obtain from the children the quality of work upon which you insist; therefore, do not accept anything but the best work of which each pupil is capable.

RELIEF MAPS   Most elementary grade children have very vague ideas about the meaning of elevation. One effective way to help the pupils get the "feel" of different elevations is to have them make relief maps. The concept of elevation and its effect upon man's activities is introduced in the fourth sequence. (See page 88.) Relief maps, however, should not be attempted there. These maps are difficult to make accurately, and the pupils do not have the necessary background. There usually is distortion in relief maps because the horizontal scale is different from the vertical scale. To help the pupil visualize the approximate elevation of the physical features, draw a horizontal line to represent the east and west extent of the region being mapped. State the number of miles represented by the line by writing it under the line. Next, estimate how much of the line would represent the height of the highest mountain in the region which the pupils are mapping. There will have to be some distortion in the vertical scale. Emphasize the importance of keeping the elevation of the surface as nearly accurate as possible. Misconceptions about topography are often the result of making relief maps without using a definite scale for elevation.

In the intermediate grades, a thickness of one-eighth inch of the relief map-making media should represent 1,000 feet in elevation on a desk-size map. In junior high grades, elevation should be more exact. One-eighth inch thickness should represent 2,000 feet in elevation. When forming mountain ranges with the map-making media, drive small nails or strong pins into the cardboard or wood base used for the map to show the height of certain peaks. These will serve as guides to the elevation for the entire range to be constructed.

A misconception which many children have, and which should be corrected, is that high elevation figures indicate mountains and low ones, plains. The elevation of some parts of our Great Plains in the United States exceeds the elevation of the Appalachian Mountains. Call attention to the way mountains usually slope into foothills and plateaus, and then into plains. There are few places in the world where the mountains rise abruptly from the plains.

MAKING THE RELIEF   Have the pupils prepare an eight and one-half by eleven-inch outline map of the country or region which they will use in making the relief map. They will need a physical-political map, such as those found in a textbook or atlas, as a reference for their work. Staple the outline map to a piece of corrugated cardboard and slide the cardboard and map inside a transparent plastic bag. Smooth the bag over the map and fasten any excess plastic material to the underside of the cardboard with transparent tape. (Many of the mixtures used in the making of relief maps contain water. The cardboard curls when it becomes damp, causing the map to crack. Placing a plastic bag over the map and cardboard keeps the cardboard dry and the outline of the map visible.)

If the salt and flour mixture is used, a thin layer can be spread over the entire map. Later, mountains and plateaus can be added. A pointed meat skewer makes an excellent tool with which to shape the coastline and to trace the irregular courses of rivers. Let the first layer dry overnight. Apply additional layers to the map the next day. When the map is completely dry, it may be painted and finished. (See suggestions for maps, page 111.) A piece of black tape placed along the edge of the cardboard so that about one-fourth inch of it shows, will give the map a finished look.

There are several combinations of materials which can be used for relief maps.

1. Salt and flour. Two parts of salt to one part of flour. Add water until the mixture has the consistency of bread dough.

2. Sawdust and liquid flour paste. The liquid flour paste should be of a thin, creamy consistency. Add enough sawdust to achieve the bread dough, or mortar, consistency.

3. Liquid starch and detergent. Four tablespoons of liquid starch to one cup of powdered detergent. Dry the map well; then, paint with tempera colors. Apply clear shellac or varnish for a finished appearance.

4. Layers of corrugated cardboard from cardboard boxes. Make patterns for the different elevations by tracing the contour lines (usually shown by a change of color) of a good physical-political map. Then cut out the layers of cardboard. Let each layer of cardboard represent the same number of feet in elevation. If the thickness of the cardboard is to represent 1,000 feet and the contour line shows an increase of 2,000 feet, then two thicknesses of cardboard will be needed. A change of color does not always indicate the same increase in elevation. These cardboard layers build up the topog-

raphy most accurately. Cover the entire map with a thin coat of plaster of Paris to round off the abrupt drops in elevation which the cut edge of the cardboard makes. When the plaster of Paris is dry, paint it the conventional map colors. This type of map takes more time but the results are well worth the effort.

5. Nonoil base clay maps. These maps may have beaverboard or heavy poster paper for a base. The skill and accuracy needed to make this type of map and the many ways these maps can be used in the classroom contribute to their effectiveness. The clay comes in brown, yellow, or green colors, allowing different altitudes to be shown in the standard colors used by map makers. These maps may also be painted with tempera paint.

6. Powdered asbestos. This is inexpensive and is an excellent material for making relief maps.

CLOTH AND CRAYON MAPS   An effective map may be made with wax crayons and muslin. Trace the map on the cloth and then go over the pencil lines with wax crayon. Press the map on the wrong side with a warm iron. Cover the ironing surface to avoid marring it with melted wax. Fringing the borders of the muslin map adds variety and provides a necessary finishing touch.

A FUN MAP MADE WITH CRAYONS AND BLACK PAINT Draw a map on art paper. Trace the map with heavy crayon. Boundaries might be put in with yellow crayon, rivers in blue, cities with red. Other features may be added, such as mountains, lakes, products, depending upon what you wish to show. Draw a margin around the map. Paint the area within the margin with black tempera paint (or with watercolor), right over the crayon. The paint will slide off the crayon and a decorative map will emerge. There is little educational value in making this map, but there are times when the pupils should do work for the sheer pleasure involved in doing it.

ORNAMENTAL MAPS   Cloth maps make interesting homework projects and wall decorations. Trace the outline map on a piece of cloth. Colored cloth is very effective. With an outlining stitch, put in the states, provinces, rivers, and cities. The maps should also show interesting facts and relationships whenever possible. A land use or a product map may be made by sewing the symbols in various colors.

DISTRIBUTION MAPS   Large distribution maps for class use may be made by enlarging smaller maps and showing distributions by means of dots. The large-sized dots may be kept the same size by punching a hole in a piece of cardboard with a punch and using the cardboard pattern to make each dot. The space covered by the hole can be completely filled in with colored pencil. Desk-sized distribution maps, made by the pupils, are valuable visual aids for showing relationships. Be sure to have the pupils give an interpretation of any map they make.

SUGGESTIONS FOR THE TEACHER

A MAP STENCIL can be made by projecting a map on wrapping paper. Along the outline make holes about an inch apart with a large needle. When needed, place this wrapping paper stencil against the chalk board and gently pat the outline with an eraser covered with chalk dust. It works!

A MAP for classwork can be made on an inexpensive window shade. Such a map is convenient because it is easily rolled up.

IT TAKES only a few minutes to draw a map on the chalk board—or on wrapping paper—if it is projected with an overhead or opaque projector. Wrapping paper maps can be used for several years if they are rolled or stored flat.

The Development of Hypothetical Maps

The teaching of the hypothetical map is one of the best devices for introducing new geographic concepts and correcting faulty ones. No two pupils have the same difficulties and this device gives the teacher an excellent opportunity to do individual work with the members of the class. This unit of work will result in a class having a much better knowledge of geographic fundamentals and principles, and it will increase their understanding of geographical relationships. There can be no memorization of facts because no two pupil-made hypothetical maps will be identical. The land use map, which the pupils make as a part of the hypothetical map project, provides an excellent means for introducing elementary concepts in economics.

Hypothetical maps may be adapted to any grade level by eliminating or adding concepts. The following work is planned for an eighth grade class. It is a useful project for drawing together and checking all of the concepts which have been taught in sequences one through seven.

MOTIVATION

"How many of you have lived in, or had a long visit in another state or country? What did you like about it? What did you dislike? Have you ever tried to picture a land where everything was as you would like it to be, a place where you might find beautiful sunny beaches and rugged mountain scenery, and where the people all earned a good living because the best possible use was made of natural resources? That would be an ideal land, wouldn't it?

Let's plan such a country. We will make a set of two maps of our imaginary country. We must place this country on the surface of the earth where it will not touch another large land mass. The first map will be the physical-political map, and the second will be a land use map telling how the people will use the land to supply their needs. You can see why we have to locate our island countries in latitudes where people can earn a good livelihood. There must be a standard of living in our hypothetical countries equal to our own.

We are going to have some fun along with our work. You may name your island anything you wish, and you may make it in any shape. Let's see how much originality you have in working out a clever map. Perhaps someone will want to have an 'Animal Isle' and make it in the shape of an animal's head; or 'Flower Island' and give all of the surface features, land forms, water bodies, cities, and so on, the names of flowers. Pirate Land, Disease Island, or Cartoon Country have interesting possibilities, too.

After we have completed the two maps, we will also write a brief description of our island country, such as we might find in *The World Almanac*. This will prove that you understand all that you have placed on your maps. Let's advertise our island and try to interest people in coming to live on it by making travel folders similar to those used by the travel agencies.

Here is a list of the natural and cultural items to be placed on the physical-political map:

1. cape	10. latitude	19. desert
2. peninsula	11. longitude	20. five cities
3. sound	12. plains	21. canal
4. island	13. plateaus	22. railroads
5. isthmus	14. mountains	23. scale of miles
6. strait	15. falls	24. profile
7. bay	16. lake	25. arrows showing
8. a swift river	17. delta	wind direction."
9. a meandering river	18. swamp	

Show the entire list so that the students will grasp the over-all plan for the project. From this list select a few items each day for which you will develop understandings. There must be sound reasons for placing each item on the maps. To have the students try to place all of the items at once without the study of relationships causes confusion and results in much extra checking for the teacher.

DEVELOPMENT

It is necessary to develop the work slowly, step by step. This provides an excellent opportunity for the teacher to discover and correct the inaccurate concepts which the pupils may have concerning geographical terms. Many students will be seeing geographic items and relationships for the first time. It is one thing to read meanings from a physical-political map, and quite another to place natural and cultural items on a map so that certain relationships will exist. Such work necessitates understanding and application of geographic fundamentals. This requires thinking, and thinking takes time!

THE PHYSICAL-POLITICAL MAP

1. "The first seven items on the list refer to land forms and water bodies which affect coastlines. About what cape have you heard? *Cape Cod, Cape*

Kennedy, and so on." The teacher points to these on the world map. "Why are these called capes? Cape *comes from the Latin* caput, *meaning head or point. Capes are points of land extending out into the sea.* Name some peninsulas about which you have heard. How does a peninsula differ from a cape? Peninsula *comes from two Latin words which mean "almost an island.* Would capes and peninsulas be an asset or a liability to a country?"

Continue in this manner with the remaining five items. Then summarize the day's development by giving the definitions of each of the seven items orally, or in the form of a quiz, to see if the pupils understand the meanings of the terms. Have the pupils open an atlas or textbook to a physical-political map. Then have them trace the coastlines of several countries with their fingers to actually "feel" how irregular coastlines are. For application work of this day's lesson, have the pupils sketch a simple outline map which will include the seven items discussed in the lesson. This outline map need not be the one they will use for their final map. It is merely a way to check whether or not the pupils have the terms clearly in mind.

2. "How many of you have decided what shape your island will be?" Check the outline maps. "Today we must decide where in the world to place it. We cannot place it on any of the continents or large islands. How does latitude affect man? What effect will latitude have upon your island?

We know that later we will place rivers on our maps. We want to be sure that our islands will be in a latitude where the winds will bring rainfall. We shall need to review the generalized wind belts to find what winds will affect our islands and the conditions we shall find in different latitudes."

Generalized wind belts (see page 247) should not be taught as such before the seventh sequence. The fifth sequence pupils will be familiar with the westerlies from their study of the United States, and their islands should be placed in that latitude. Work on Latin America will include knowledge of trade winds and the equatorial calms. If the hypothetical map is taught in the fifth or sixth sequence, be sure to have the pupils place their islands in a latitude with which they are familiar.

3. "What three kinds of surface are shown on the physical-political maps you have seen? How are differences in surface indicated? We shall have to be very careful in planning just where the plains, plateaus, and mountains will be placed on our maps. Why? *Effect on precipitation, the courses of rivers, location of lakes, swamps, use of the land, and so forth.*

Look at the physical map of the world. What do the colors indicate? Notice that the color bands are very uneven, wide in some places and narrow in others. Trace with your finger the edge of a color band. Do you see how rivers have worn the land to lower elevations? Notice the differences in color along the courses of the rivers. In what other ways is the elevation of the land changed? What color is used for each type of surface?" The teacher should draw a simple

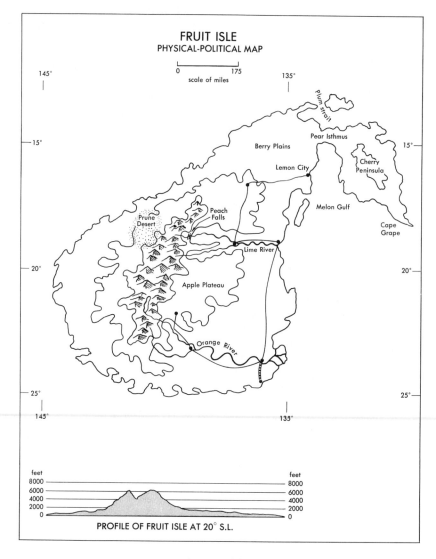

Figure 22

profile to make sure that the students are seeing elevation and not just color.

"Have you decided in what latitude you are going to place your island? From what direction will the wind bring moisture? Keep in mind that a desert must be placed on the map. What causes deserts? What is the surface of a desert region like?" More children have incorrect ideas of deserts than of any other item. A physical-political map of southern Argentina will show desert areas on three types of surface.

"Deserts may be found behind a mountain barrier, in the horse latitudes,

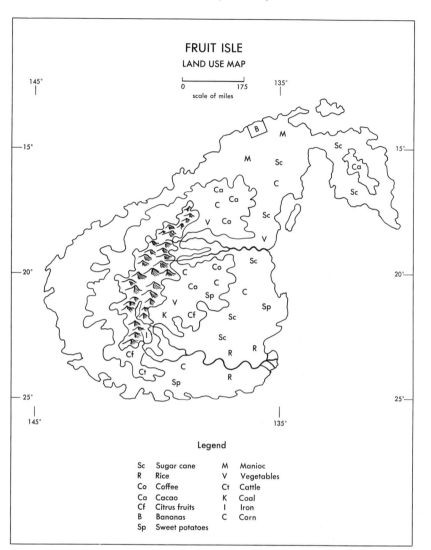

Figure 23

and in areas where the rain-bearing winds have lost their moisture before reaching a region. If you plan to have the desert in the rain shadow of the mountains, in what direction will you plan to have the mountains extend? In placing the mountains be sure to leave plenty of well-watered land for the people to use to earn their living.

4. Are you sure there will be water for your rivers? Will the region where the rivers rise receive rainfall? One of these rivers will have a delta. What does this tell you about the course of the river and the surface of the land through

which it flows? Your second river must flow through an area where the color bands are very narrow. What does this tell you about the surface of the land and the rate of flow of the river? Where might there be a waterfall on this river? How will the people use the falls? What is the map symbol for falls?

5. What are swamps? How are they caused? Where are swamps likely to occur? What is the symbol used to show swampy areas? Find swampy regions on a physical-political map. Of what value have some swamps been? How are lakes formed? Study a physical-political map to see where some of the lakes are located. How do they get water? What are some of their many uses?

6. There are many factors which influence the growth of cities. You cannot place cities or railroads on your physical-political map until you develop the land use map. You must show a need for both cities and railroads.

7. Each of you will have a different scale of miles for your map. Two parallels of latitude must be indicated at the margin. There are approximately seventy miles in one degree of latitude. If the parallels are five degrees apart, the space between the parallels will represent five times seventy miles or 350 miles." See pages 59 and 85.

8. "Draw a simple profile of your island under the map." See The Making of Profiles, page 93. "This is a test of your ability to read elevation on a physical-political map and to transpose that information into the graphic form of the profile."

If the teacher has had the class, as a whole, check these maps frequently, there will be less for him to check individually. At the beginning of the class period, ask questions to see if the students have the natural items correctly placed: "How many have located their islands in the westerlies? In the trade winds? From what direction will the winds blow? Have you placed the wind-direction arrows?" And so on. This will often help correct many minor errors and will save time when the teacher checks the work of individual students.

Have the pupils color the kinds of surface roughly on the practice map so that it is easier to correct. Follow the standard coloring for physical maps: mountains, tan or brown; high plateaus, orange; low plateaus, yellow; plains, green.

Many of the pupils will finish the assignment at approximately the same time. As a result, there may be congestion at the teacher's desk as he does individual checking. Have the pupils sign a paper when they are ready for a check and correct their work in the order in which they have signed. They can return to their desks, and while waiting, make two copies of their checked outline map, one on oak tag or art paper for the final map, and one on scratch paper on which they will plan their land use map.

LAND USE MAP—AN ECONOMIC APPLICATION OF GEOGRAPHY

9. "Now we must plan how the people on this island can earn a living. Do you have an outline map of your island on scratch paper? Put in the natural regions and color them lightly. We need to show surface because various kinds

of crops grow at different elevations. We shall need to learn what crops grow in the equatorial calms, the trade winds, the horse latitudes, and the westerlies." See Appendix H. "I don't believe that any of us will place our islands in the polar latitudes and so we will exclude them from our list. What effect will elevation have upon the kinds of crops raised? What will grow on the plains, low plateaus, and high plateaus in each of these latitudes? What use can be made of the mountain areas? We are planning a high standard of living; consequently, we will need minerals to be used in manufacturing to provide jobs. You may choose two minerals. Think of your location. Can nearby countries supply you with the same minerals which you have chosen? Would it be better to select minerals which are difficult to obtain, or minerals which would add to the economy of your country?"

THE ECONOMY OF THE ISLAND 10. One definition of the economy of a country is the use of the natural resources to supply the needs of the people. As the students list the needs of the people and try to work out a plan to supply them, they become impressed with the fact that most of our wants are supplied from the earth. They become aware of the great number of workers at home and in foreign lands who are involved in supplying our needs. Interdependence becomes reality instead of remaining just another word. Have the pupils list needs of the people, such as cotton, wool, synthetic fibers, leather, rubber, wheat, corn, rice, vegetables, citrus fruits, milk, meat, glass, paints, copper, steel, and so on.

"Which of these commodities can we supply on our islands? Those we cannot supply we will have to import. We may need to manufacture in order to provide work for our people. In this case we will import some raw materials."

In the same manner discuss and name the natural resources of the islands, the subsistence crops, the cash crops, the manufactures and the cities where products are made, and the imports and exports.

Now the pupils are ready to plan the land use map. A surplus of agricultural products must approximate the value of the needed imports. On the map place symbols for crops and minerals where they will be grown or found. Use pictorial or nonpictorial symbols, remembering that the symbols must all be the same size. To keep them uniform, draw the symbols within the confines of a hole punched in a card.

11. Discuss the reasons which determine the growth of cities. Below are listed a few of them. Have the students add to the list.

a. railroad center	f. industrial center
b. near a source of cheap power	g. agricultural center
c. lake port	h. near mineral deposit
d. river port	i. break-in-bulk
e. seaport	j. health resort

12. "Now it is necessary to think of the products we need to manufacture on the island. Where would a city be located which would manufacture these products?"

After cities are placed, plan the routes of railroads which will carry the products made or grown on the island to ports or to other markets.

"What products will be exported? What raw materials or manufactured products will need to be imported?"

After working out these concepts on the scratch land use map, place the cities on the physical-political map. The railroads should be red lines. Then make the final land use map which should also have a key, a scale of miles, and parallels and meridians.

SUMMARY

The description written by the students summarizes the information given on the two maps. Have the students write the description in encyclopedic form following a definite outline. They should give the size of the island in miles, north and south, and east and west; surface; climatic conditions; leading industries; chief crops, exports; imports; cities; and scenic spots. Writing this summary not only requires the ability to read back the information placed on the maps, but it also gives an opportunity to practice the many geographic skills used in making the maps.

APPLICATION

The travel folder is supposed to advertise the island in such a manner that it will attract tourists, prospective home-seekers, and industrialists. This work can be assigned as work for extra credit. It also provides additional enrichment work for the better students. Have a few commercial travel folders brought to class. Discuss their merits. Posters can be made to illustrate scenic spots on the islands. Perhaps some students will enjoy making rainfall, population, land use, or even salt and flour relief maps of their islands.

TESTING

For a test, have the pupils answer the following two questions about A, B, and C, described below.

---

1. What climatic conditions would be found here?
2. What might the people do for a living?

Region A. A wide plateau stretched for hundreds of miles. The latitude is 30° to 36° N.

Region B. The latitude of this land is from 40° to 50° S. In the western part, a high wall of mountains extends north and south for hundreds of miles along the coast. In the eastern part there is a rolling plateau.

Region C. This country extends from 15° to 25° N. A high mountain range in the southwest extends northwest and southeast. North of the range is a wide plateau which slopes gently to a plain.

Every pupil will benefit by doing this work. Teachers will be amply repaid for their efforts by the interest created and by the amount of information gained by the class. Maps used in any class thereafter will take on more meaning because they will be better understood.

Map Reading Readiness in the Primary Sequences

Just as there is a need for reading readiness before the child begins to read, so is there a need for map reading readiness. Pupils need many understandings before maps have meaning for them, and much work can be done in the primary grades to prepare pupils for the map reading work which is begun in either the third or fourth sequence. A map should never be used as an end in itself. It should be used to develop geographic concepts. We must plan activities which will encourage our pupils to increase their powers of observation and which will require them to do critical thinking about what they see.

In the first sequence, the teaching of the concept of direction is begun as a prerequisite for map reading and interpretation. By planning several outdoor lessons, the attention of the children can be directed to the different positions in which the sun can be seen at different times during the day. By observing their shadows at noon (in the Northern Hemisphere), north can be determined. Questions such as the following can be asked to strengthen the concept of direction.

- Where do we see the sun early in the morning?
- Where is the sun at noon?
- Is the sun ever directly overhead where we live?
- Where is the sun in the early evening?

Placing N, S, E, and W labels on the walls of the classroom helps to orient the children to directions indoors.

Plan a series of lessons and activities which require a knowledge of directions so that the children will feel a need for knowing them. Ask them questions, or give them directions, such as these:

"Take three steps to the north and five steps eastward. What will you find in front of you? If John takes ten steps south and six steps west, whose desk will he be near? In what direction do you walk from the school to your home? What direction do you walk to go to the school office?"

An interesting game for primary sequence children revolves about two boys who pretend that they are "bump cars," such as are seen in amusement parks. Have them begin this game by standing side by side at the front of the classroom. Choose two other children who will "drive" the "cars" by taking turns in giving them directions. The first "driver," while seated at his desk, might say to his "car," "Car One, take six steps to the north and three steps to the east." The driver of the second car might then say, "Car Two, take four steps to the south and five steps to the east." The game should continue in this manner, each driver trying to bring his car as close to the other driver's car as he can, without colliding. If a collision occurs, a new driver is selected for the car which bumped.

These activities, and others similar to them, will help to make the pupils conscious of direction on the surface of the earth. While the pupils are becoming acquainted with surface direction, we must be certain that they also come to an understanding of the true meaning of "up" and "down." (See page 42.)

At the beginning of the first year, time is usually spent acquainting the children with their school home. After they are thoroughly familiar with the building and grounds, they are ready to take their first step toward simple map making, a short trip beyond the school grounds. Remember, as primary pupils study their environment, they should be helped to see the relationship between cultural and natural features. Helping children to discover relationships requires planning and guidance on your part and you should make certain that the pupils study the human activity before they study the natural conditions to which the activity is related. For instance, the children might observe the location of a steel mill before learning why it was built on a riverbank. Later on, when you help them to understand one or two simple reasons for the location of the mill, they will have begun the study of relationships. Discovering relationships can become one of the most exciting aspects of geography for children.

Take the first field trip in the immediate vicinity of the school. Perhaps the initial trip might be made for the purpose of noting where several of the children in the class live, where the public buildings are located, the different types of homes in the neighborhood, the construction of new houses and the work being done by the builders, different modes of transportation, and hills, valleys, and trees, all of which make up their world. When the class returns to the classroom, discuss where they went, the direction in which they walked from the school, where they had crossed the street, where there were traffic lights, hydrants, mailboxes, and so on. As they discuss what they saw, help them to understand the relationships connected with their observations.

At the close of the discussion, the teacher should suggest that the children make a record of the trip which they have just taken. Before the first map on paper is made, it would be advantageous to have the children reconstruct their route in a sand table. Changes can be made easily in the sand as the children revise their thinking about cultural and natural items which they have seen en route. There is kinesthetic value in the sand table experience, also. If a sand table is not available, tape two or more strips of wrapping paper together to make a large, basic map (six feet by eight feet, or more) of the streets in the immediate vicinity of the school. More streets may be added as the horizons of the children widen.

All maps in the primary grades should be made either on the floor or on a low table to help the children establish the relationship between the cardinal directions on maps and directions on the earth's surface. Maps placed on the floor or low tables are easier for the children to work with and they can "finger walk" or actually walk on the streets of the map during map activities. The hanging of maps too soon often results in the children confusing north with "up," and south with "down." In drawing the first map, discuss the cardinal directions and mark them on the paper. Decide the direction of the streets and then, with the help of the children, draw a basic map with chalk or tempera paint. This basic map should show the street in front of the school and no more than one or two parallel and intersecting streets. Now, have the children place wooden blocks or small boxes on the map, in their correct locations, to represent homes and buildings. Three dimensional reproduction is most helpful in bringing about understanding of difficult concepts. For instance, the children will understand better why bridges have to be built high if they try to move toy boats under a block bridge made too low on their basic map.

The basic map on paper can be used several times during the year and can be enlarged to include a broader area as the school year progresses. In a lesson on safety, the teacher and children can locate fireboxes, traffic lights, hydrants, stop signs, and safety islands on the map. In other lessons the children might discover why gasoline stations are built where they are, how the street pattern is related to the topography, and why one location for a supermarket is better than another. Near the end of the year, the children might draw pictures on art paper of things that they have seen in their environment—homes, buses, trucks, cars, trees, stores, firehouses, children on bicycles—and then cut them out and paste them on the map. It is important that this map represent something which they have actually seen and with which they are familiar. (After this initial map making experience, the observations made by the children will be much sharper, particularly if they know that they will be making other maps or adding to the initial map.) When completed, the map may be hung, preferably on the north wall of the classroom. Maps which have been developed in this manner should be reproduced in a much smaller scale and duplicated by the teacher so that each child may have a copy of the map he has helped to make.

Children living in rural areas need this mapping experience as well as those who live in urban areas. Rural areas can be mapped in much the same way, although the scale and the plans for the field trip would necessarily be different. The children would need to be taken by cars or bus because the area which would include the homes of several of the children is so much greater than that in the vicinity of an urban school. If there is a local vantage point from which a great distance can be seen, it will be of great help in visualizing the checkerboard pattern of the rural community and its surrounding farmland. Before the trip, you will need to go over the route very carefully to discover what relationships can be observed between man's activities and the environment, and what geographic concepts can be introduced. It probably will not be possible to cover the whole area in which your pupils live in a single trip. You should, therefore, start with the area adjacent to the school because this is familiar to all of the children. For the first map, plan the trip to include the highway which passes the school and, perhaps, a side road which crosses the main highway. Add to the map during the year as you do more exploring. A committee made up of children who live on a side road may be able to report and record very accurately the number of farms, the land use, and other things of interest along the road they use.

After the first field trip through the countryside, ask the children questions such as those which follow.

"What direction did we travel on Route _____? Was the land flat, rolling, or hilly? Which kind of surface is easier to cultivate? Whose farms did we pass? What kind of farms are they? How do you know that they are dairy farms? What breed of dairy cows did we see? What crops did you see growing along the road? What work was the farmer doing in the field? How were the different farm buildings on the farms used? Through what community did we pass? What public building did we pass? How many of you noticed the gulley where heavy rains had carried away the soil? Why were there ditches beside the road? We crossed a stream. Does it have a name? In what direction does it cross the field? Why? What roads did the main highway cross?"

Such questions are not foreign to the experience and knowledge of most children growing up on farms. If you are a primary teacher in a rural community, you will have an excellent opportunity to introduce simple concepts pertaining to topography, weather and climate, and man's activities, all of which will be valuable in the children's later formal work in geography. Such concepts as the following (and many others) ought to be part of the geography readiness program in the primary grades:

◈ The surface of land may be flat, rolling, or hilly.
◈ Streams flow across the land.
◈ Plants grow on the land.
◈ Plants grow when there is no frost.
◈ Farmers raise several kinds of crops.

Now the children are ready to make a map which will reproduce, on paper, the field trip which they have taken. Place the cardinal directions on a piece of paper larger than that which was suggested for use in the urban school. Have the children determine the directions of the roads which they traveled, and of any side roads they may have passed. Then put the roads on the map with black tempera paint. Decide how to show the location of farms, fields, and other landmarks. At first, use small blocks to show the groups of farm buildings; later, symbols can be used. If there is a rural community along the highway, have the children indicate it on the map with small blocks placed along several of its streets.

In the second sequence in an urban area, the map (still made on the floor) may include a longer trip, as well as the area adjacent to the school. The trip may be to a public building, a supermarket, or to a farm. As the area mapped increases in size to include other trips which the children have taken, the original area mapped decreases in size, the houses becoming small rectangles or squares. Do not try to map all of the borough or city in detail. Simply put in the route taken, the destination, and an occasional well-known landmark such as a park, a public building, or a gasoline station seen en route and with which the children are familiar. Symbols are decided upon as they are needed. The maps now become less pictorial and more abstract. In rural areas, second graders should be familiarized with routes leading to the nearest larger community where some

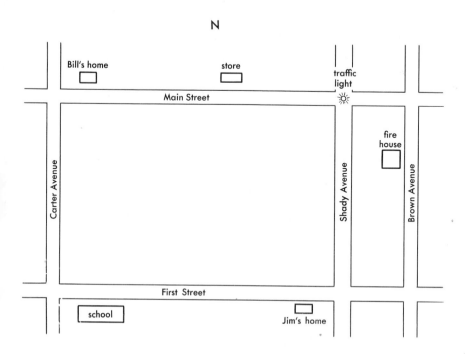

Figure 24

members of their family may work. If such a trip can be arranged, a new map should be made, using a different scale. Have the children decide on symbols which may be needed for farm buildings, schools, stores, and other cultural features. Remember that a map symbol does not stand for a word and that a child does not necessarily understand a symbol even though he can name it. When children use symbols, place a key or legend in the lower left hand corner of the map. The important consideration in the making of maps in the primary grades is that the map should represent something which the children have actually seen.

For additional practice in map making, have the children draw simple maps of routes taken in going to school, to the nearby store, or to a friend's home. In many of the stories which the children read, or which you read to them, trips are described in such a way that simple maps may be drawn of the route taken by characters in the story. Draw a simple map on the board and have the children answer questions concerning it.

Jim made three trips from his home yesterday: to school, to the store, and to the firehouse.
1. On which trips would Jim need to cross the street? —————
2. What direction would Jim walk from his home to school? —————
3. What directions would Jim walk, along the nearest route, from his home to the store? —————
4. What directions would Bill walk, along the nearest route, from his home to to the firehouse? —————
5. Bill and Jim decide to visit the firehouse after school. Which boy would have the greater distance to walk home from the firehouse? —————

7

Use all available tools

The Selection and Use of Pictures

Good teaching always facilitates learning, but regardless of the manner in which we teach or the tools which we use, our pupils must do the learning themselves. All we, as teachers, can do is to create within them the desire to learn and to show them ways to learn. To teach pupils how to read and to interpret pictures will put into their hands a learning tool which will serve them for a lifetime. The first requisite of all effective geographic thinking is to acquire clear-cut imagery of geographic content being studied. This is best gained through actual field work. To take pupils to the places which they study certainly would be ideal, but aside from the occasional, well-planned field trip in the immediate area of the school, such excursions are usually quite impossible to arrange. Pictures are the finest available substitute for actual geographic field work.

Of what value are pictures in the teaching of geography? Well-chosen pictures not only serve to introduce new concepts, but they also bring into focus those which have been learned in the past and give additional meaning to concepts being developed. Pictures give a clearer understanding of relationships much more quickly and with less effort than any other tool.

While the basic reason for the use of pictures in geography is for the purpose of developing accurate concepts, there are additional values in their use which need to be mentioned. Pictures help to give substance to far-away places and people. When the pupil hears or reads about them, they sometimes seem unreal because they are unfamiliar to him and the conditions about which he reads are outside of his experience. Faulty interpretation of the descriptive material which he reads may give him incorrect concepts because the mental image he builds depends upon associations and experiences recalled by the words. Well-chosen pictures help to clarify his ideas and provide him with the images we want him to have. They also help to correct any misconceptions he may have acquired.

In a picture of terraced hillsides on both sides of a narrow valley in Java, two men are shown transplanting rice. Each little terrace has its mud wall, or dike, about a foot wide and high enough to hold the water. There are little gates placed at intervals to regulate the flow of water through each terrace and from one terrace to another. In the narrow valley a group of steep-roofed houses are shown crowded together so that they take up a minimum amount of space. Around the houses a few palm trees are growing. What can we learn about this part of the world from the picture? What relationships can we find? One key item which is shown, and which will help the children place the landscape, is the palm trees. They indicate that this landscape is in a semi-tropical or tropical climate. The rice, which the two men are transplanting on the terrace, is usually grown in regions which have heavy rainfall or easily available irrigation waters. Rice produces more food per acre than any other plant in regions with a frost-free climate because two—and sometimes three—crops can be grown each year. We can conclude that there is a dense population because most of the hillsides in the picture are terraced. Rice is seen growing on all of them, and rice requires much labor. The way in which the houses are grouped together indicates that every bit of land must be used for food production; no land around the houses is allowed to lie idle. The steep, wide roofs of the houses give the villagers protection from heavy rains and hot sun. The shadows of the lightly clothed men working in the rice fields are very short and sharp, indicating that the sun is directly overhead. The picture must have been taken at about noon. The absence of other workers would seem to indicate that the fields have been deserted until after the daily rain.

What are the relationships we can find in the picture described above?

The planting of rice ———→ (is related to)	1. the need for food.
	2. dense population.
	3. heavy rains.
The terracing of the land ———→	1. the need for land.
	2. the use of hillsides.
The climate of Java ———→	1. the position of the sun nearly always overhead.
	2. daily rains which occur in the low pressure area near the equator.

The growing of palm trees ——————→	1. the frost-free climate. 2. the need for shade. 3. the large number of products obtainable from the tree.
The steep, wide roofs ——————→	the need for protection from the hot sun and heavy rains.
Living in houses crowded closely together ——————→	the great need for land on which to raise food.

One of the chief values of pictures is the contribution they make to the pupil's geographic vocabulary. So often our pupils do not acquire an accurate idea of what we are trying to teach them due to their misinterpretation of the geographic terms and expressions which we use. If we use pictures to help clarify the meanings of geographic terms and expressions, there is very little chance that our pupils will misinterpret them and they will become part of their vocabulary and thought. How many times have we seen the eyes of a child light up as he finally understands, with the help of a picture!

Another value to be derived from the use of pictures is the stimulation of geographic thought. Pupils who can be taught to think geographically will live much fuller lives as a result of their increased understanding of what they see in the world around them. Before a pupil can answer questions about the lives of the people shown in a series of pictures, he must first recall all that he knows about the region. As relationships between the human activities and the environmental factors depicted are brought to his attention, his concepts expand and are reinforced and he is able to do critical thinking about the area. This careful examination of pictures often gives rise to thought-provoking questions which spur the pupil on to further research, and to draw inferences from what he sees in other pictures. He is also induced to use pictures to help prove that the conclusions at which he has arrived are correct.

Pictures are essential in teaching the meaning of map symbols. Every child must be able to visualize what each symbol represents before he can interpret the symbols on the map. Pictures illustrative of the various map symbols should be selected with care so that the children will be forming clear concepts of the various natural and cultural items shown on maps. The symbols should be taught, of course, as they are needed by the pupils.

There is an emotional value to be found in the use of pictures which should not be overlooked. We always want our pupils to understand, respect, and admire, some things in all people, even those of the most primitive cultures. While a first glance at many pictures of primitive living conditions may fail to excite admiration, we want our pupils to be able to understand why the conditions exist, and to have sympathy and respect for those who do a great deal with the little that they have in environmental resources. For instance, a popular magazine recently carried a large picture of an Arab child with a bit of the desert showing in the background. The child was clad in flowing robes which appeared to be far from clean. From beneath a tattered head covering peered bright, intelligent eyes. Tangled strands of matted hair hung around the child's face. At first glance, the viewer would be tempted to exclaim, "My, what a dirty child!" But one who has been trained to think geographically questions the obvious and tries to find reasons for conditions shown. How could this child be clean when every drop of water that his people could get would probably be needed for cooking and drinking purposes? The supply of water might be many miles away. Seldom would the child be able to have the luxury of a bath and clean clothing. Why is his hair matted and stringy? The wind, sand, and heat suggested by the background are to a large measure responsible. When money is almost nonexistent, how can money be spared for a comb? "If we lived there," we might ask our pupils, "would our problems be similar? This boy's bright eyes would seem to indicate that he is intelligent. He will not know about many of the things that we do because he lacks education as we think of it, but he *does* know how to survive in desert lands. How many of us could do that? Would you like to have him for a friend?" In speaking of a picture such as this, in the manner suggested, we have built sympathy, understanding, and an appreciation of the problems of an entire people. Best of all, we have taught our pupils not to make quick judgments from a casual glance at a single picture.

Selection of Geographic Pictures

Today we have many sources of pictures but most of the pictures which are available have little geographic value. A picture, to be of value in the teaching of geography, should show topography, give some indication of the type of climate, illustrate how man works and lives in the region portrayed, and be suitable for the maturity of pupils using it. What are the criteria for selecting geographic pictures?

Geography pictures must be selected for their geographic quality. There are several qualities of geographic pictures, depending upon the relationship which they show. In pictures of high geographic quality, the relationship of man's activities to his natural environment is shown. This is described as a natural to cultural relationship. In a picture showing harvesting of wheat on vast areas of rolling land in Nebraska, the harvesting of wheat with a heavy combine would be related to the dry harvest season and to the rolling land on which the large combines can be used. (C–N.) Pictures of medium geographic quality might show or suggest the relationship of natural items to the natural landscape. For example, the forest growth on the slopes of the Cascades would be related to the mountain barrier and to the moisture laden westerly winds. (N–N.) Medium geographic quality pictures also include how human activities are related to cultural landscapes. A picture of trucks filled with raw cotton, standing in front of a cotton gin, might suggest that the need for a cotton gin is related to the raising of cotton. (C–C.) Pictures of low geographic quality are usually those which portray a natural or cultural item with little or no landscape to suggest a relationship. Pictures of a building, a festive costume, an animal, or a plant—such as a banana plant—are of low geographic quality because they do not show relationship. However, these pictures have a definite place in the geography lesson. They are needed to build and enlarge geographic concepts.

As you select pictures to be used in the teaching of geography, be sure that they are truthful. They must be typical of the region as it is today, not atypical, and show life as it is being lived there now by most of the people. The pictures should not be of the unusual or bizarre. Pupils are quick to assume that pictures of the unique or atypical represent the entire landscape of the country, or the activities of the people. Pictures more than five years old can create incorrect concepts of the country, too. A five-year-old picture taken in Europe would show many changes, whereas a five-year-old picture taken in Mongolia would reveal little change. Nevertheless, changes in the world take place constantly, even in some of the most remote areas. For this reason, in order to convey true concepts of people and lands, your picture file must be kept up-to-date.

Select pictures for specific purposes. Perhaps a picture is needed to introduce the concept of how cacao pods develop on the trunks and large limbs of the tree, and another picture is required to expand the concept of how transportation is related to topography. Only these two pictures are selected and used in the lesson, regardless of how many interesting pictures are available. Pictures should never be selected simply because they show scenic views or cultural items of the region under study. Each picture must contribute to the solution of the problem being discussed, the development of a concept, show relationship, or assist in building vocabulary.

To be worthwhile, the pictures must be selected for key items which illustrate points to be considered. Photographs are usually taken for a definite reason: to show some particular thing, the way work is done, the way people live, or natural or cultural conditions in a region. Each picture has a center of interest or principal idea. Often the background will contribute much to help the pupils understand the relationships shown in the picture. Direct the attention of the pupils to the most important items in the picture. Then ask for the factors which have contributed to the center of interest. We want the children to form the habit of looking for reasons which account for the obviously true fact or relationship portrayed. There should be key items in geographic pictures which provide clues to the elevation, the amount of rainfall, or the latitude. In an application lesson on latitude, the teacher might have several pictures of lands in different latitudes. Each should have a key item which would indicate what might be found at that latitude the world over. For example, at 0° to 20°, palm trees might be the key item; at 30° to 40°, corn or winter wheat might indicate the latitude; at 60°, coniferous trees; furbearing animals, travel by dog sled, or caribou might suggest regions near the North Pole. Key items are important in identifying countries, industries, and landscapes.

Pupils can get much information from pictures if they can read meaning into them. We should never take for granted that they all "see" the same things in a picture. Pupils must be taught how to read pictures for the geographic information they contain and the relationships which they suggest. There are many significant things pictured which will be passed over as unimportant unless we call attention to them and explain their meaning. The pupils will need help at first in judging the size of objects, in estimating distances, and in determining the amount of rainfall the region receives. (See page 130.) They will need to know what certain key items in the landscape indicate. In a farm picture, for example, a silo attached to a barn usually indicates that the farm is a dairy farm. Shadows always create interest in pictures. They can disclose direction and the approximate time of day when the photograph was taken. Concepts such as these make picture reading an interesting exercise and the interpretation of pictures challenging.

In teaching the pupils how to read pictures, we might ask them to name some of the things they see in the picture. Next, ask:

"What are the people doing? What tells you this is true? In what way does the method of doing the work differ from the way we may have seen it done here in the United States? What would you judge the climate of this place to be? What tells you this? In what ways does the surface affect the lives of the people living here?" If there are houses in the picture, ask the pupils to explain how the style of house is related to the environment. "Is this a large or a small house? What do you see in the picture which gives you an idea about relative size? Now, we'll check what we have learned from this picture with the information we can find in our textbooks and with other sources to see whether our assumptions are correct." The teacher can direct the attention of the pupils to important items in the picture which he wants to emphasize in order to give them the understandings he wishes them to have. In other words, we ask, "What do you see? What does it mean? Are our conclusions correct?"

The effective use of pictures in the teaching of geography requires that they be used as integral parts of the lesson. Always give the pupil something definite and worthwhile for which to look. It may be for some information which will aid the class in the solution of a problem, or perhaps for an inference to be drawn from what is seen in the picture. Be certain to check to see if the pupil has the required information. If you fail to check, he feels that he has been given an insignificant task and that it is of no importance whether or not the work is done. Ample time should be provided for the discussion of each picture, for answering questions concerning it, for drawing conclusions, and for writing arrow statements (relationships).

The discussion should raise questions which can be answered only by further investigation. There are always a great many "whys" involved in the study of pictures. It is these "whys" which provide the opportunity for further interesting work by the pupils on their own. Many inaccurate concepts can be corrected through the study of pictures. We must remember to use few (possibly only three or four), rather than many pictures as we plan a particular lesson. Too many pictures tend to confuse pupils and lead to the scattering of interest rather than the concentration of it. Consider, too, the use of pictures with captions. Some teachers prefer uncaptioned pictures so that pupils will read the picture rather than the caption. Others cover the caption with a pertinent question of their own.

When discussing a picture, be sure that all of the pupils can see it clearly. When mounted or unmounted pictures are shown only at the front of the room, very few pupils can see them well enough to note details in the background. Such details are often important in understanding relationships. Ask the question you wish to ask about the picture; then, walk along the aisles with the picture so that all of the pupils may see the answer to it. After all of the pupils have seen the picture, call for the answer to your question. (For the use of an opaque projector in this connection, see Other Audio-Visual Aids, page 185.) Pictures can be used in all parts of the unit but care must be taken in their selection so that the purpose for which they have been chosen may be achieved. Pictures, when used in the motivation, help to orient the pupils to the environment which they are going to be studying, enabling them to get the "feel" of the region, sense its characteristics, and recognize that the region has a geographic personality of its own. In motivating a unit of work, the curiosity of the pupils may be aroused by showing them pictures of human activities with which they are not familiar. Often key questions which require answers will take form in their minds as they study a picture. In talking about a picture of a village east of the Caspian, for instance, the teacher might ask:

"Why would these people use this unusual means of transportation (horse with arch yoke and cart)? Is this a mark of poverty or of practicality? Why do you think so? Notice the dress of the people. What would you judge the climate of this place to be from the type of clothing the people are wearing? What might be one reason for this type of dress? What are these people transporting? In what direction might traffic be moving?" Judge by the shadow. "In what way has western civilization touched this remote place?" In order to answer these questions, the pupils will feel the need to obtain more information and they will be motivated to read more reference material.

Another way to introduce a unit with pictures is to compare and contrast two or more regions. For a unit on Mediterranean lands, have several pictures showing the landscape and activities of the people of Southern Italy, California, and Central Chile. The teacher can motivate the work by saying, "These pictures are of countries which will have a Mediterranean climate. Let us see in what ways these countries are similar. As we study, whenever we find differences, we shall try to find reasons for them." The teacher will provide each member of the class with a chart similar to the one which follows. The pupils will fill in the charts as they discuss the pictures and read reference materials.

MEDITERRANEAN-TYPE CLIMATES	SIMILARITIES	DIFFERENCES
Southern Italy Southern California		
Southern Italy Central Chile		
Central Chile Southern California		

In the development or problem solving part of the unit, pictures are almost indispensable for introducing and developing geographic concepts which may be new or not clear to the pupils. We cannot depend upon their imaginations. If relationships can be seen in pictures they are much more easily understood. Inferences drawn from map study or reading materials can be quickly checked and verified with pictures. Pictures are valuable in solving problems which confront pupils as they study. In studying remote lands, such as northern Alaska, pupils might come to the conclusion that, since there are no natural sources for hydroelectric power near the northern interior, homes there would not have electric lights. A picture of the interior of an Eskimo home, appearing in the *National Geographic Magazine* or some other source, might show that this is not true. The pupils would then have to be led to the conclusion that electric power can be produced by small, gasoline-driven generators which can be found in the most remote places of the world. Pictures help to verify facts.

In giving special reports, pupils will have a more attentive audience if they make the talk interesting by using pictures to illustrate specific points. Pupils should be taught to look in the direction of any picture which they wish their audience to observe. The attention of the class is thus drawn to the picture. Pictures should not be passed about among the class members during a report since they distract class attention from what the speaker has to say.

Pictures are excellent to use in summarizing the work covered in the unit. Several pictures of the region just studied, which show relationships, are selected by the teacher. Individual pupils are each given a picture and are asked to explain why the relationship shown in it exists. Another way to use pictures to summarize the material learned, is to have collected a set of uncaptioned pictures of the region. As the teacher holds up each picture from the collection, pupils are asked to identify it and to locate, on a large map, the place where it belongs.

There will be many ways to check the concepts developed by the pupils through the application of the facts they have learned to new and different situations. Pictures provide an excellent means for doing this in the application step of the unit. Plan a picture journey with the pupils. On the chalk board or on wrapping paper draw a large outline map of the region which has been studied. Have the pupils plan the route of the journey to be taken and plot it on the map. Place numbers along the route at various places for which you have pictures. Ask the pupils to select pictures which show what they would see at each numbered location and place them correctly on the map.

Testing with pictures is perhaps one of the best uses to which they can be put. A picture test appeals to the pupils. The picture test is easy to answer and can be checked quickly by the teacher. It provides both the teacher and the pupils with many opportunities to check and correct wrong concepts. There are several ways to test with pictures. One way is to select and mount ten, or fewer, pictures on heavy construction paper. Below each picture place a question about the picture, together with several possible answers. Each pupil is provided with an answer sheet on which appear the numbered, multiple-choice answers for each picture's question. After studying the picture, the pupil underlines the correct answer on his answer sheet.

Another equally good method is to pass the mounted pictures, without captions, to part of the class, and to provide each pupil with a question sheet such as that which follows.

These are pictures of various parts of Australia. Each numbered question below corresponds with one of the numbered pictures. Can you answer the questions on the lines provided?

1. These animals are found only in Australia. What are they? ——————
2. This is a mining town in Western Australia. It is located in a desert. What town is it? ——————————————————————————
   What are they mining here? ——————————————
3. Sheep raising is the leading industry. Give three ways, which you can see in the picture, that sheep raising in Australia differs from sheep raising in England.

   ————————————————————————————————
   ————————————————————————————————
   ————————————————————————————————
4. Where is this bridge located? ——————————————————

5. This is a new city in Australia. It was designed by an American. What is the city? ————————————————

6. These plants (bananas and pineapples) grow in Australia. Name the Australian state where we might find them. ————————————————

7. Identify each of the cities on this map. (Seven locations on an outline map are circled.) ————————————————

8. These boats are unloading iron ore in southeastern Australia. The steel mill is back of the mill yard. Name this important steel center. ————————

9. This is the climatic graph of one of Australia's large cities. Which city has these climatic conditions? ————————————————

10. This is a picture of one of Australia's chief exports. There are two places where this picture might have been taken. Name one. ————————

It will take planning to administer this test, for rarely does one have more pictures on a single subject than he has pupils in his class. Give the picture test to half of the class and provide a second part of the test for the other half. Have a few more pictures than there are pupils taking the picture test. Each pupil has a duplicated sheet with a numbered question for each picture. The number on the picture corresponds with the question number on the sheet. The pupils pass the picture to pupils in back of them on a signal given by the teacher. Some questions may require a little more time to answer, but the pictures should be passed on signal. At the end of the test, the pupils who have not completed the questions for certain pictures may get them and finish up the test. The next day reverse the parts of the test, having the pupils who tried the picture test work on the second half of the test. This type of test is one of the best ways to check the concepts of children.

Sequential Development of Picture Reading Skills

In the fourth sequence, we expect our pupils to develop the ability to recognize in pictures the natural items which are characteristic of the regions or areas studied, as well as the cultural items. We also expect them to recognize items which serve to set the region apart from all other regions. We also teach them how to read into pictures probable geographic relationships. For example, if the picture shown is of persons in loosely flowing clothing who are taking down tents and packing possessions on camels, we would expect our pupils to infer that this is a picture of nomadic grazing, that it is a dry region, and consequently that there is not enough pasturage in one place to last any great length of time. The herds must be moved frequently to fresh pasture and to watering places. Tents are the most convenient kind of shelter when people must move every few weeks or days. Fourth sequence pupils are also taught how to identify the landscapes of various regions and to associate particular types of landscape with particular geographic regions. (For example: In which of the following places was the picture taken? a. Congo b. Sahara c. Italy d. Holland.) We also expect to make them conscious of the landscapes which they see when they travel, not simply as passing scenery, but as a part of a geographic "book" which they are learning to read.

In the fifth sequence we expect our pupils to develop the ability to identify such cultural items and human activities as crops (small grains, corn, sugar cane, tobacco, vegetables, orchard fruits); farm operations (plowing, planting, harvesting, irrigating, filling a silo, making hay); certain types of manufacturing plants (iron and steel mills, shipbuilding yards, meat packing plants, saw mills, hydroelectric power plants, dams, paper pulp mills); types of transportation (railway yards, canal locks, tunnels, bridges, electrified railroads, passenger steamboats, freighters); and certain items characteristic of the various types of mining (coal mines and shafts, derricks, open pit mines). We also expect them to recognize landscapes characteristic of certain types of activities in specific regions of the United States, such as lumbering in the Pacific Northwest, farming in the Corn Belt, and ranching on the Great Plains; to recognize landscapes characteristic of certain regions in both the United States and Canada; to read into a picture (i.e., to draw inferences) the meaning of relationships of human activities to natural environments; to read from pictures the relations of various land forms to climatic conditions, such as rainfall; to match a given set of pictures with a given list of places; to arrange pictures of farm or other activities into groups according to seasons; and to arrange a set of pictures of the United States in order from east to west, and from north to south.

Sixth and seventh sequence pupils, in addition to knowing all that has been listed for fourth and fifth sequence pupils, must also be able to select from a given set of pictures those which are typical of a specific country that has been studied, to display increased facility in reading into pictures geographic relationships, and to recognize scenes characteristic of the great cities of the world.

Teaching with Statistics

Statistics are often avoided by teachers because their application demands careful planning and clear thinking, but they have an important place in geographic education, helping the teacher to arouse the curiosity of the pupils, stimulating their asking of questions, helping them to obtain necessary information, furnishing proof for statements found in geographic reading material, and assisting in conveying concepts needed to reach some geographic understandings. The latest statistics must always be used so that our pupils will receive an up-to-date picture of the country or region being studied. The many changes which occur from year to year in the economy of countries and in world patterns of distribution will be very evident when these statistics are compared with those of earlier years. Children should be made aware that these changes take place. The geography of a region changes constantly, and textbooks a few years old may not present true pictures of the country or area under study. We can easily correct this situation by consulting a book of reliable statistics, such as *The Statistical Abstract of the United States, The Statesman's Year-Book,* or *The South American Handbook,* and noting any changes which have taken place, before we begin to teach the unit each year.

Probably the greatest contribution of statistics to geographic education is in showing the pattern of distribution of such geographic factors as climate, population, minerals, crop production, and trade movement. When changes do occur in world patterns, they are evident in the statistics of the countries involved. A prolonged drought may make changes in the list of a country's exports, in its crop production statistics, and even in its population distribution. To account for these changes, the pupils are motivated to do interesting research, with the result that they have additional practice in thinking through newly discovered relationships.

Statistics are fascinating to pupils if they are presented in a challenging and interesting way. The ability to read and interpret statistics is developed slowly and cumulatively. At every opportunity the teacher must bring statistics to the attention of the pupils with the idea of having them search for the facts behind the figures in order to discover their meaning in relation to human activity. There needs to be quite a bit of background teaching done to enable our pupils to "read between the lines," and they must have some knowledge of geographic fundamentals, but it takes skillful questioning on the part of the teacher to lead his pupils to draw inferences and arrive at conclusions. At first, the work in interpreting statistics must necessarily be simple, but as the pupils develop their reasoning abilities, the level of difficulty may be increased. In spite of the amount of work connected with it, the teaching of the interpretation of statistics is very rewarding because there are very few kinds of work which will promote logical thinking to the degree that this does.

How shall we develop the ability to interpret statistical material in geography? Statistics, like all reading material, must be graded according to the readiness of the pupil to understand the concepts involved in them. A child in the fourth sequence, although interested in "big" things and the statistics related to them, has little use for concepts which involve quantitative comparisons. Consequently, this work is usually introduced in the fifth sequence. At the beginning, the pupils must be taught to read the usual and unusual facts which appear in tables of statistics. Next, they must be able to recognize statistics which will help them to solve problems. Finally, they need constant guidance and adroit questioning from the teacher as they are taught to look for the implied facts with which they will be able to draw conclusions. By studying the statistics of a region, they should become able to explain the human activities taking place there and to point out interesting trends by comparing recent statistics with older ones. None of this is difficult if we proceed slowly from statistics which require simple interpretations to those which are more difficult.

Begin the fifth sequence work in statistics by giving the pupils a list of large cities in the United States—or of a section of the United States— together with the population for each. Ask them to find the five or ten largest cities and arrange them in order of size, from largest to smallest. If the class were studying a section of the United States, such as the New England States, the children could be asked to arrange the states of the section in order, according to area, or in order, according to population.

TABLE 1   Statistics Concerning the New England States (1960)

STATES	AREA IN SQ. MILES	POPU- LATION	CITIES	POPU- LATION
Maine	33,200	969,000	Boston, Mass.	697,000
New Hampshire	9,300	607,000	Bridgeport, Conn.	157,000
Vermont	9,600	390,000	Cambridge, Mass.	108,000
Massachusetts	8,200	5,149,000	Hartford, Conn.	162,000
Rhode Island	1,200	859,000	New Bedford, Mass.	103,000
Connecticut	5,000	2,535,000	New Haven, Conn.	152,000
			Providence, R.I.	208,000
			Waterbury, Conn.	107,000
			Worcester, Mass.	187,000

Source: *Statistical Abstract of the United States* (Washington, D.C., U.S. Government Printing Office, 1965).

As a second step in developing the ability to read and interpret statistics, give the pupils a list of states and the amount or value of production of a certain crop or mineral and have them arrange the states in descending order of production or value of the crop. In the list, be sure that figures have been rounded off to the nearest whole numbers. The teacher will ask questions about the facts presented in the table until the pupils are able to discover for themselves what the facts imply. As they discover implications, have them write their interpretations beneath the list. An example of how to make use of a statistical table follows.

TABLE 2   Chief Cotton Producing States and the Amount of Cotton Produced in Each (Number of Bales of 500 Pounds Each) 1964

STATE	TOTAL BALES	NUMBERS ROUNDED OFF	YIELD PER ACRE IN POUNDS
Alabama	895,000	900,000	518
Arizona	835,000	840,000	1,069
Arkansas	1,580,000	1,580,000	611
California	1,820,000	1,820,000	1,174
Georgia	620,000	620,000	470
Louisiana	595,000	600,000	549
Mississippi	2,240,000	2,240,000	736
South Carolina	550,000	550,000	491
Tennessee	675,000	680,000	648
Texas	4,125,000	4,130,000	349
All others	1,421,000	1,420,000	
Total	15,356,000	15,360,000	

SOURCE: *Statistical Abstract of the United States* (Washington, D.C., U.S. Government Printing Office, 1965).

"Let us see what we can learn about the production of cotton in the United States from this statistical table.

✓ What was the total production of the United States in number of bales of cotton in 1964?
✓ What state leads in the amount of cotton produced? Approximately what part of the total cotton crop did this state produce? Why was this possible?
✓ Where in the United States are most of the states on the list located? Let's put a chalk mark on the map showing the location of each of the states listed. Where do we find most of them?
✓ What must be true about the length of growing season and the amount of rainfall which these states receive? *Average two-hundred-day growing season, twenty to sixty inches of annual rainfall with a dry harvest season.*
✓ What two states in this list would be exceptions in having these conditions?
✓ How do you account for their large production of cotton?
✓ Why would Florida not be a large producer of cotton?
✓ In the last column to the right, the yield of cotton per acre for each state is given. What interesting facts can you find about the amount of cotton per acre the states produce? Can you account for the differences in the yield per acre among the states?"

Many relationships are implicit in the foregoing table and, as the teacher studies it with his pupils, he will want to discuss some of them. For instance, the yield per acre is related to many factors such as soil fertility, irrigation, mechanization in planting and harvesting, and so on.

Statistics become even more interesting for pupils of the sixth and junior high school sequences. By the time they reach junior high school, they will realize how much information can be obtained from statistics if they have had training in the interpretation of them in their former sequences. Their widened experience and increased reasoning ability, which result from their study of the world, enable them to become more proficient in reading between the lines and in drawing correct inferences. Suppose that in the study of a country of western Europe, oats is mentioned as a crop raised there. The teacher asks:

"Just why would the people raise oats? For what purpose are oats used? We know that corn and wheat are very important grains in the world, but are there many oats grown? Let's look at this statistical table to see if we can discover the answers to these questions."

TABLE 3   Chief Oat Producing Countries of the World
(Oats Measured in Metric Tons)

World Total	48,300,000
United States	14,000,000
Canada	7,000,000
France	2,900,000
Poland	2,800,000
West Germany	2,300,000
United Kingdom	1,500,000
Australia	1,300,000
Sweden	1,200,000
Argentina	900,000
Finland	800,000
East Germany	800,000

SOURCE: Figures rounded off from *1964 Statistical Yearbook* (New York, The United Nations). Copyright, United Nations, 1965. Reproduced by permission.

- "What is the world's production of oats?
- What countries are the two greatest producers of oats? What part of the total production did they grow?
- On what continent are these two countries?
- Look over the list and tell me on which continent most of the remaining countries are located? *Europe.*
- There is quite a difference in the amount of oats produced by the second and third largest producers. What must be considered? *Size.*
- How does the area of France compare with that of the United States? *The*

United States is about seventeen times the size of France. How does Poland compare in size with the state in which you live? Knowing the area of the country and the amount of its production helps us to determine whether or not this grain is an important crop in the country.

⟡ On this world map we shall circle the countries which are the chief producers of oats and see what that will tell us." Have a pupil encircle the chief oat-producing countries.

⟡ "What do you notice about the growing of oats in the southern hemisphere? I wonder why this is true?

⟡ Look again at the map and see if we can learn under what conditions oats will grow best. What type of climate does the north-central United States and south-central Canada have? *Short summer, humid continental.* What type of climate do the countries of Western Europe have? *West coast marine.* What conclusion would you draw concerning the climate in which oats will grow well? *Oats grow well in cool, moist climates.*

⟡ In what part of Australia do you think oats would be grown if they require a cool, moist climate?

⟡ What is the chief use of oats? *Feed for cattle and horses, as a grain and sometimes as hay. It is also a principal source of food for human consumption.*

⟡ Using an outline map of the world, make a distribution map to show the production of oats throughout the world. Use the figures given in the table." See Distribution Maps, page 82.

After this lesson in the reading and interpretation of statistics, the pupils will have a much better understanding of the importance of oat production to the world. They will have experienced inductive reasoning, made their own discoveries, and enlarged several geographic concepts.

POINTS TO BE REMEMBERED WHEN USING STATISTICS

❖ Be sure to use reliable sources and the most recent statistics. Pupils should be taught to record the sources of the statistics which they use. (See Bibliography, page 285.)

❖ Be certain that the concepts gained from the statistics contribute to the major understanding being developed. Never use statistical work as "busy work."

❖ Make statistics less cumbersome by rounding off numbers. This will facilitate handling and make it far easier to compare amounts.

❖ The inferences sought should be based upon well-founded concepts which have already been mastered.

THE USE OF STATISTICS IN DEVELOPING A UNIT   Statistics may be used in any part of a unit. Wherever there is a need for the information which statistics can provide, or wherever they can add to geographic understanding, they should be used in the unit. They are especially effective in the motivation of a unit because they build a readiness to learn by stimulating curiosity as well as providing information about the area to

be studied. Often the challenging questions asked by the pupils suggest problems to be solved as they continue their study.

Suppose that you are about to begin the study of Japan. Plan to motivate the unit with statistics. Give each pupil a list of the exports and imports of Japan, together with the value of each.

TABLE 4   Value of the Principal Exports and Imports of Japan

EXPORTS		IMPORTS	
Total Exports	$6,673,191,000	Total Imports	$7,938,000,000
Iron and steel	910,000,000	Petroleum	1,154,000,000
Ships	476,000,000	Machinery	825,000,000
Cotton fabrics	310,000,000	Chemical products	458,000,000
Clothes	252,000,000	Cotton	439,000,000
Metal products	236,000,000	Lumber	438,000,000
Fish and shell fish	223,000,000	Iron ore	420,000,000
Radio receivers	214,000,000	Wool	376,000,000
Automobiles	181,000,000	Wheat	262,000,000
Textile machinery and		Nonferrous metals	255,000,000
sewing machines	153,000,000	Sugar	249,000,000
Rayon fabrics	151,000,000	Iron and steel	
Optical instruments	144,000,000	scrap	235,000,000
Toys	93,000,000	Coal	211,000,000
Chinaware	79,000,000	Corn	209,000,000
Plywood	69,000,000	Soybeans	185,000,000
Chemical fertilizers	57,000,000	Iron and steel	176,000,000

SOURCE: Compiled from *The Statesman's Year-Book*, 1965–66 (London, Macmillan & Co. Ltd.), 1965.

The teacher asks, "Do you like puzzles? Hidden in these statistics are many puzzling and interesting facts about Japan. Let us see how many things we can discover about this country by studying the list of exports and imports." The teacher writes facts and inferences on the board as they are given by the class.

- "Compare the total value of exports with the total value of the imports. How can Japan buy more than she sells, that is, how can her imports exceed her exports? How can the deficiency be made up? *Japan receives many manufactured parts from other countries which her workers assemble and which she then returns in the form of completed products. She thus exports labor, although her people never leave home. In addition, one of her principal sources of income is tourism, in which she is, in a sense, exporting services.*
- What must be the chief industry of Japan according to the exports? What does the list of exports reveal about the type of work in which Japan excels? *Technical; requires skill.*

- Into what categories will most of Japan's imports fit? *Raw materials and food.* From what countries will most of Japan's imports come?
- What does the large export of iron and steel tell you about Japan? To what extent is Japan self-sufficient in the raw materials needed for the steel industry?
- Examine the list of exports. For which of the manufactured products does Japan have the raw materials?
- Japan must sell her manufactured goods. Where will her markets be?" Consider the buying powers of the different countries.
- Explain why the value of imported raw cotton is much greater than the export of cotton fabrics.
- "What conclusion can you draw about the ability of Japan to feed herself?"
- Suggest a reason why Japan imports so much petroleum. *Thirty-seven percent of Japan's supply of energy is derived from petroleum. Energy derived from petroleum is increasing while that produced from coal is decreasing.*
- "What general statements can you make about Japan which you have already discovered through the study of her exports and imports?"

"As we were studying these statistics, questions may have come to your minds which you would like to have answered. Let us list some of them and try to find answers for them as we continue our study." The pupils will ask questions similar to these:

- How important to Japan is her trade with the United States?
- Why isn't Japan able to feed her people?
- What natural resources does Japan have?
- Why does Japan make manufactured goods if she has to buy the raw materials for them?
- Why is Japan's economy so much better than that of other Asian countries?

This motivation makes it possible for the teacher and pupils to work together to plan where they need to do further research and how they will do it.

JAPAN: LAND USE GRAPH

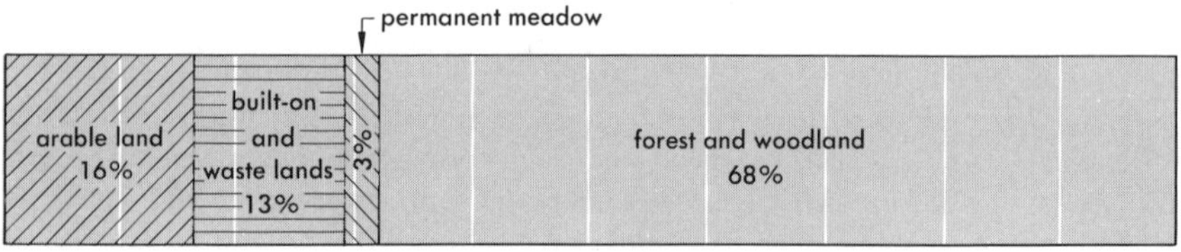

Figure 25

In the development or problem-solving part of the unit, solutions are sought for the problems set up by the class. Statistics are often used to prove a point, to provide additional information, and to supply figures for the making of graphs and distribution maps to illustrate relationships.

In trying to solve the problem of why Japan cannot feed herself, statistics can be very helpful. Statistics relating to area, population, and density of population are basic to an understanding of this problem. Statistics for Japan may be compared with those of California. Land use statistics, such as arable land, 16%; permanent meadow, 3%; forest and woodland, 68%; land built on and waste lands, 13%, will help to show how Japan is handicapped agriculturally. Translate these statistics into graphic form by drawing a simple, single bar graph to show the land use. The graph will make the statistical table more meaningful. Then ask questions similar to those which follow. Why is there so little arable land in Japan? (Refer to a physical-political map.) Why is there so little land in permanent meadow? Where would the forest and woodland be found? A study of the amount of the principal crops grown will lead to a study of the methods used by the Japanese farmer to produce Japan's food. The problems which he has to face will mean further research into the factors which favor and those which handicap agriculture.

TABLE 5   Amount of Principal Crops Produced in Japan (1961)

CROP	METRIC TONS
Rice	12,400,000
Sweet potatoes	6,300,000
Irish potatoes	3,900,000
Barley	2,000,000
Wheat	1,800,000
Soybeans	400,000
Maize	100,000

SOURCE: *The Statesman's Year-Book, 1965–66* (London, Macmillan & Co. Ltd.), 1965.

As the development of the unit proceeds, statistical tables on the several topics will add immeasurably to the geographic understandings and concepts which you wish your pupils to have about Japan.

The foregoing work illustrates the use to which statistics can be put in the development or problem-solving stage of a unit.

If the statistics on exports and imports are not used elsewhere, they may be used in summarizing the unit. Ask the pupils to account for the different exports and to tell from which part of the country, or from which city, they came. Imports show the needs of a country. Have the pupils account for the needs of the country just studied and tell from which country the imports come.

If you feel that you must test the pupils with regard to the statistics which you have used in the unit, please remember that statistics change from year to year, and that, therefore, a memory test is never to be used. Rather, you must test your pupils on the insights which they have gained from their study of statistics, insights which are capable of application to the statistics of any country at any time. Test the pupils' ability to think inferentially and analytically and avoid measuring their ability to commit to memory long lists of products and mere numbers.

The following lesson outlines procedures which may be used to make the study of statistics enjoyable, challenging, and enlightening, and demonstrates how statistics can become the focal point in the teacher's plan.

THE MYSTERY COUNTRY, A LESSON IN THE READING AND INTERPRETATION OF STATISTICS.[1] Give the following statistics of an unknown country to the pupils. The purpose of the lesson is to discover, with the aid of maps, the globe, and climatic graphs, to which country in the world these statistics belong. There should be a seasonal precipitation map of the world, a world physical-political map, and a globe where the pupils can refer to them at any time during the lesson. The pupils should have their textbooks or an atlas opened to a physical map of the world.

[1] Much of the material presented in this lesson appeared originally in *The Journal of Geography*, Vol. 51 (1952), "The Mystery Country—A Lesson in Reading Graphs and Statistics" by Linnie B. James. The authors are grateful to *The Journal of Geography*, and to Dr. Herbert H. Gross, ed., for permission to quote and abstract from that article. All of the statistics have been brought up to date, and changes in the method of teaching the lesson have been included here.

TABLE 6   To What Country Do These Statistics Belong?

Area	103,736 square miles
Population	2,594,420
Density of population	23.3 per square mile

LAND USE	ACRES	PERCENTAGE OF CULTI- VATED LAND
Total Area	66,390,700	
Unimproved land (native grasses, bush, unproductive)	44,396,435	
Total cultivated land	21,994,265	
Pasture	18,247,832	82.3%
Field Crops	2,561,194	13.3%
Plantations (conifers, eucalyptus)	1,041,476	3.6%
Orchards (90% apple, pear, peaches)	31,881	.2%
Lying fallow	111,882	.6%

DISTRIBUTION OF IMPORTANT CROPS	ACRES	PERCENTAGE OF EACH CROP TO TOTAL CROP AREA[a]
Total	2,561,194	100%
Grasses and clover for hay and silage	988,882	34%
Turnips and swedes	459,620	20%
Green fodder	246,315	9%
Wheat	207,860	8%
Grasses and clovers for seed	187,612	7%
Lucerne for hay or silage	159,274	6%
Barley	103,961	5%
Oats	73,075	4%
Peas	29,971	2%
Potatoes	25,045	1%
All others	79,579	4%

PASTORAL PRODUCTION

Sheep	51,291,898
Beef cattle	3,567,768
Dairy cattle	3,128,437
Pigs	771,450
Horses (estimated)	25,000

EXPORTS[b]

Total Exports (U.S. Dollars)	$1,018,054,800
Wool	379,601,600
Frozen meats (beef, veal, lamb, pork)	252,232,400
Butter	153,109,600
Cheese	49,120,000
Hides and skins	42,509,600
Milk (dried, condensed)	17,318,000
Sausage casings	16,780,400
Newsprint, paper	16,125,200
Casein	15,884,400
Woodpulp	7,700,000
Apples	6,899,200
Seeds (grass and clover)	4,827,200
Fishery products	4,365,200
Canned meats	3,567,200
All others	48,014,800

IMPORTS

Total Imports (U.S. dollars)	$878,253,600
Machinery (exclusive of electric)	103,118,400
Motor vehicles	98,560,000

IMPORTS (*Cont.*)

Iron and steel products	70,361,200
Electrical machinery	66,715,600
Petroleum and petroleum products	64,069,600
Textiles and textile fibers	45,228,400
Metal manufactures, excluding machinery	31,217,200
Raw sugar	26,882,800
Chemicals	20,344,800
Medicines and pharmaceuticals	15,758,400
Tractors (agricultural and industrial)	15,408,400
Textile yarn and thread	15,139,600
Paper	14,616,000
Wheat	10,712,800
Fruit (canned, fresh, dried)	10,054,800
Tea	7,196,000
All others	262,869,600

PRINCIPAL INDUSTRIES AND VALUE OF PRODUCTS (U.S. DOLLARS)

Meat freezing and preserving	$358,982,400
Butter, cheese, milk products	252,193,200
Motor and cycle repairs	118,420,400
Machinery, including agriculture	100,242,800
Clothing manufacture	100,007,600
Saw milling, planing	93,424,800
Motor vehicle assembly	90,272,000
Metal products	66,007,200
Printing and publishing	49,518,000
Sheet metal working	47,544,000
Joinery and wood products	42,282,800
Wool scouring	39,648,000
Chemical fertilizers	36,223,600
Footwear	34,353,200
Furniture	33,107,200

ᵃ Percentages are rounded and approximate.

ᵇ Export, Import, and Principal Industries and Value of Products statistics are from *The Statesman's Year-Book, 1965-66.* These statistics, orginally expressed in pounds, have been rounded off and converted to United States dollars.

SOURCE: Unless otherwise noted, source of statistics is the 1965 yearbook of the country under study.

MOTIVATION

"Do you like mystery stories? Do you ever listen to them on television? Usually the detectives do not make up their minds about the solution to the mystery until the last available clue has been found. Today I am giving you some statistics to study. They are about a country which you have not studied. On these sheets there are many clues which point to the name of the country. We are going to be detectives and find out the name of the country to which these statistics belong. You may look at all of the maps and the globe as much as you wish. However, wait until all of the evidence is in before you tell us what country you think we are talking about. Even good detectives sometimes make mistakes, you know! We will want to prove to our own satisfaction that we are right, over and over, before we say which country we think the answer is. I will ask for the name of the country at the close of the lesson. As we find clues, I will write them on the board for all of us to see."

DEVELOPMENT

1. "Look at the first page of statistics. How large is this country?

2. This country is about the size of Colorado. Would you consider it to be a large country or a small one?" Teacher writes on the board: small country about the size of Colorado.

3. "Name a state, county, or city with which we might compare the population of this country.

4. What is the density of population? How does this compare with the density of population of the United States?

5. Is this country densely or sparsely populated?" Teacher writes the second clue: Sparsely populated.

6. "Why isn't it always safe to judge a country by its density of population?

7. Now, let's find out how these people use the land. About what part is under cultivation? Approximately one-third?" Teacher writes the third clue: About one-third of the land is under cultivation.

8. "Examine the part of the table which tells us about the cultivated land. What do you think is the chief industry of this country? What tells you this?" Fourth clue: Grazing is the chief industry.

9. "What do the orchards tell you about this country? Notice what kinds of fruit are chiefly grown. In what kind of climate do hardy fruits grow?

10. 'Plantation' has a little different meaning in this mystery country than it has in ours. In the mystery country it means areas of planted trees. What trees have been the chief ones planted? It must be that the inhabitants need much soft wood if they are growing coniferous (cone-bearing) trees.

11. What does 'lying fallow' mean?

12. What part of the cultivated land is devoted to crops? If we learn what the crops are which the inhabitants raise, we will be able to judge what kind of climate they have.

13. What can we find in the third group of statistics which will tell us something about the country and the climate? *Most of these crops are used by livestock. If hay is grown, some parts of the country must be too cold for the pasturing of livestock out of doors during the winter. Root crops, turnips and potatoes, need cool, moist climate. Barley, also, needs moist climate.*"

14. The teacher explains the meaning of lucerne and swedes. "Why would our mystery country raise lucerne and swedes?

15. We agree, then, that some of the parts of this country must have a cool, moist climate?" Fifth clue: Some parts of the mystery country have a cool, moist climate.

16. "Look at the fourth group of statistics. What interesting facts do you find here?

17. Many countries of the world might have a moist climate. It might help us to eliminate some of them if we could learn whether the mystery country is in the northern or southern hemisphere." The teacher shows the pupils large climatic graphs like those which follow.

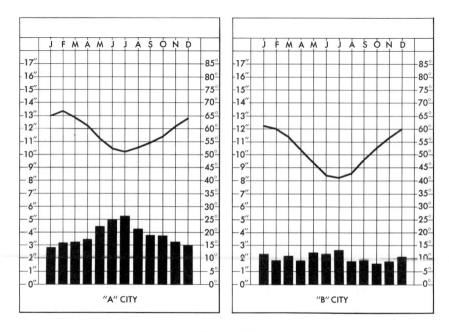

Figure 26

"These are climatic graphs of two of the cities of this country. Are these cities in the northern or southern hemisphere? How do you know? If this country is south of the equator, which of these cities is the farther south? How do you know?" Sixth clue: In the southern hemisphere.

18. "We still have some more clues hidden in these pages but let's glance over those which we have so far." Review the clues, reading them aloud to the class.

19. "Now we are ready for the exports and imports. What is true of most of the exports as far as major groups or classifications are concerned?

20. What is the leading industry as shown by the list of exports?

21. What other industries seem to be important?

22. To what factors is dairying usually related? Look at the three dairy

products exported. Do you think from the kind of dairy products listed that the market would be close to the mystery country or far away from it? In what way is the raising of pigs related to the making of these kinds of dairy products? *Whey from cheese, buttermilk from the making of butter, to feed the pigs.*

23. Notice that frozen lamb is exported. Do you recall whether the same conditions are required for mutton sheep that are required for wool sheep? *Must have better pastures for meat sheep.*

24. What must be true, then, with regard to precipitation?"

25. Refer to the graphs. "What do the climatic graphs suggest regarding the distribution of the precipitation? What effect would this have on the pasture lands?

26. The pattern of distribution of rainfall is similar in both parts where these cities are located, isn't it? 'A' City is on the western side of the mystery country and 'B' City is in the eastern part a little farther south than 'A' City. Can you tell me from which direction the wind blows?" Seventh clue: Rainfall evenly distributed throughout the year. This country receives over forty inches of rainfall in some parts. Winds will probably blow from the west. Why does 'B' City receive less rain than 'A' City?

27. "Now, let's look at the import list for more clues. Compare the amount of total exports with the amount of total imports. Is this a sign of a well-balanced economy, or a poorly balanced economy? What would conditions be like in the mystery country if she imported more goods that she exported? Could such a condition continue for a very long time?

28. What type of goods are most of the imports? *Manufactured.* Then manufacturing must be less important in the mystery country than are grazing and agriculture?

29. What is implied by the large amount of iron and steel products which are imported by the mystery country?

30. What is indicated by the large quantities of petroleum and petroleum products which are imported?

31. What does the importation of paper imply? *Tractors?*

32. What does the importation of unrefined sugar and tea tell you about the climate?

33. Look at the list of chief industries of the mystery country. To what are they related?"

SUMMARY

"Now let's read our clues over again to see if you think that we have enough clues to tell us the name of the mystery country."

1. Small country about the size of Colorado.
2. Sparsely populated.
3. About one-third of the land is under cultivation.
4. Grazing is the chief industry.
5. Some parts of the mystery country have a cool, moist climate.
6. In the southern hemisphere.
7. Rainfall evenly distributed throughout the year. This country receives over

forty inches of rainfall in some parts. Winds blow from the west. Must be in the belt of westerlies.

8. Exports raw materials and foods; imports manufactured goods.
9. The balance of trade shows a sound economy.
10. Manufacturing is less important than grazing and agriculture.
11. There must be good means of transportation.
12. There must be a lack of sufficient softwoods for paper.
13. Does not have a frost free climate in any part.

"To what country do you think these statistics belong? *New Zealand. 'A' City is Auckland. 'B' City is Christchurch.*"

CONCLUSION

"Having discovered what the mystery country is, our task will be to read about it and find out if our clues are correct. We shall want to find out why so much machinery and iron and steel are imported and from what countries these things come. We will want to know why so much meat is frozen for export and to what countries it is sent. We will also want to know more about the people who live in this beautiful country. They have been described as people who work hard and play hard. As we continue our study of New Zealand, we will discover what games the people of New Zealand play, what their favorite foods are, and what their school life is like, among other things."

Graphs

Nearly a hundred billion dollars budgeted for national expenditures, over a hundred million tons of pig iron and steel produced annually in the United States, 43,050,000 metric tons of fish caught in the coastal waters of several countries—astronomical figures! These figures are so large that their meaning is difficult for us to grasp. They would be much easier for us to understand if they were presented in graphic form. If we saw the different items of our nation's budget shown in relation to the whole budget, in a circle graph, the billions of dollars involved would seem less incomprehensible. If we saw pictured in two simple graphs the amount of steel produced in the United States compared with the amount imported, we might better understand the problems confronting management and labor. A bar graph, showing the amount of fish caught by the chief fishing nations, would lead us to wonder why they are the chief producers. Immediately, the relationship between the amount of fish caught and the locations of the producing countries would be seen. Graphs are convincing when they picture amounts which are difficult to conceptualize. Thus we see that graphs make important facts clearer, make possible the comparison of data, and show relationships which are difficult to grasp in table form.

The ability to read and interpret graphs is an important part of every child's education, not only for the information which they provide, but also for the opportunities which they offer for the development of critical thinking. Growth in the ability to read and interpret graphs depends upon the readiness of the pupil to understand the concepts involved and upon the skill with which the teacher presents the material. This growth is slow and cumulative as practice continues. The teacher must guide the pupils in the interpretation of graphs until they become proficient enough, through practice, to discover facts and to draw inferences themselves. Every pupil should learn how to present quantitative data in graphic form after he has progressed in the reading and interpretation of graphs. In teaching pupils how to make graphs, the teacher must give specific instructions for each step until the skill is learned.

The making of graphs related to geography can be a waste of time unless they contribute information which can be used to help reach geographic understandings. They must always be an integral part of the lesson if they are to be of value. For example, there is a definite need for three graphs in the teaching of the cotton-mixed farming region. Graphs should be made to show the acreage planted in each of the states in the region in comparison with the total acreage, thus indicating the relative importance of cotton as a crop. A second graph showing the yield of cotton per acre in the chief cotton-producing states would lead the pupils to do further research in order to find the answers to such questions as why Texas' yield per acre is less than the yield per acre in Mississippi, and why California has the greatest yield, per acre, of all. The third graph, depicting the amount of cotton produced by the chief cotton-producing countries of the world, will show the place of the United States among cotton producers and perhaps suggest a reason why we have difficulty in disposing of our raw cotton. Our continued surplus of cotton, in turn, is one of the factors which has encouraged the development of mixed farming in this region, an inference which can be drawn by the pupils under the direction of the teacher. Each graph contributes to an understanding of the cotton-mixed farming region of the United States because it pictures the facts in a much more easily comprehended way than reading descriptive materials can do, and the facts are presented in a much shorter time.

Sequential Development of Graphs

In the geography readiness program of the primary grades there will be little opportunity under the topics of sun behavior, weather, direction, and seasonal change to use graphs beyond the daily recording of the temperature or summarizing, graphically, the monthly weather calendar. In a graph which summarizes weather conditions, bars of solid color could be used, but the pictorial symbols used on the weather calendar, when they are enclosed in bars, will have more meaning for young children. (See Figure 27.)

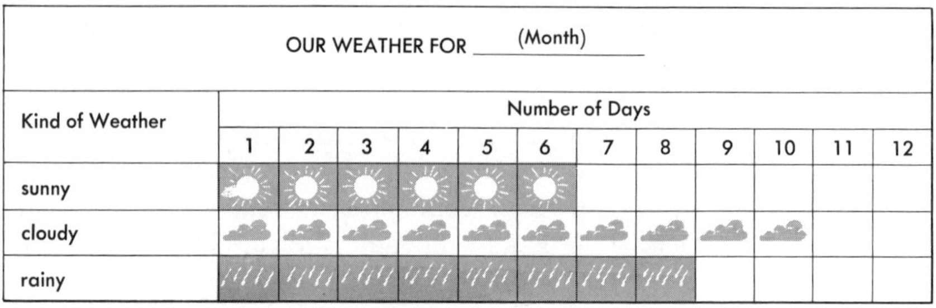

OUR WEATHER FOR _____(Month)_____												
Kind of Weather	Number of Days											
	1	2	3	4	5	6	7	8	9	10	11	12
sunny	☀	☀	☀	☀	☀	☀						
cloudy	☁	☁	☁	☁	☁	☁	☁	☁	☁	☁		
rainy	🌧	🌧	🌧	🌧	🌧	🌧	🌧	🌧				

Figure 27

In the third sequence, if a chart showing length of day has been kept (see page 41), readings taken about two weeks apart which show the increase or decrease in the hours of daylight could be shown in graph form. (See Figure 28.)

Statistical material is difficult for primary children to understand because they have had little formal arithmetic. However, some teachers do introduce simple pictorial and bar graphs on subjects which pertain to the life of the pupils, such as the number of books which they have read, a comparison of the number of boys with the number of girls in the class, or numbers of items in the various collections made by the children. None of these can be classified as geographic. The primary sequences, unfortunately, offer only limited opportunity for the natural growth of the ability to do geographical graph work.

Graph work in the intermediate grades can be begun shortly after the reading and interpretation of statistics work. Geographic graphs may be made which will give information about population, crop production, amount of natural resources in a region compared with the amount in another region or country, value and amount of manufactured products of a region, exports and imports, and so on. Your pupils will find some of these graphs in their textbooks and in other reference works. Take time to point out the practical value of graphs. Follow this discussion with practice in reading and interpreting graphs in much the same way that statistics are interpreted. (See page 141.) Ask such questions as those which follow, modifying them according to the complexity of the graph and the mental ability of the pupils.

- What is the title of the graph?
- How recent are the figures (statistics) used in the graph?
- What is the unit of measurement?
- What comparisons can you make?
- What relationships between approximate quantities do you see?
- What inferences can you draw from the facts shown in the graph?

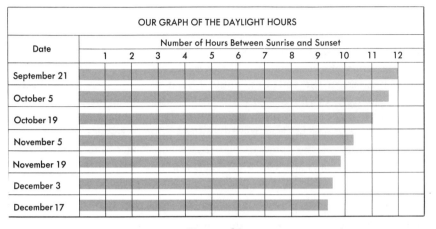

Figure 28

When your pupils are ready to make graphs, explain that graphs picture amounts and that they make it easier to understand the amounts. Show examples of the several kinds of graphs: pictograph, broken bar graph, bar graph, line graph, and circle graph. Note the differences among the graphs and discuss the possible merits of each kind.

It is important that graph making be taught in progressive steps and that each type of graph be thoroughly understood before the next is undertaken. Make the transition smoothly from one type of graph to the next so that real learning takes place. "Hang new knowledge on old pegs of experience." The pupil needs definite instruction regarding the mechanics of graph making as he learns how to change statistics into meaningful graphs. For each new type introduced, it is a good plan for the teacher to make the first one along with the pupils, the teacher doing the work, step by step, at the blackboard for all to see. When a graph has been finished, require the pupils to write an interpretation under it. Without thinking through and writing the interpretation, the graph is of little value to our pupils.

Pictographs

A pictograph expresses ideas clearly and simply by means of pictures or symbols. It shows approximately amounts or numbers of items, but not exact amounts. Pictographs are used extensively in the intermediate grades because they appeal to children and their meaning is quickly understood. The pictures or symbols should be easily associated with the items they represent, whether they be people, crops, or dollars. Each symbol must be identical with all others in size and shape and must represent the same amount. When teaching children to make their first pictographs, round off the numbers used so that the amounts will be easily divisible by the unit of measure selected. At first the symbol should be used to represent multiples of ten: 1, 10, 100, 1,000, 100,000. When the skill has been learned, different units of measure may be used. In these first pictographs, fractional parts involved in the statistics should be reduced to common fractions—halves, quarters, or thirds—with which the children can work more easily. Drill will be necessary to teach the children how to determine the number of symbols necessary to show the amount or value of the commodity. Start at the bottom of the table of statistics where the number of items is smallest. It is usually less confusing for the pupils to determine how many symbols will be needed if the smallest number is considered first.

TEACHING THE PICTOGRAPH   Place the following statistical table on the board, using only the names of the states and the rounded figures, leaving room for the later insertion of the figures given under the Symbols column.

TABLE 7   Value of Cotton Production in the United States
and in the Chief Cotton-Producing States

STATE	VALUE	VALUE IN ROUNDED NUMBERS	NUMBER OF SYMBOLS NEEDED[a]
Total Value	$2,356,597,000	$2,350,000,000	23½
Texas	595,990,000	600,000,000	6
Mississippi	343,850,000	350,000,000	3½
California	324,918,000	325,000,000	3¼
Arkansas	242,530,000	250,000,000	2½
Alabama	133,802,000	133,000,000	1⅓
Arizona	131,859,000	131,000,000	1⅓
Tennessee	102,600,000	100,000,000	1

[a] Where each symbol represents $100,000,000.
SOURCE: *Statistical Abstract of the United States*, 1965.

"We have been studying about the growing of cotton in the southern states. I wonder just how valuable cotton is to these states? Look at the statistical table on the board. Of how much value was Tennessee's crop? It is difficult for us to picture $100,000,000 isn't it? We know what five dollars, ten dollars, or even twenty dollars looks like, but it isn't easy to imagine a pile of money containing a hundred million dollars. But we do have a way to picture these large amounts of money so that they are easily understood. Graphs are used to show large amounts. Some of you may have seen graphs in newspapers

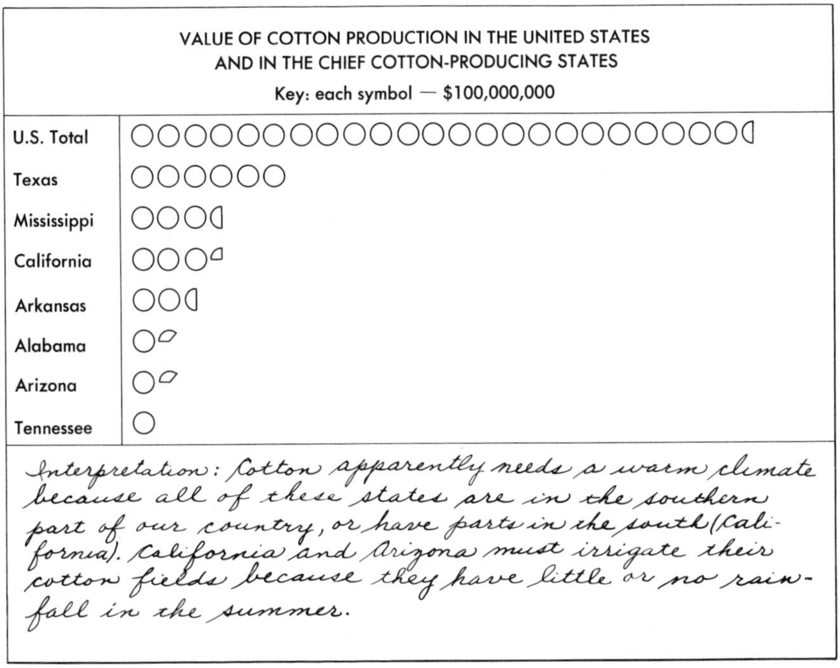

VALUE OF COTTON PRODUCTION IN THE UNITED STATES
AND IN THE CHIEF COTTON-PRODUCING STATES
Key: each symbol — $100,000,000

U.S. Total	○○○○○○○○○○○○○○○○○○○○○○○○○○○○○◖
Texas	○○○○○○
Mississippi	○○○◖
California	○○○◔
Arkansas	○○◖
Alabama	○◔
Arizona	○◔
Tennessee	○

Interpretation: Cotton apparently needs a warm climate because all of these states are in the southern part of our country, or have parts in the south (California). California and Arizona must irrigate their cotton fields because they have little or no rainfall in the summer.

Figure 29

or magazines. There are several kinds. We are going to learn how to make a pictograph, or picture graph, to show the large amounts of money which these states get for their cotton. In a pictograph we draw symbols which resemble the item for which amounts are shown in a table of statistics. Each symbol will represent a certain number of the items. In this table we are expressing value in dollars, so the items to be shown by symbols are dollars. If we were representing the number of bales of cotton produced, we might use little bales of cotton to represent the amounts. Here, however, we have dollars. Have any of you seen silver dollars? What symbol could we use to represent silver dollars? Yes, we could use a circle. We shall draw circles in our pictograph to represent the various amounts of money shown in the statistical table. Here are some buttons which you can use as models of the silver dollar. You will trace around them later. If we let one circle represent $100,000,000 worth of cotton, how many circles or symbols for dollars will we need to show the value of Tennessee's cotton production?"

After working the number out with the pupils, the teacher places a figure, equal to the number of symbols needed, at the right of the rounded number in the table on the board. It will be necessary to do this for only the first few pictographs done by the pupils. We want them to be able, eventually, to do the necessary calculations themselves. "How many circles will we need to show the value of Arizona's cotton? Alabama's? California's? Mississippi's? That of Texas? The United States?"

Where it is possible to do so, show the total production, total value, or other total, first on the pictograph. This provides an additional concept of the whole in relation to its parts. Be sure to draw a vertical base line along the right side of the names of the states, countries, or products, and keep the symbols in alignment, one beneath another vertically, as they are entered on the graph so that comparison is as simple as possible. The teacher will need to help the pupils with the interpretation which is written beneath the pictograph, at least until the pupils have formed the habit of making inferences. The first graph completed by the pupils and teacher should be similar to that shown in Figure 29.

Broken Bar Graphs

After the pupils have become proficient in reading, making, and interpreting pictographs, they are ready for broken bar graphs. Have the pupils read aloud the amounts shown on a previously made pictograph. In some cases, difficulty will be encountered by them as they attempt to determine the amount represented by the fractional part of the symbol shown on the pictograph. The pupils might refer to their pictograph of fish caught in the world and in the coastal waters of several countries of the world. (See Figure 30.)

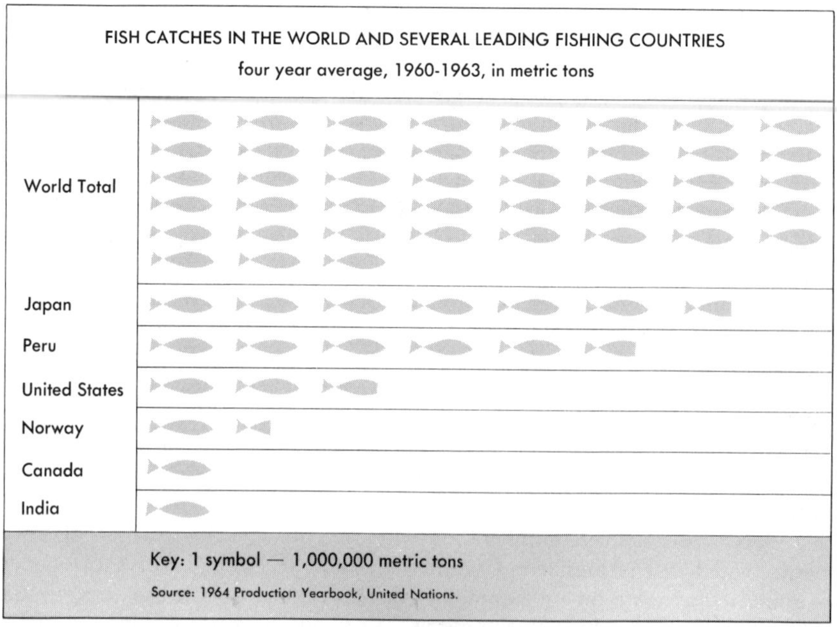
FISH CATCHES IN THE WORLD AND SEVERAL LEADING FISHING COUNTRIES
four year average, 1960-1963, in metric tons
World Total
Japan
Peru
United States
Norway
Canada
India
Key: 1 symbol — 1,000,000 metric tons
Source: 1964 Production Yearbook, United Nations.

Figure 30

"How many metric tons of fish did Norway produce? How many symbols are there? Yes, there is one complete fish and approximately one-half a fish. Norway produced one and one-half times a million metric tons, or one and one-half million metric tons. How many fish symbols does the United States have? Yes, two and almost another whole fish symbol. Can we tell exactly what part of a whole fish this partial symbol is? No. It is too difficult. Why do we have trouble telling the exact amount shown on the pictograph? What kind of symbol could we use which would be more accurate when it is divided? *Square*. Let's remake this pictograph about fish production and see if it would be easier to read if we let a square represent a million metric tons of fish instead of a fish symbol."

The teacher should have placed the following statistics on the board:

TABLE 8   Fish Catches in the World and Leading
Countries: Four Year Average 1960-63 in Metric Tons

		ROUNDED NUMBERS
World Total	43,050,000	43,000,000
Japan	6,616,000	6,660,000
Peru	5,671,000	5,660,000
United States	2,857,000	2,750,000
Norway	1,446,000	1,500,000
Canada	1,067,000	1,000,000
India	1,035,000	1,000,000

SOURCE: *Production Yearbook 1964*, United Nations.

In rounding the numbers for the first broken bar graph, be sure to use only easily recognized common fractional parts.

"Let's take these statistics and see how many squares we will need to show the amount of fish caught in the world and each country. If each square represents one million metric tons of fish, how many squares will we need to show the amount of fish India caught? *1.* Canada? *1.* Norway? *1½.* The United States? *2¾.* Peru? *5⅔.* Japan? *6⅔.* The world? *43.*"

On the chalk board the teacher draws several horizontal lines, and a base line (a line from which you start to count) separating the countries from the symbols. The teacher, using three-inch squares of colored paper, places them to show the amount of fish caught by each country, leaving a half-inch space between each square as it is placed, hence, the name "broken bar graph." Place numbers above the first row of squares to show the amount or number of squares. Remember, each square or number represents a million metric tons of fish. (See Figure 31.) When the graph is

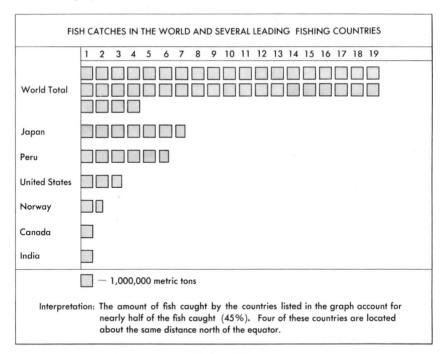

FISH CATCHES IN THE WORLD AND SEVERAL LEADING FISHING COUNTRIES

— 1,000,000 metric tons

Interpretation: The amount of fish caught by the countries listed in the graph account for nearly half of the fish caught (45%). Four of these countries are located about the same distance north of the equator.

Figure 31

finished, have the pupils give an interpretation of the meaning of the graph. The teacher will write this interpretation under the graph on the board. When the pupils make their own first broken line bar graph, give them quarter-inch-square graph paper and have them fill in the squares they need to show with pencil, leaving a square between each symbolic square. Later, after they have learned the technique, they may make their own squares leaving less space between them.

THE MAKING OF BAR GRAPHS   The next step in the mastery of graph making is to teach pupils how to make the bar graph. Make a broken bar graph on the chalk board. Use three-inch squares of colored paper for symbols. Place a loop of masking tape on the back of each square so that the squares may be placed on the board and moved about. (Whenever you use abstract symbols, such as squares, be sure that the pupils constantly keep in mind what these symbols represent.) After reading and interpreting the broken bar graph, suggest that the squares might be placed so that they would touch. At this point, the teacher moves the squares about on the board so that they touch, and a solid bar is formed. Count the symbols with the pupils and place the unit of measure in figures above the bar at the end of each square. (See Figure 32.)

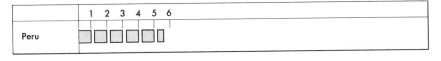

Figure 32

The effectiveness of the graph depends upon its clarity; hence, the bars must be distinctly shown. When making graphs on squared paper, have the pupils leave a row of squares between the figures of the column headings and the first bar, and between the bars as they are made. Be certain to have the pupils write an interpretation under each graph.

In the sixth sequence, after the pupils are familiar with percentage, simple bar graphs showing land use may be made. Land use graphs add much to the understanding of a country's personality. Draw a rectangle five inches long and one inch wide. Divide this bar into ten parts. Let each part equal ten percent of the total. Then, using the statistics given below, show how the land is used. Color and label each part and include an interpretation beneath the bar. (See Figure 33.)

LAND USE OF BRAZIL

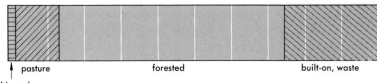

pasture   forested   built-on, waste

cultivated

Interpretation: Only a small portion of Brazil's land is cultivated or in pasture land. Almost two-thirds of Brazil is forested and approximately one-fourth is waste land and land containing buildings. Brazil could apparently support many more people.

Source: 1964 Production Yearbook, United Nations.

Figure 33

Line and Circle Graphs

The line, or "trend" graph, is the most accurate of all graphs. It is often used to show changes in quantities during fixed periods of time. Thus, a line graph on the production of cotton in ten year periods of time would be an interesting one to discuss and to make inferences about. What could be the contributing causes to the sharp increases and decreases in production which are shown by the direction of the line? The climatic graph showing the trend of average monthly temperature throughout the year is also a line graph.

The circle, or "pie" graph, has less value in geographic education than most of the other graphs. Although quantitative comparison can be made by using this graph, other types of graphs which can be more easily made show the same facts and make the same comparisons possible. Circle graphs are easy to read but difficult to make accurately. They show totals, or whole amounts, and the segments show fractional or percentage parts. To show these parts which make the whole will require that the statistics used be converted to percentages or fractional parts of the whole, if the parts are to be drawn accurately. This conversion in itself is difficult for pupils of the intermediate sequences. The problem of accurately dividing the whole circle into the required parts requires the use of a protractor. Since a circle is equal to 360° and the whole equals 100%, three and two-thirds degrees will equal about one percent of the circle. It can be seen at once why the operation is difficult. The common fractions, ½, ¼, ¾, ⅓, and so on, can easily be separated from the whole circle, but the others are difficult. However, pupils familiar with the use of the protractor and with percentage will be able to make accurate circle graphs after careful instruction. Circle graphs relating to geography might be made to show the area of various countries, and the production of crops such as sugar, coffee, and tea in several countries.

Climatic Graphs

In the sixth sequence the pupils will need to apply concepts which they have previously learned about rainfall and temperature to climatic conditions in other lands. It is an easy step from the rainfall and temperature charts suggested for the fifth sequence in Teaching the Concept of Rainfall, page 266, to rainfall and temperature graphs because of the similarity in form. Have the pupils make the graphs on quarter-inch graph paper. Each graph must be fourteen squares wide and nineteen squares from top to bottom. Place the temperature figures in the first column at the left, writing the figures across the horizontal lines, never in the squares themselves. Number the bottom line 0°. This is the base line for climatic graphs. Then proceed up the column, numbering by fives. Place the letters representing the months in the top row of squares across the vertical lines. Use only the initial letters of the months. The J for January is placed across the first line to the right of the column of temperature figures. Place dots opposite the correct temperatures on the lines representing the months.

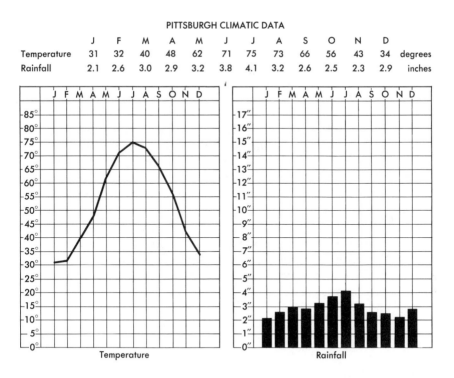

PITTSBURGH CLIMATIC DATA

	J	F	M	A	M	J	J	A	S	O	N	D	
Temperature	31	32	40	48	62	71	75	73	66	56	43	34	degrees
Rainfall	2.1	2.6	3.0	2.9	3.2	3.8	4.1	3.2	2.6	2.5	2.3	2.9	inches

Figure 34

Find the temperature given for January. Place a dot opposite the correct temperature on the January line. Do the same with the temperature figures for the other months, remembering that each temperature figure is an average temperature for the entire month. Connect the dots with straight lines. The resulting temperature curve will often tell the approximate location of a place north or south of the equator and whether or not there is a seasonal change. It can also indicate the length of the growing season.

On the rainfall graph, the amount of rainfall is shown by vertical bars or columns which are drawn along each line representing a month. Leave space between the bars. The inches of rainfall are numbered by ones in the first left-hand column. Be sure that the bottom line in this column is numbered "0 inches." Many facts about a country can be learned by studying the amount and distribution of rainfall as it appears on a rainfall graph. (If the rainfall comes only in the winter season, there will be need for irrigation. If the annual rainfall is from thirty to forty inches and it is evenly distributed throughout the year, the country will probably have agriculture.) (See Figure 34.)

Making graphs can be a waste of time unless pupils do some critical thinking about the information shown on the graph. Insist that an interpretation be written below each graph. For example, under the graph showing the temperature of Pittsburgh, the pupil might write, "Pittsburgh has hot summers and mild winters. It has four seasons." Under the rainfall graph, he might write, "The annual rainfall is 36.2 inches, distributed evenly throughout the year. In the vicinity of Pittsburgh, all other things being favorable, agriculture could be carried on."

In the seventh sequence, the temperature and rainfall graphs are superimposed to make a combination graph. This graph requires fifteen squares because an extra column is needed for the rainfall figures. These are placed in a column at the left side of the graph, while the temperature figures occupy the column along the right hand side of the graph. Seventh sequence pupils are able to glean much more information from climatic graphs because of their additional maturity. They can estimate the approximate length of the growing season from a climatic graph, for instance, by noting the number of months having an average temperature of about fifty-seven degrees or above. Figure 35 illustrates how teachers may show their pupils the ease of use and advantage of combining the two graphs, rainfall and temperature.

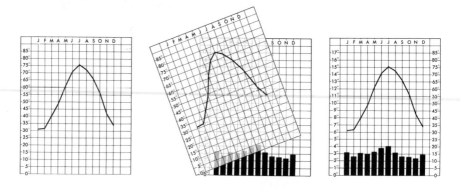

Figure 35

To show the pupil how simple it is to combine the two kinds of graphs, have ready, on regular paper, a rainfall graph of any given place. On a sheet of semitransparent paper have ready a temperature graph of the same place. Show the two graphs to the class side by side. Then carefully slide the transparent temperature graph over the rainfall graph, showing how the two graphs can be drawn on a single sheet of paper. Point out that the figures for temperature will have to be placed in a column down the right hand side of the combination graph.

Junior high school pupils will also be able to read the topography of

the country as well as its approximate location north or south of the equator, the amount and distribution of the rainfall, and the temperature of the place from a climatic graph. The following sample lesson is presented as an illustration of this work.

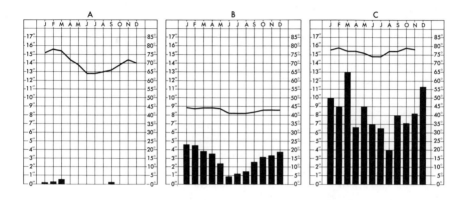

Figure 36

The graphs shown in Figure 36 should be enlarged by the teacher and placed side by side on oak tag in the order shown. Each graph shows climatic data from a city, that on the left being a west coast city, the middle graph a city in the interior, and the graph on the right side, a city on the east coast.

The teacher will need to guide the thinking of the pupils and may proceed in the following manner:

"Do you know that you can tell something about the surface of a country by studying climatic graphs? It seems impossible, doesn't it? I am anxious to see how many of you will be able to draw a simple profile of the surface of this country after you have studied these graphs with me. These three graphs show the climatic conditions of three cities in the same country. They are located at approximately the same latitude. The one on the left is in the western part of the country; that in the middle is near the central part; and the one on the right is in the east. Let us try to locate the country in reference to the equator by studying the temperature line. We will need to know approximately how far the country is from the equator in order to determine the wind direction. Is this country north or south of the equator? *South.* What tells you this? Is this country near to the equator or far south of it? *Near the equator. The curve in the temperature line shows only slight change in seasons.* From what direction will the winds come if the country is near the equator? *Southeast trade winds.* What would cause the heavy downpour in the eastern part of the country? *Mountain barrier.*

Notice the temperature lines on the graphs. How do they differ? If these places are in approximately the same latitude, what other factor might influence the temperature? *Elevation.* Notice how much lower the temperature is on Graph B. What might be the cause of this? *Mountain elevation.* Notice, too, that there is little seasonal change in temperature, that it remains about the same throughout the year. How does the amount of rainfall in Graph B differ from that shown for the city on Graph C? What could lessen the amount of rainfall received by City B? *Loss of moisture over mountain barriers.* Compare the temperature line on Graph A with that on Graph C. What difference do you see? *Graph C shows very little variation.* How do you account for the great difference in the amount of rainfall shown on Graphs A and B? *Maybe there is another mountain barrier.*

Now, let's summarize our clues about the surface of the country at this particular latitude. In the east we thought that the southeast trade winds would bring moisture. There must be a mountain barrier somewhere inland from the east coast which caused so much rain to fall. *Nearly 100 inches.* Then, as we pointed out with Graph B, we knew that this city must be on high land, perhaps on a plateau between mountain ranges, because the rainfall was less than that shown in Graph C. We decided that Graph A was of a city which was at a lower elevation than City B, and perhaps separated from the rest of the country by another mountain barrier which caused this land to be a desert in the western part. Now, let's see how well we can visualize the surface of this country. Draw a sea-level line on a piece of paper, and above it sketch a simple profile of the country." See Figure 37.

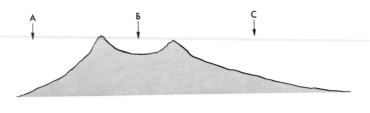

Figure 37

After the pupils have sketched the profile, have two or three of them put their sketches on the board. Then have them trace with their fingers along a world physical-political map south of the equator to see if they can discover a country which this profile would fit. After they have made their deductions, and if they have not discovered the country, tell them the name of it and have them use physical-political and seasonal rainfall maps to find out how accurate are the profiles which they have made. Also have them check the inferences which have been drawn throughout the lesson.

The country sketched is Peru. If the teacher had divulged the name of the country at the beginning of the lesson, the pupils would not have depended upon their own powers of deduction to discuss and determine the topography. The actual cities are Chiclayo in Graph A, Cerro de Pasco in Graph B, and Iquitos in Graph C.

This lesson is an excellent one for promoting geographic thinking. It tests the pupils' knowledge about map interpretation as well as geographic concepts concerning climate.

POINTS TO BE REMEMBERED WHEN MAKING GRAPHS

✧ Graphs must contribute to the geographic understandings being developed.
✧ Graphs must be accurate, neat, and their meaning should be clear.
✧ Graphs must have a title as brief as possible, yet one which is immediately understood.
✧ Graphs should show the total amount with which individual items can be compared. If production of selected countries is given, then world production should be shown; if the production of several states is shown, include that of the United States as a whole.
✧ Graphs must have a common base line to be used as a starting point for each item indicated. To present a true picture, this base line should start at zero.
✧ Graphs must have a key or legend which tells what each symbol represents.
✧ Graphs must have vertical or horizontal scales, or both, whichever the type of graph requires.
✧ Picture the amounts shown in graphs in ascending or descending order for quick reading.
✧ Credit should be given for the source of the statistics used. Give the date of the statistics, also, wherever possible.

RELIABLE SOURCES OF STATISTICAL MATERIAL   *Statistical Abstract of the United States; The Commodity Yearbook; The Agricultural Yearbook; The Statesman's Year-Book; The World Almanac; The South American Handbook;* and *The Statistical Yearbook of the United Nations.*

8

Use all available tools, continued

Charts and Posters

Charts and posters, whether teacher or pupil made, or obtained from commercial firms, are always worthwhile and useful tools in the teaching of geography. Each of the three types of charts, and all of the various kinds of posters, makes a unique contribution to the teaching-learning process. If they are commercially printed, be certain to examine them critically to see that the information shown is suitable to the interests and maturity of your class. There is no value in bringing material to their attention which is too difficult for them, or which does not contribute to the lesson they are studying. If they are teacher or pupil made, follow the few, simple suggestions for making them which are given here.

Charts are useful in geography for showing relationships, simple processes (as in a flow chart), and for summarizing information about cities, countries, resources, and products. It is frequently a time-saving device for the teacher to make and use charts to which he can refer as he teaches. Information can often be presented more clearly, and certainly much more quickly, by means of charts than by having the pupils listen to explanations or read pages from the textbook. We must remember that many of our pupils are picture oriented and learn more from charts than from the printed page. The chart made by the teacher may be an enlargement of one taken from a book or magazine, or it may be original. It is a simple matter to trace, on a large piece of paper or cardboard, an enlargement projected from an opaque projector, but it is equally easy to make one's own charts.

There are three types of charts which can be made by pupils to illustrate geographic understandings, and which apply learned facts. A chart which shows relationships, the most effective of the three, might illustrate with pictures or silhouettes, that the manufacture of steel is related to deposits of coal, access to iron ore, deposits of limestone, and a supply of water. Simple flow charts show the major steps in processing a product. An example would be a flow chart which traces wheat from the field to the home. The illustrations might include a sketch of a wheat field, a grain elevator, a flour mill, a bakery, a retail store, and finally a scene at the table in the home. Charts which summarize learned material would include such things as a chart showing the exports of Argentina, or the uses of coal.

Your pupils may make charts on standard-size art paper or on cardboard of various sizes for use in their own class work. They should remember that the purpose of a chart is to present information in a clear, concise, and effective manner. The following criteria for charts will help them to do their work in the best possible way.

POINTS TO BE REMEMBERED WHEN MAKING CHARTS

✦ One does not have to possess artistic ability to make charts. However, a sense of proportion, balance, and color harmony all help one to make attractive charts.

✦ Keep your chart simple. A good chart presents only one idea or thought. It may be a relationship or a comparison, but it should tell a story at a glance.

✦ Make your chart eye-catching and as attractive as possible. Use contrasting colors to emphasize primary and secondary details. Size variations of the objects on the chart can also help with emphasis.

✦ Space is important. Do not put too much on your chart. It loses its effectiveness if it appears crowded. Have wide margins and, if you make your chart for classroom use, be certain that it is large enough to be seen clearly from all parts of the room.

✦ Before you make your chart, plan it on scratch paper. Make certain that the paper you use for planning is the same shape as the piece of cardboard which you will use for the final chart. When your plan is completed and approved, sketch it lightly on the cardboard, observing spacing and arrangements similar to those on your plan.

Posters have their own special use in the teaching of geography. Colorful, commercial travel posters may be used to motivate interest in a region which is about to be studied. Discussion of the posters will frequently raise problems and questions which the children will want to solve or answer. The posters add atmosphere and a decorative touch to the classroom after their initial use is passed. They may be obtained from railroad companies, steamship lines, airlines, and from many of the foreign information agencies. Frequently, a small charge is made for them, which may range from a few cents to a dollar.

Children enjoy making posters of their own, however. An unusually good time to engage in this activity is during the summary or application part of the unit. Posters help to reinforce key learnings and also measure the effectiveness of your teaching. Pupil-made posters might advertise foreign products, call attention to scenic places, or encourage tourists to visit interesting lands. They also give purpose to a review of the known facts about a country.

After studying the Netherlands, the teacher might ask, "What first comes to your mind when I say 'The Netherlands' to you?" The answers should be listed on the board: dikes, canals, Delft, dairy products, tulips, windmills, large ships, bicycles, diamond cutting, Dutch chocolate, cleanliness. After discussing these items as possible subjects for posters, remind the pupils that each poster will have only one key idea. Suggest that the posters be made to advertise products or to interest tourists in visiting this country. Ask the pupils what key ideas they are able to suggest for each of the items listed on the board. Encourage them to be original. Next, discuss the criteria for good posters. Give each pupil a nine-inch by twelve-inch piece of newsprint on which to plan his poster. When the plan is approved, have them put their poster ideas on art paper for completion.

Pupils and teacher alike should keep in mind that posters must convey their message in as few words as possible since they are read hurriedly by people as they pass by. Therefore, if they are to be understood at a glance, their key words should stand out from all other words. This can be accomplished by means of contrast in colors or by size of print. The eye of the reader should be immediately drawn to the center of interest in the poster; hence, it must stand out sharply from its background. Aside from these eye catching details, encourage the pupils to keep their posters simple in design. Teach them the value of color and the importance of providing adequate space for the message and the margins.

Textbooks: Masters or Servants

When a child dislikes geography, the reason he usually gives for his dislike is that all he is asked to do is read. Is this really all that can be done with geography in the classroom, giving the pupil reading assignments? What is wrong? Geography is such a dynamic subject. Is it the fault of the textbook that many pupils dislike it? Possibly; but far more likely it is the ineffective use of the textbook by the teacher which is to blame. The pupil has not been motivated to read the textbook, and he feels no immediate need to learn anything about geography. Perhaps the subject matter which he has been assigned is filled with concepts with which he is unfamiliar, or the topic itself may be far removed from his life. The teacher may not have used in the lesson the interesting facts or anecdotes about the subject which create a desire on the part of the pupil to learn more. There may have been no activities in connection with the work of the text which required that the textbook be read for information. But probably the chief reason for the pupil's dislike of work in a textbook is that the teacher has ignored the relationships which are implicit in the study of geography and has insisted upon the memorization of facts for which the pupil has no particular need and which may not even be true at the time he is memorizing them. Facts change from year to year, and relationships need to be revised with every change in man's use and occupancy of the land.

Although today's schools have many tools to aid the teacher, the textbook is the most important geographic tool available to the teacher of geography. It is basic to geography instruction and education, and while there are things which may be said both for and against the use of textbooks—things which may strengthen or weaken good teaching practices— the attitude of the school administration most frequently determines the way in which textbooks will be used. Will the textbook *be* the curriculum in geography which must be covered during the school year, by "teaching the text" page by page, from beginning to end? Or will the teacher be instructed to "teach children" instead of the textbook, and be allowed to use the text according to their needs? Will the textbook be used as a curriculum guide, or will it be used as a resource book?

Textbooks are a great help to inexperienced teachers, and to teachers who, with little or no geography background, have had the teaching of geography thrust upon them on the first day of a new term. The textbook acts as a guide for these teachers by providing them with an overview and a limited amount of subject matter which should be taught during the school year. The textbook is usually organized into parts convenient for both pupils and teacher. The teacher's manual, which accompanies the textbook, and an annotated, teacher's copy of the textbook will be helpful to such teachers until they master geographic fundamentals and concepts.

But textbooks should never be used to determine the content of the geography curriculum. Textbooks are printed for general use by thousands of school children in all parts of the United States. Although many of them are well organized and attempt to develop concepts and skills logically, they are not designed for any specific class of pupils where one is likely to find widely divergent abilities and interests. Usually there is far too much subject matter in a textbook for all of it to be taught well during one school year. Every page of most textbooks contains many opportunities for the development of concepts and showing of relationships which are vital to an understanding of the subject matter. It takes time to develop concepts and show relationships. To attempt to do so with an entire textbook is folly. Is it not common sense to teach less but to teach it well? Let us, then, not try to "cover" the book; let us, instead, teach children, teach fewer concepts, and teach them both well!

Geography textbooks, in attempting to include subject matter about a large part of the world, give too little detailed information for a good understanding of the subject. Often the pages are filled with facts, but the relationships, which make the facts true and interesting, are not present. Geography, as we have written so often, is a study of relationships and if they are missing in a geography textbook, the teacher must develop those which are needed for the complete understanding of the facts. By adhering too closely to the text, the teacher often robs the pupils of the opportunity to do their own thinking and to ask questions, since the textbook author too frequently provides, in all too conclusive form, all of the answers.

Why do teachers continue to adhere slavishly to the textbook, page by page, in their teaching, when they know that such practice is contrary to the best knowledge about learning? Is it because they are unwilling to spend the time and energy to obtain the background necessary to make geography interesting? It is because they do not understand how to teach geography by using the textbook as a tool? Whatever the reason, let us consider some suggestions which will help all of us break the habit of rote textbook teaching.

At the beginning of the term, go through the geography textbook very carefully, noting the subject matter and tracing the development of skills and geographic concepts. Use the material presented in previous chapters of this book as a guide in determining whether or not skills and concepts are developed logically. If the book which you must use with your pupils contains too much material for all of it to be taught well, select only those topics or units which will help you best to introduce and develop the geographic concepts which you want your pupils to grasp. These concepts should, of course, be part of a living geography curriculum, developed by you and your colleagues for your own school district in terms of the needs and abilities of the clients your district serves. They should be appropriate to the sequence for which you are planning the year's work. After deciding which country is best suited for the development of the concepts of the topic or unit, you are ready to plan the relationships about the country which will lead to an understanding of the topic.

One of the topics to be taken up in your sequence might be latitude.

A concept related to this topic would be the understanding that latitude is one of the chief determiners of man's activities. One country which might be studied in order to help the pupils develop this concept would be Chile. The relationships which would lead to an understanding of the topic of latitude, which you would write out and then teach to your pupils, might be similar to those which follow.

A. The climate of Chile ————→ 1. latitude.
2. mountain barriers.
3. Humboldt Current.
4. Westerlies.
5. sun position.

B. The importance of ————→ 1. deposits of natural nitrates.
Northern Chile to 2. deposits of other minerals, such as
the whole country copper, silver, and iron ore.
3. lack of rain.
4. its location near the coast.
5. the export of iodine, nitrates, copper, and iron ore.

C. The concentration of————→ 1. the Mediterranean climate.
population in Central 2. the availability of irrigation waters.
Chile 3. the patriarchal system of life on the haciendas.
4. the raising of sheep on mountain slopes.
5. the emergence of a small middle-class caused by employment in the large cities of Valparaiso and Santiago.

D. Life in Southern ————→ 1. the Marine West Coast climate.
Chile 2. the mountainous surface.
3. the lack of crop land.
4. the rugged fiord coast.
5. the heavy rainfall associated with the Marine climate and mountain barriers.
6. lumbering and the raising of sheep.
7. the discovery of oil near Punta Arenas.
8. isolation due to the lack of connecting roads and railroads.

Having written these relationships, you are now ready to "clothe" them with information which can be found in the textbook and in other reference materials. Write the relationships separately on three-inch by five-inch cards. List on the cards the pages and paragraphs of the textbook which will provide information about the relatonships. These cards may be filed for future use and other references added to them as they come to your attention. Having these page and paragraph references will save time for both you and your pupils later when the unit has been begun. When you have done this, you have begun to teach systematically; you have a skeleton upon which to hang the "meat" of your geography course.

Remember that it is not necessary for the pupils to read every page in the geography textbook. It certainly is not conducive to efficient teaching to have them spend their time reading material which does not contribute to the topic under study. Textbooks are a means to an end, but they are not an end in themselves. You should, of course, use the textbook whenever it can make a contribution to the understanding of concepts, but such use does not relieve you of the responsibility for motivating a lesson, or for the step-by-step development of relationships. The teacher must provide motivation for the relationships he is going to teach in the development part of each lesson. He must create within the pupil a desire to know more about the subject. He must make the pupil want to turn to his textbook to find some of the answers to the questions which he has been asked, or which he is asking.

In the development portion of the lesson, the teacher teaches the relationship which he has previously written. If a relationship is written on the board without comment and the pupils are told to read their texts to discover why the parts of it are true, they cannot help adopting a passive attitude toward learning since all of the thinking has been done for them by the teacher and the textbook. How much more interesting it would be if the pupils helped to develop the various points in the relationships by having them discover things for themselves as they are urged to use physical-political and rainfall maps and read descriptive paragraphs and short stories! Which method will help the pupil remember longer? Which method will teach him to do logical thinking?

We must understand that many vivid and vital details necessary for geographic understanding must be omitted from textbooks because of the lack of space. It is up to you to supply the additional material. You may find only one page of material about a country such as Switzerland in your geography text, but it will take a full two weeks, or more, to develop concepts, make graphs, begin appropriate activities, and do the additional reading required to make the pupils see Switzerland as a real country in which warm, friendly, and industrious people live. The average textbook simply does not supply enough information about any one subject; it cannot. Consequently, it cannot be the only source of information for the pupil.

There are several ways to make the reading of the material in the textbook meaningful. Having the pupils draw sketches of what they see as they read certain descriptive paragraphs in the textbook is an excellent device to use. They must "see" the picture mentally before they can put it on paper. This activity promotes more careful reading of the text. For instance, if a relationship concerning Central Chile were being studied, have the pupils read the description of the hacienda and make a sketch of what they would see there, or draw a plan of one that is described by the text-book.

Ask the pupils to look for relationships in the material which has been assigned for reading. Relationship recognition is not for the exclusive use of the teacher. We want our pupils to be able to discover and write relation-ships, too. Have the pupils write their relationships in arrow statement form. Make this exercise more like a puzzle by saying, "On page seventy-six there are five relationships suggested. Let's see how many good detectives in this class can find them and write them out." Let your pupils experience the joy of discovery.

When the pupils are given questions which must be answered by using material from the textbook, be sure that they are application ques-tions rather than factual ones. Instead of asking them to list the products of Central Chile, have them pretend to be children living on a hacienda there. Ask them to make a work calendar, naming the months, and tell what type of work they might be doing each month and what crop they might be helping their fathers to plant, cultivate, or harvest. Ask questions which require the pupil to see himself living in Central Chile and reacting to life there as a child of Central Chile might react. "Would you encourage your father to learn to drive the new tractor which the owner of the hacienda has just purchased? Why?" "Will you worry about the lack of rainfall in the winter? Why?" Pupils are interested in questions like these and will be willing to do research to answer them, not only because they are permitted to use thought, but also because they present problems which their own experience can help solve. On the other hand, questions which require only short, factual answers, gleaned from the printed text (usually word for word) are generally meaningless to the pupil and the answers are soon for-gotten.

Probably the best uses which can be made of the textbook are to sum-marize the material which the teacher has developed, and to review the whole unit of work. When the pupils go over the textbook material as a summarizing activity, it will have meaning for them because the teacher has developed the concepts and relationships which explain why the text-book material is true. The textbook can also be very helpful to the slow learner who must work at his own rate of speed and needs the opportunity to go over the material several times. However, even his work is made profitable and interesting by the teacher who not only encourages thinking, but by means of his planning and questioning, teaches how it is done.

In conclusion, be certain that you take time to acquaint your pupils with the textbook at the beginning of the term. Go beyond the usual rou-tine of pointing out the title, the index, the table of contents, and the names of the authors. Instead, use part of the "get acquainted" period to show the pupils what kinds of information they can expect to find in the geography text and where it is located. Ask them to think of ways in which they might be able to use some of the statistical material in the textbook, or when they might wish to consult certain maps and for what reason. Ask them to talk about how their geography textbook differs from all other textbooks which they might already have used in their school careers. Discuss with them how you intend to use the geography textbook, as a guide or a resource book, and a tool of learning. Finally, discuss with them the geography curriculum, or course of study, and how the geography textbook will fit in with it. No one likes to be on a journey, in real life or through twelve years of school, and not know where he is going or what he is being prepared for. We have found that pupils work much better, and with greater comprehension, if they are given some idea of how the work they will do in this sequence is related to what they have done in past sequences, and how it prepares them for their next—and all subsequent—sequences. Great thinkers are able to see wholes as well as the detail of parts. We cannot expect our pupils to become logical thinkers by constantly showing them only the parts.

CRITERIA FOR GEOGRAPHY TEXTBOOKS   To give the geography teacher and his pupils the best possible service, a geography textbook should be of top quality in three areas: binding, format, and content. The binding of the textbook should be such that it will lie flat as the pupil reads and as he studies maps within the text. Too often the signatures which comprise the textbook are sewn through the pages near the spine of the book, rather than along the back of the spine. Such texts cost less to produce and they seem to have a longer life, but the inconvenience which they cause both pupils and teacher is great enough to warrant extra expenditure for a desirable binding. Such matters as the color of the cover of the textbook and the quality of the paper and its "glare" potential depend upon the taste and wisdom of the teacher. Attractive covers, with pictures in color, may do very well for a story book, but a geography textbook is more than a story book. The usefulness of such covers is considered later when pictures are discussed. The teacher alone must decide whether picture quality should be sacrificed through the use of noncoated, nonglare paper, since there are no conclusive studies on the subject. The binding, nevertheless, concerns the user more than any other aspect of the physical make-up of the geography textbook.

The format of the textbook includes such things as the arrangement of pictures and maps, spacing and size of type on the page, and appropriateness of both to the sequence in which the book will be used. It includes the table of contents, the definitiveness of the index, and the attractiveness of the book as a whole. Here, again, decisions about the desirability of a textbook, with relation to its format, are entirely matters of appropriateness and wisdom, and the needs which the teacher foresees. Haste in considering these matters may bring regrets for the teacher—and pupils—which will last for the life of the textbook.

The most important matter to consider in the selection of a geography textbook is its content. The wise geography teacher will note whether or not the authors are recognized in the field of geography and, particularly, whether they write from firsthand experience or only from secondary sources. At least one of the authors should have experience in the field of education and, essentially, in classroom teaching at the level for which the textbook is intended.

The wise teacher will also examine, carefully, large portions of the text to determine whether or not the authors have stressed relationships. Every word of the text should contribute to the development of understandings and concepts through emphasis upon geographical relationships. He should note whether or not there is a gradual development of concepts and skills in terms of complexity and difficulty. The number of concepts introduced per page must also be considered, and whether or not the authors introduce and develop the concepts with sufficient clarity. Consider whether or not the authors have supplied sufficient detail to build geographic understandings. If detail is lacking, you must consider how much of your time will be used in supplying the necessary supplementary material.

Each geography textbook should give close attention to the pronunciation of place names and terms which are associated with geography. While many books have indexes which are also pronunciation guides, and some have glossaries of place names and terms, we prefer the textbook which provides pronunciation within the body of the text, immediately following the place name or term. Complex pronunciation marking procedures are not necessary, but the text should contain a guide to the pronunciation symbols used in it. They should be those which are used by the best makers of dictionaries.

Maps and pictures which appear in the textbook must also be given careful attention. As has been indicated in the chapter on maps, the geographer depends upon them and the geography teacher cannot function effectively in his classroom without them. Many times pictorial maps are included in the textbook and the symbols used on them are not correctly placed or they cover too large an area. Pictorial maps are almost completely without value and the good geography textbook is not heavily laden with them, although they are suitable for some pupils and in some instances. Of the maps which are included in the textbook, how many of them are suitable for the age level for which the book has been written? All of them should be. Are the maps as accurate as possible? Have they been carefully drawn to scale? Is there always a key or legend? Are they political maps which will have limited use, or are they physical-political maps which the pupils can be taught to read? Are the projections used the best for the purpose which the maps are to serve? Is their positioning on the page such that they can be studied with a minimum of inconvenience to the pupil? If they cover two pages, are the left- and right-hand parts carefully aligned and delineated? Are internationally accepted elevation colors used? Are the elevations clearly separated or delineated? Are the colors carefully applied to the map or do they blur? The teacher must also give strict attention to the usefulness of the maps included in the textbook. Will they help in the development of concepts and understandings? Do they contribute to the understanding of relationships? Consult the chapter on maps to review the characteristics which good maps should have. Such characteristics are applicable to those appearing in a textbook.

The criteria for the selection of pictures, found in this chapter, apply equally well to the evaluation of pictures in the geography textbook. In addition to those criteria, the teacher should consider the quality of the printing of the pictures. Colors should not run. They should not be blurred. Too often publishers sacrifice picture quality by using a poor quality of paper. The price of the textbook can be lower, but such false economy also lowers the quality of the book as a whole and reduces its usefulness for the teacher and pupils. Pictures should be of high quality, on good paper, and should contribute to the sequential development of the written text by showing relationships. They should never be merely decorations. Publishers do not encourage their authors to use pictures as decoration. They recommend not using such a picture. You may be sure that the author, rather than the publisher, has made the choice, if the picture is merely decorative.

Check the captions of the pictures. They are important. Some captions are actually distracting, leading the pupil away from the relationship that is in the picture. Other captions say little or nothing. Good captions are those which cause pupils to search the pictures for answers to questions concerning them. Some teachers prefer that there be no captions, hoping thereby to encourage their pupils to read and interpret the pictures.

Every good geography text includes a few well-chosen teaching and study aids. These should follow the pattern already suggested for the formulation of questions by the teacher of geography. Of the questions included as study aids, do most of them require brief, factual answers? Do they, instead, require reasoning ability? There should be a natural preponderance of those which require the pupil to think. Of the study aids and activities suggested, are they reasonable as to execution? Can they be completed within a reasonable length of time? Are directions for completing the activities given clearly and completely? Are they related to the concepts studied in the chapter? Do they contribute to understanding, or are they busy work?

To help you in selecting your geography textbook, ask yourself the following questions which recapitulate and summarize the foregoing discussion.

✓ Is the author a geographer?

✓ Has the author had classroom experience?

✓ Does the subject matter lead to the mastery of major understandings through the study of relationships?

✓ Are relationships emphasized?

✓ Is there enough information given in the textbook to provide your pupils with vivid mental pictures of the regions studied?

✓ Is the textbook appropriate to the comprehension level and ability of your pupils?

✓ Is the subject matter presented in a manner which will make it appealing to your pupils?

✓ Are geographic skills developed sequentially and practiced consistently?

✓ Will the book be helpful to you in your teaching? Are there enough teaching aids (maps, charts, clear pictures showing relationships, accurate statistics, profitable application work, and so on) to stimulate thinking?

✓ Are the questions easily answered by parts of the subject matter, or do they require the child to orient himself to the situation before he answers them?

✓ Will the questions appeal to the interests of the pupils or will answering them require only memorization?

✓ Is the book attractive, well made, and will it stand hard use?

So many aspects of the teaching-learning experience must be considered in evaluating a geography textbook for adoption that they cannot all be included here. There are very few geography textbooks available which fulfill completely the best list of criteria, simply because teachers have been willing to take what publishers will give to them. Teachers have not been willing to demand the best for their pupils and settle for nothing less. In final analysis, whether a good textbook or a poor one is chosen depends almost completely upon the geographic knowledge, understanding of the learning process, and the good judgment and integrity of the teacher.

Other Audio-Visual Aids

Each of us has had some training in the use of audio-visual materials but we more often abuse them than use them, in spite of our good training. We have at our disposal thousands of dollars worth of audio-visual equipment designed to aid and improve our teaching, but we seldom, if ever, use the equipment to full advantage. We fail to follow the carefully worked out instructions which accompany the printed materials we use, and improperly handle the most common audio-visual machines.

One of the most common audio-visual aids is the phonograph. Nearly every elementary school has two or more phonographs for the convenience of its teachers, and teachers use them—for music appreciation classes or to provide music for folk dancing. It never seems to occur to them that there are many kinds of recordings available. As teachers, we forget that the first phonographs were advertised as educational aids and that Edison considered both his phonograph and kinescope for use, primarily, in the schools.

Suppose your pupils are about to study lands at the north polar region. The voice of Commander Robert E. Perry, describing his discovery of the Pole, was recorded shortly after his return from his expedition and is available for your use in motivating the lesson.[1] If your classes are studying tropical islands, recordings of authentic tropical sounds are available. The study of Japan is enlivened by listening to a recording of authentic street and market place sounds.[2] Hearing them will help children to visualize what life is like in Japan. The countdown and lift-off of the first manned American space vehicle is available to spark one of your geography lessons in the study of our globe.[3] Slides with recorded comments about nearly every country on earth are at your disposal, as well as slide-record studies of the life of land and sea. Travel to Russia with Harrison Salisbury, or to Thailand with Lowell Thomas by means of slides and records helps to provide both a visual and an auditory experience for our pupils.[4] The list of such records and slides is endless. Let us, therefore, stop thinking of the phonograph only in terms of music and begin to think of it as an audio-visual aid with possible geographical application. If our school record libraries do not have the records mentioned here, plan to order them, or some similar to them, and then use them. We should also try to include in our record libraries a good selection of commercially available sound tapes of far-off places.

If we travel at home or abroad, we can make use of the small battery-powered tape recorders to record sounds of places we visit, as well as our own comments about them, to take back with us to our classrooms. These portable tape recorders are quite inexpensive and they are perfect for recording notes about the pictures we take, as well as the sounds we hear. Our own memory is refreshed if we use a tape recorder while we interview people our classes meet on a field trip. We are certain to do a better job of preparation for the field trip if we have the recorded interview to remind us of points we might forget to include in our class preparation. As we prepare our lessons for our classes, we can record commentaries about the slides or mounted pictures we wish to show; even enrichment work for our rapid learners can be prepared in advance on tape. The tape recorder is, in

---

1 *Hark! The Years*, Capitol Records, FED 282.
2 Elektra Records, (51 West 51st Street, New York, N.Y. 10019), has many sound recordings from distant places.
3 Columbia Records, XXI.
4 Columbia Records, Panorama Colorslide Travel and Nature Series.

effect, our own personal teacher aide, and there is little reason why its use should be limited to speech and music lessons when it can be so effective in our geography teaching.

The film strip and slide projector, in combination, is another more abused than used visual aid. Merely showing a film strip, even when it is accompanied by a recorded commentary, is not enough. All of us know that each showing should be preceded by class motivation. The showing of the film is a part of the development of the lesson we teach, and each such lesson is followed by summarization and application. Summarization may include discussion, but how shallow are some of the discussions which we carry on with our classes! We should remember that every frame on the film strip, and every slide that we project, is a picture. Each of these pictures should be read exactly as we read a still picture. (See reading pictures, page 134.) Neither should we forget the value of our own comments, or those of the children, about slides which are accompanied by recorded commentary. If we have visited the spot shown, we can frequently do a better job of description and commentary than that which is done by the speaker on the prepared record or sound track; we are able to sense the questions our classes will ask because we know our classes, whereas commercial firms cannot possibly take into account all of the individual class differences as they prepare materials for publication.

We do not need to be expert photographers to own a collection of first-rate slides for use in our geography classes. If we are geographers, we will take pictures which show geographic relationships. If we do not own cameras, we will frequently find slides of geographic value on sale at the places we visit, although we must be careful to purchase only those which have value, and avoid the bizarre and unusual. Slides that are collected and owned by the teacher have greater value for both class and teacher than collections owned by schools. First, in building our own collections, we are more likely to include the geographically valuable scenes. Scenes which show relationships, or which are relevant to the regions we teach, have value. Second, we will include those scenes which we really need. Commercial collections, while valuable in a general sense, do not always include the scenes we most want. Third, our own collections are always available for immediate use. School-owned collections are on call by all teachers and the slides we need may not be available at the time we must have them. Finally, we are more likely to use our own slides because we are more thoroughly acquainted with them and the areas we have visited. Because we own them, we are more likely to include them in our lesson planning. As we use them in our lessons, we must remember to treat them as we would still pictures, and not subject our pupils to a whole period of nothing but looking at slides!

The geography teacher who is also a home-movie enthusiast has an excellent means for enlivening his classes. One elementary teacher used home movies which he had taken in Bedford County, Pennsylvania, to supplement the geography textbook material on that section of Pennsylvania. His own films of the western United States were used during the study of that part of our country. Again, when field trips to remote factories, parks, rivers, lakes, and so on, were out of the question, he brought the regions to his classroom on color motion picture film which he had taken. Not all of us can afford either the equipment, the film, or the travel expenses to do as he did, but his work illustrates what we can do if we really want to enliven our teaching.

One cannot underestimate the value of the commercially produced motion pictures available for school use, if they are used properly. However, too often a film ordered by one of us for a specific purpose is shared by our colleagues. "I see that you have a film about Nigeria scheduled for today. Would you mind if I brought my class into your room to see it, too? We will not be studying Nigeria this year at all, but the children have heard it mentioned in the news reports and I thought it would be good for them to learn a little about it." Does that sound familiar? And what can we say in response to the question? We have our lesson planned; we have previewed the film; we have motivation and development carefully worked out, and stopping to call another class to come to our room will only break the train of thought which we hope to establish; the visitors have no knowledge of our teaching methods, none of the background which we have developed, and cannot possibly participate in the discussion to follow the showing of the film; finally, bringing thirty more children into our classroom will make the room stuffy and the seating arrangements uncomfortable. In addition to all of these things, we suspect that the request made by our colleague could be freely translated, "I have absolutely nothing planned for today and having my class see your film will help to pass the time until dismissal." If we are teachers, we must do our own planning and generally rely upon ourselves, not our colleagues.

In many elementary schools, an unwise choice of films and poor scheduling of them (usually without any previewing on the part of the teacher) results in children seeing the same films over and over as they pass from one sequence to the next. Films should be scheduled by wise teachers for use in specific sequences so that there is no repetition in viewing.

Films are not "entertainment breaks"; they are teaching tools and learning aids. They must be previewed before they are shown. In some cases, as a result of our preview, we may decide to show only a part of a film, or none of it. We may decide to shut off the sound entirely and deliver the commentary ourselves. No film is really too advanced for our classes, generally speaking, if we shut the sound off and describe the film ourselves in vocabulary suitable to the level of our pupils. In our preview we may make note that a particular frame should be shown in "still" position. Have you ever used the "still" device on the motion picture projector?

Too frequently, showing a film means exactly that, showing every foot of the film. In reality, we would be far better off if we were selective in our planning and used our time more wisely by showing only those portions of a film which contribute to the reaching of our objectives. Why show twenty-five minutes of film when our previewing has disclosed that five minutes of the film will suit our purposes? As we preview the film we should plan how to motivate interest in it and formulate the four or five questions for which the children will seek answers as they watch it. List the questions on the board before showing the film. After the children have watched the film, the class discussion should focus on these questions. A short quiz, related to the questions, should follow the discussion as application work. Using a film as a part of the geography lesson can be a waste of time unless there is planning similar to that which has been described.

One recently developed audio-visual aid which has found rapid acceptance in the public schools is the overhead projector. The device is useful for projecting transparencies of maps, charts, and pictures on a wall or screen. It has the additional, but questionable, advantage of permitting the teacher to face his class while the image is projected to the front of the room behind him. A roll of transparent plastic is attached to the projector's table, upon which the teacher may write or draw with a grease pencil. The material is instantly projected. In addition, separate transparencies can be shown, written upon, and attention called to certain details, without difficulty on the part of the teacher. It is an easy task to learn how to use this machine and to make the transparencies for it. However, its real value lies in the multiple-layer, multicolor charts, graphs, and pictures which can be projected from it. To learn to make these overlays and to use this versatile projector to its greatest extent, one should take advantage of the courses offered, usually free of charge, by the manufacturer. It has been our experience to note that most teachers use only the single sheet transparencies, or the writing roll, of this expensive machine. They might just as well be making use of the opaque projector which has been the geography teacher's "good right arm" for many years. Older models of the opaque projector were sometimes cumbersome to handle, but even this disadvantage was offset by the many educational uses which could be made of the machine. No special preparation of materials for the opaque projector is necessary, although the room should be fairly dark for projection. Photographs, maps, graphs, statistical tables—any printed material—can be placed on the projecting table of the opaque projector and an enlarged image of it shown on a screen, wall, or blackboard. A map projected upon the blackboard with the opaque projector can be traced there by the teacher for later use in his classes. (The overhead projector offers a similar useful advantage.) The movable pointer which is attached to most opaque projectors is useful in directing the attention of the class to details of the projected image.

These are only a few of the audio-visual aids which can be used to enhance geography lessons. Models are especially helpful in motivating interest in geographic problems since they help the pupil to visualize. Layouts and dioramas serve well as application work, since they help to determine whether or not the pupil has understood the geographic concepts and relationships which he has been taught. The wise geography teacher will use as many audio-visual aids as possible.

SELECTED REFERENCES RELATING TO THE USE OF AUDIO-VISUAL AIDS

Christensen, D. E., "Experimenting with Geography Teaching by Television," *Journal of Geography* (February, 1965), 59–64.

Grilzner, C. F., "Geographical Filmstrip—A Neglected Teaching Aid in Higher Education," *Journal of Geography* (March, 1965).

"Overhead Projector—Use in Televising Geography," *Journal of Geography* (October, 1964), 319–322.

Wittich, Walter A., and Charles F. Schuller, *Audio-Visual Materials* (New York, Harper & Brothers, 1953).

9

Plan your work

Good teaching requires careful planning. As we plan the work in geography, we need to think in terms of the geographic concepts that we wish to introduce and develop during the year, as well as the units which will provide vehicles for them. For example, Switzerland would be an excellent unit topic to use to illustrate the effect of elevation on people. Similarly, the study of Chile would show the effect of latitude on human activity. If the course of study in your school system is already established and you have no choice in the selection of the units to be taught, carefully analyze the material to determine which new geographic concepts can be introduced and extended through a study of the countries included in it, and plan how to introduce them. Three sets of plans should be made. The first plan is the over-all plan for the year in which we select the units which we believe will be of greatest interest and benefit to the pupils. To write this plan we must become acquainted with what the pupils have had in previous years and consider how our plan will fit in with what they will have the succeeding year. In this year-long plan we must also approximate the amount of time which we expect to devote to each unit. The second plan includes guidelines for each of the individual units. It may require six or eight weeks to cover the work planned for a single unit, and each unit plan may have to be broken into smaller segments, depending upon the length of the unit. Third, there are daily plans, drawn within the context of the unit plan, which are made each day for the work of the following day.

Each of these three kinds of plans is made with a different purpose in mind, and all three of them must be made by the geography teacher.

The purpose of unit planning is to devise a series of related learning experiences around a central theme, thus avoiding a fragmented program of separate and unrelated lessons. We are all familiar with units of work because the unit method is the accepted method for teaching today. Prepared units may be obtained from many publishers and industrial firms. The prepared units are helpful to the inexperienced teacher because they provide background information and teaching suggestions. However, the prepared geography units usually fail to emphasize relationships. The sequential development of geographic skills is often neglected, too. Many of the materials suggested in the prepared unit plan are not readily available for classroom use. The units have been written with no particular class of pupils in mind, and frequently they fail to make provision for individual differences. Consequently, they are not always appropriate for your own class.

Although it is a tremendous amount of work, it is better for you to write units which provide for the interests, needs, and individual differences of your pupils, remembering that you must make changes each year as the make-up of your classes changes. As you make your own plans, you will be acquiring a background for the unit you will teach, increasing your ability to see relationships, and developing your own creativity.

The geography unit is a body of well-organized material which leads the pupils to a mastery of a major geographic understanding. It includes much more to be learned than content. Plans for the development of geographic skills and for opportunities to practice those skills must be made, and the use of various geographic tools must be taught. The teacher cannot "give" pupils the understandings included in a unit; he can guide the thinking of the pupils as they develop concepts. The pupils must do the learning themselves. Remember that material should never be included in a unit merely because it is interesting; every part of the unit must contribute to the major understanding being taught. It takes courage to exclude merely interesting material, and imagination to include only that which is essential.

Writing the Unit

1. Prepare yourself before you begin to write a unit. Build as comprehensive a background for it as you possibly can. You must have a rich store of knowledge about your unit topic if you wish to interest your pupils and present them with a total picture. You must know more about the

topic than you will be required to teach to your pupils, and your broad knowledge will help you to check the accuracy of materials which the pupils will bring to you from other sources. You must have ready, accurate answers for the questions they will ask. Your background reading should certainly have included the general article on the unit topic which appears in an encyclopedia, as well as specific reference works related to it. It will be necessary for you to check the *Reader's Guide* for recent magazine articles about the unit topic so that you will have the most up-to-date information. Geography is the story of the present as well as the past. Examine your basic textbook carefully to determine how much of its material you can use to develop concepts and relationships. Be certain to take notes as you read. Finally, read units on the topic which have been developed by others. You may find worthwhile suggestions in them.

2. Visit a children's library to learn whether books and pictures about the country or region you are planning to study are available. You may need a vivid description of the land, a story telling the way the people live, or a few paragraphs which explain some of the problems the country might have, to teach a relationship or extend a concept. Keep a list of these books on index cards, and file them.

3. Make an outline of all the information which you feel will be necessary to bring about comprehension of the major understanding of the unit. Refer to it frequently as you plan the relationships you will teach.

4. Make a list of the maps, globes, graphs, pictures, and projectors which you will need as the unit progresses. Planning ahead assures that you will have them available on the day you wish to use them. Check, also, to see if the materials which you will need for class work are available.

There are several kinds of units and many different formats for the organization of them. The format used here is suggested for a teaching unit, but others are equally good. You must use common sense in writing a unit, understanding that not all parts of a suggested unit outline will be applicable to every unit topic.

FORMAT FOR A TEACHING UNIT IN GEOGRAPHY

I. The Objectives
   A. the major understanding or geographic personality of a region to be developed
   B. major objectives to be reached
   C. specific objectives to be reached
   D. relationships to be developed
   E. geographic concepts to be developed
   F. vocabulary peculiar to the topic
   G. map and picture reading skills to be acquired
   H. attitudes and appreciations to be developed

II. The Development of the Unit
   A. motivation and problem raising stage
   B. teacher-pupil planning period
   C. development or problem solving stage
   D. summary
   E. application
III. Testing
IV. Evaluation

I. The Objectives

Objectives must be stated in terms of measurable or observable positive changes in the behavior of your pupils. Behavior, used in this sense, implies (among other things) changes in attitude, appreciation, and understanding, and the acquisition of a usable store of knowledge.

A. WRITING THE MAJOR UNDERSTANDING OR PERSONALITY OF A COUNTRY OR REGION   A major understanding or geographic personality is a statement or explanation of the outstanding relationships developed about the region. In describing an individual's personality, you state his outstanding characteristics, those which are of major importance in making him what he is. The geographic personality or major understanding of a region describes the outstanding adjustments which its inhabitants have made to their environment, adjustments which serve to distinguish it from other regions and which give it a character of its own. The changes which man has made in the environment are also noted as a part of the geographic personality.

Your goal is to have your pupils master the major understanding. When you are organizing a unit, the first question which should come to your mind is, "Just what worthwhile understandings do I want my pupils to have after they have studied the relationships that exist between man and his environment?" The answer to this question comprises the major understanding of the country or region. The major understanding is for you, alone. Writing it out helps you to organize your thinking and keep the goal of the unit in mind.

THE MAJOR UNDERSTANDING OF INDIA

India, today, has many problems to solve, some of which are related to geography. India is about one-half the size of the United States and has approximately 500 million people. It has the second largest population in the world. The world's highest mountains, the Himalayas, are in the northern part of India. South of this wall of mountains are the wide plains of the Indus, Ganges, and Brahmaputra valleys. The alluvial plain of the Ganges River is one of the most populated areas of the world. Peninsular

India is chiefly a plateau region. Each type of surface creates conditions which the people must try to change or to which they must adjust. The climate of India is dominated by the monsoons which bring heavy rains during the summer and little or no rain during the winter season. Too much or too little rainfall means famine for the people.

Most of India's people (about seven-tenths) are farmers who live in small villages. It is necessary to increase agricultural yields, but the small farms, primitive methods, and the lack of fertilizer and good seed stand in the way. Irrigation is essential because food can and must be raised during the entire year. Rice, wheat, millet, and barley are the chief food crops, but other important crops, such as jute, cotton, tea, oilseeds, and sugar cane are grown.

India has rich mineral resources, the most valuable of which is coal. Manganese, copper, iron, bauxite, gold, mica, and other minerals are mined and contribute to the economy of the country. The dominance of agriculture has hindered the development of manufacturing, but the lack of capital and the low buying power of the people have also been influencing factors.

Many of the Indian people are skilled craftsmen, creating articles of gold, silver, ivory, pottery, and hand-loomed cloth. Steel is manufactured in several mills and there are many factories which manufacture cotton, silk, woolen, and jute goods. Calcutta, Bombay, and Madras are manufacturing and trade centers.

The most serious problem facing India today is to raise the living standards of its people.

These are the key understandings upon which the unit study will concentrate.

B. *MAJOR OBJECTIVES TO BE REACHED*   An objective is what the teacher hopes to attain through his teaching. Sometimes this is confused with the word "outcome." An outcome is what the pupils have actually accomplished when teaching has been completed.

A major objective is a general statement of the overall goal, or aim, of the teacher. As the major objective of the teacher who is teaching a unit on India, he would want to help the pupil to understand India today and to have him know and appreciate the problems of India's people.

C. *SPECIFIC OBJECTIVES TO BE REACHED*   Specific objectives deal with particular geographic concepts and relationships essential to the development of the unit. They refer to all of those skills and understandings with which your pupils will be acquainted when the unit is completed. The thoroughness and comprehensiveness of your teaching can be checked against the list of specific objectives which you write.

In writing a unit about India, two of your specific objectives might be to teach something about the many problems which a densely populated country faces, and to teach the effects of the monsoon climate on India.

D. *PREPARING THE RELATIONSHIPS*   The major understanding is written in general terms. The relationships implied by it need to be developed. Writing out these relationships will aid you in organizing pertinent materials in a logical and sequential manner, and will help you to eliminate materials which do not contribute to the major understanding. When you are ready to teach a given relationship, you will have prepared it in advance. You will be able to present it in a clear, concise manner which the pupils will understand. They like the precision of relationship study. It makes memorization unnecessary and challenges their thinking. Relationships may be written out in paragraph form, but you will find the arrow statement a much easier form with which to work. The relationships which you write for the study of India might include the following:

India's advantageous location
——————————————————————————→
(is related to)

1. nearness to the chief trade routes around Asia.
2. nearness to the sea, which affects climate and promotes trade.
3. nearness to the equator which assures a frost-free climate except in the high mountains.
4. the Himalaya Mountains at the north, which keep out the cold winds.

The climate of India ——————→

1. distance from the equator.
2. nearness to the sea.
3. location in a large land mass.
4. monsoons, a result of high and low air pressure.

The inability of the people of India to raise enough food ——————→

1. lack of land to farm.
2. the huge population to feed.
3. undependable monsoon climate.
4. small farms, often divided into widely separated plots.
5. poor methods of cultivation.
6. lack of fertilizer and good seed.
7. lack of irrigation water.
8. poverty of the people.
9. reluctance of the farmers to try new methods.

The slow development of manufacturing in India ——————→

1. dominance of agriculture.
2. slow breakdown of the caste system.
3. lack of capital to start industries.
4. low buying power of the people.
5. lack of education, therefore, few skilled workmen for factories.
6. need of additional water power.
7. kinds of raw materials available: cot-

ton, jute, iron, coal.

8. need for improvement in transportation facilities.

The dense population of ⟶ 1. the easily worked, level land.
the Ganges plain   2. monsoon climate.

3. alluvial soil.

4. availability of irrigation waters.

5. wet-rice agriculture.

6. raising of jute on the delta land and wheat in the northwest half of the plain.

7. belief in the sacredness of the Ganges.

Relationships which should be worked out in addition to these are (1) the growing of crops such as tea, jute, and cotton; (2) the cultivation of tropical plants on the Malabar coast; (3) the growth of several large Indian cities; (4) the poverty of the people; (5) foreign trade; and (6) many problems which India has.

Natural environmental items are never the only cause, or reason, for any human activity. The culture and the characteristics of the people are factors in human activity, also. Hence, we can say that a study of relationships between man and his environment helps to explain his activities. (The repetition of this, and other thoughts related to the study of relationships is intentional. It is our intention that you become increasingly aware of relationships as you carry on your work.)

E. GEOGRAPHIC CONCEPTS   The purpose of the unit is not only to develop new concepts, but also to reinforce and enlarge the understanding of those concepts which have been taught previously. The subject matter of a unit merely clothes the concepts which are peculiar to it. Geographic concepts are dynamic, major ideas. We must remember that they grow and change with the accumulation of geographic knowledge. They may pertain to rainfall, agriculture, sun position, planetary winds, latitude, longitude, climate, elevation, atmospheric pressure, or any number of factors. In the unit about India, the study of the three different types of irrigation used there will help to extend the pupils' concept of man's demand for, and his use of, water. The concept of population density, as it is applied to the Netherlands, is quite different when it is applied to India. The population problems in these countries are not similar, due in part to the cultural heritage and present governmental policies of the two peoples. Thus, it can be seen that before a pupil can generalize about any concept, he must have had many experiences which clarify and broaden his acquaintance with it.

F. VOCABULARY   This topic is self-explanatory, since you will merely note, and make provisions for teaching, any new words with which the pupil must be familiar in order to enhance his geographic understanding. We suggest that you use a philological approach in introducing new words, explaining the meaning of the root word and calling attention to some of its history and other words formed from the same root.

G. *MAP AND PICTURE READING SKILLS*   This material is discussed in Chapters 5 and 7.

H. *ATTITUDES AND APPRECIATIONS TO BE DEVELOPED* It is assumed that you will naturally be concerned about the attitudes which your pupils develop and their appreciation of the world about them. J. Russell Smith in an address before the National Council of Geography Teachers at Columbus, Ohio in 1946, said:

> There are two enduring things that you may hope to plant in the minds or spirits of children. The most important of these things that endure is attitude. Attitudes help to decide how we interpret the facts of life. Attitudes are perhaps our most important residue. The second important residue of the geography class may be a few big ideas about countries, peoples, and places.

These observations are just as true today as they were in 1946.

How you teach the unit about India and *what* you teach will determine what your pupils think about India and her people and how they will feel toward them and the country. Our attitudes are based entirely upon the information which we possess at any given moment; our appreciations are related to the experiences which we have had while acquiring our attitudes. Both of them contribute to our understanding, or misunderstanding.

II. The Development of the Unit

A. *MOTIVATION AND PROBLEM RAISING STAGE*   The most important part of a lesson or unit is its motivation. The success of your teaching depends upon it. Little or no learning takes place without it. The motivation should create a feeling of curiosity and mild frustration on the part of the pupils. As the unit begins, they should feel a need to know the material which you plan to present. You must motivate them to find the answers to challenging questions or to solve problems. You must motivate them to consult maps, to do research, to read reference material, and to do creative work in order to satisfy their curiosity and relieve their frustration.

The motivation is much more than a simple statement or two which you might use to stimulate interest. You must build readiness for the work which is to be done. This readiness may consist of orienting the pupils by means of map study, or a reference to a few well-chosen pictures. You may build an interest through true stories or fiction, or through challenging questions which are left unanswered. Some information concerning the unit topic must be included in the motivation. No child or adult is interested in a topic about which he knows nothing. Similarly, pupils cannot ask questions, or express curiosity, about a topic or country with which they are completely unfamiliar. Yet we find teachers who ask, "What would you like to know about this country?" when their pupils haven't been given enough information to enable them as ask intelligent questions. As you motivate the unit, set up problems which are real and meaningful to the pupils, and whose solutions will require the understanding of the relationships which you have already planned. Each unit will have many such problems. If your pupils have been given sufficient background information about Latin America, for instance, you can see the possibilities in the question, "To what extent does Latin America affect our daily lives?" A question like this motivates further study and helps to give purpose to your own work. Another motivating question for work related to Latin America might be, "If you were on the board of directors of a large manufacturing concern, what would you list as points for and against investing money in an industrial plant in Brazil? What are some of the factors which would affect market conditions there? What are some of the items which would find buyers there?" Such questions provide real situations with which the pupils can work. The solutions to the problems which they raise are also real and involve concrete facts and geographic relationships which will be remembered long after the study of Latin America has been completed.

There are many ways to motivate a lesson or unit. Using a current event is a sure way to create interest, but be certain that the event will in some way have a bearing on geography. An exciting story about the country and its people, interesting pictures, artifacts from the country, or talks by people who have lived or visited there, will promote interest, as well as stimulate your pupils to raise questions.

B. *TEACHER-PUPIL PLANNING*   Do you give your pupils a share in planning their work? Far too few teachers do so. If you could know how much the rapport between you and your pupils will improve, and how the drive of the pupils will be increased because of active interest and purpose, you would quickly allow your pupils to have a share in planning most of their work. Teacher-pupil planning does much to eliminate the idea that the pupils are working for you. When planning is shared, you become an advisor or consultant instead of a dictator. It is also surprising and stimulating to discover how much freshness and interest the ideas of your pupils will bring to your teaching. If you scoff at this idea because you think that your pupils will make foolish proposals, consider for a moment the possibility that your teaching methods might be prompting them. If you have not used teacher-pupil planning before, then you must develop the idea gradually with your class. Your first attempt may be nothing more than asking them their opinion about how it would be best to place a graph on their papers. You might ask them to suggest ways in which a bulletin board display might be arranged. Whatever your initial act may be, you will find many such opportunities every day for planning with your class. Allowing your pupils to have an opportunity to make choices is a beginning.

At the close of the motivation, after some of the problems have been set up, you will begin to plan with your pupils how the work of solving the problems should be carried out. Together, you might follow these steps:

1. Let the pupils discuss what they already know about the subject.
2. Let them list questions about the subject which they wish to have answered. They evaluate and organize them in terms of problems they wish to solve. If the pupils have been properly oriented in the motivation, there will be worthwhile questions raised. The teacher is still the advisor and should act as a guide, helping the pupils to ask clear questions which will contribute to the major understanding. As a member of the group the teacher will add his own questions which will cover material omitted by the class. All of the questions should be listed. Discuss with the pupils the value of each question toward an understanding of the country. The trivial questions will be eliminated and others may be combined. Whenever possible, use the phrasing of the pupils in listing the questions. They will then be more easily understood by the pupils and have more meaning for them.
3. The pupils are permitted to discuss where they can find information which will help to answer their questions and solve their problems.
4. Let them help to decide how different phases of the work are to be done, whether by the class as a whole, by committees, or by individuals. As part of their discussion, let them list worthwhile activities which would clarify geographic concepts and relationships, such as the making of layouts, climatic graphs, sketches, bar graphs, and so on.
5. Summarize the points of their discussion and proceed with the work.

MOTIVATION FOR INDIA

"I have some very interesting things in this brown paper bag. They are products which we import from a country that we are going to learn about. Let's see if you have any idea about the country from which they came." Teacher removes jute and a piece of burlap from the bag. "What kind of fiber do you think this is? I doubt if any of you have seen it before, but would you like to guess what it is? Hemp? Sisal? No. This fiber is jute. It grows a long distance from here." Teacher writes "jute" on the board. "Jute is used for many things which you may already know about. This is burlap. It is made from jute. In what other products have you seen this kind of fiber? *In twine, in the backs of linoleum and carpets, and so on.* Can anyone guess what kind of metal this is? It is manganese. Our steel mills use a quantity of this mineral in every ton of steel they produce." Teacher writes the word on the board. "If the United States is the world's greatest producer of steel, how important do you think a supply of manganese would be to our country? I wonder why they put manganese into steel? Does anyone recognize this next mineral? *Mica.*" Write word on the board. "How is mica used? Many of the boys will know. It can be split so thinly that it takes ten thousand sheets of it to make an inch of thickness. It is used in electronic, radar, and electrical equipment. How important do you think it would be to our economy?" Teacher takes from the paper bag a tea bag, pepper corns, cashew kernels, and an envelope of sugar, and writes each name on the board as he calls it to the attention of the class. "Does anyone have any idea which country would send these products to us? I have already said that the country is a long distance away. What kind of climate would it have to have to produce tea and sugar? Yes, frost free. Pepper is a spice, isn't it? This country produces pepper corns. Have you any idea where the early explorers obtained spices?" Continue this form of questioning. The pupils will soon guess India.

"India is very important to the United States and we are sending billions of dollars as well as millions of tons of wheat to help this young nation. You see, this country is only about twenty years old, although it has one of the oldest civilizations in the world. There are many reasons why we want to be good friends with India, so we will have to learn a great deal about this country if we want to understand her problems.

Now, let's find out where India is. Open your textbook to the map of the world and find India. Jane will find India on the wall map of the world and Jack will find it on the globe. Jack, measure the distance from New York to Bombay with this tape measure." On a sixteen-inch globe, one inch represents five hundred miles. "Jane, will you please measure the distance on the map with this strip of paper? Why is there a difference in the two measurements? Which one will be the more reliable? *The one made on the globe.* What direction is India from where we are? Stand and point in the direction you would travel to reach India. We can think of India as being both east and west from us. Which direction would be longer? How could we travel to India to visit? *By air or by ship.* It would take twenty-two hours to fly to Calcutta and twenty-seven days by ship through the Mediterranean Sea. Why would it take so much longer by ship? Would there be any difference in the fares? *Very little. The trip would cost about $1,200, round trip.*

Turn to your map of Asia. In what part of Asia is India? Does this location have any advantages? Look at the world map for a clue. *India lies in the pathway of world trade.* What great disadvantage does this location have? How far north of the equator is India? Trace the Tropic of Cancer across India. This is the point farthest north where the sun can be seen directly overhead at noon on one day of the year. What does this tell you about the climate of India?

Now look carefully at the boundary line which separates India from Pakistan. Do you notice that Pakistan is divided into parts? Twenty years ago, all this land was India, and it was owned by the United Kingdom. Read the

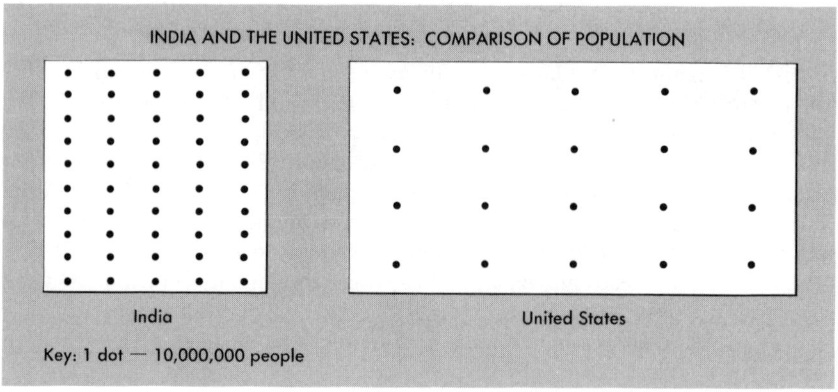

INDIA AND THE UNITED STATES: COMPARISON OF POPULATION

India

United States

Key: 1 dot — 10,000,000 people

Figure 38

last paragraph on page ———— in your textbook to find out why India has come to be separated into two countries." Teacher writes new words on the board: Moslem, Hindu, and so on. "Of course this division created many problems among the people because the two countries are different in many ways. You will study both of them later and find how each country is developing its land. There are several religious groups in India, but these two are by far the largest.

Now, let's see how many people there are in India. Turn to the statistical section at the back of your textbook. What is the population of India? Of the United States? Look at this chart. One rectangle is half the size of the other. It represents the area of India; the larger rectangle represents the area of the United States. Each dot stands for ten million people. How crowded they are!" See Figure 38.

"What problems will India's overcrowded population cause?" Teacher lists them as the pupils give them. "There will be many problems: not enough food, not enough land for the people to work, no employment for many people, low incomes, a shortage of money for education, poor sanitation, and lack of proper medical aid. These are problems which many of the newer countries all over the world are experiencing. Wouldn't it be worthwhile for us to see if we could help to find solutions for some of these problems? I am going to tell you just a little about the problems of the Indian people. Later, when we know much more about the country, perhaps we can suggest something which might have some value in solving some of India's problems.

Most of the Indian people have only one meal a day. One of your school lunches would have as much value as the amount of food that many people in India eat in two days. The Indian government is working on this problem, hoping that in the near future all the people may be able to have two meals each day. Having only one meal a day affects the health of those Indian people who are unfortunate enough to be in this situation. You must understand that not all of the Indian people have only one meal a day, but the majority of the people are in this situation.

Seven out of every ten people live on the land. The average farm is only one and one-half acres. A farm of seventy acres in the United States is able to support one family. In India that much land would have to support forty-seven families.

The average wage in India is $1.25 per week, or about $60 per year. Your father couldn't buy so much for you if he earned only $60 per year, could he? Yet these Indian fathers and mothers want things for their children just as your parents want things for you. They want their children to learn to read and write, because at the present time only about one-fourth of the Indian people can read and write. All of them are eager to learn, but there is not enough money to improve education at the present time. There is only one doctor for every ten thousand people, and in some parts of India there is only one doctor for every twenty-five thousand people. It is no wonder that the life expectancy of an Indian citizen is only about thirty-five years. About half of the children die before they are ten years old. The life expectancy here in the United States is about seventy years at present, and very few of our children die in infancy.

Let's try to find out why this country has these problems and see if we can suggest any solutions. We will begin with their problem of not having enough food. What information will we have to obtain in order to understand this problem?" Teacher lists the answers on the board: surface of India; climate; effect of the monsoons; necessity for irrigation; the principal food crops and where they are grown; cash crops raised; small farms; farming villages; method of farming; and the efforts of the government to improve farming methods to increase yields.

"We can now make plans together to see how to work out this problem." See Teacher-Pupil Planning, p. 195.

Now that you have read this motivation for the study of India, ask yourself these questions:

- ✓ What drive of the children was enlisted at the first?
- ✓ How was the vocabulary of the pupils increased?
- ✓ How was the location of India established?
- ✓ What relationships were noted?
- ✓ How is a sympathetic attitude toward India and her people built up?
- ✓ How is the textbook used?
- ✓ What skills were strengthened? (Map reading, interpretation of charts, measuring of distances.)
- ✓ How were the problems for further study set up?

C. DEVELOPMENT OR PROBLEM SOLVING STAGE   In the development part of the unit, geographic relationships are developed, new geographic concepts are introduced, and skills are strengthened as your pupils solve the problems which were recognized by them in the motivation. It is the "work" part of the unit in which they gather information which will help solve their problems. Too many teachers rely completely on the geography textbook, teaching the material in the book and insisting that parts of it be memorized. This is not problem solving, nor does it make use of other geographic tools. The futility of using this method of "teaching" is evident when you realize that geographic facts, such as population figures, the sizes of cities, crop production figures, and principal exports and imports, are constantly changing. It is not very consistent on our part as teachers to insist that our pupils memorize facts which are likely to change in a short time. Our task is to teach lasting concepts, concepts which may grow and change but which will still be applicable in new situations, and to increase the ability of our pupils to think logically. It is much more sensible to use the problem-solving method in teaching geography since it places emphasis upon logical thought processes, concept development, the importance of understanding relationships, and the use of many geographic tools.

The problems to be solved must be real, interesting, and make sense to your pupils. Try to word them in such a way that the pupils will feel involved in them. Instead of asking them to list the agricultural problems which India has, ask, "If you were an East Indian boy or girl and lived in a small farming village, what conditions related to farming would worry you and your father?" The problem, as it is stated, will require the pupil to become involved as a person, even though on a suppositional basis, and he will remember the facts which come to light as he participates in the discussion because of his involvement and the opportunity which he has to apply facts already learned. Using problems to teach geography is more interesting because solving them means that the pupils must do something —read, sketch, make graphs, discuss, reason, and so on.

When you and your pupils have decided on the problems which must be solved, they decide what information is needed to work out a solution and where they will have to look to obtain it. Work periods devoted to gathering information can be handled in many different ways. Your pupils may work together as a class, as committees, or as individuals to gather, interpret, and present information in class discussions or in individual and committee reports. In assigning committee work be sure that you give them clear directions and that each pupil understands what he is to do. References and assignments may be written on cards and handed to each pupil or committee. It is senseless to assign topics which are fully covered by the textbook which the pupils use. Each topic should be a special one in the sense that the information about it will not be available to the entire class.

It is your responsibility to help each committee member to prepare his report. Help him to outline its main points, suggest visual aids which will make his talk more interesting, and encourage him to give the report in his own words, using his note cards only for reference purposes. Ask him to summarize his report for you, privately, before he presents it for the class. Insist that he stay within the time limits for oral reports which have been established by the class. Have him prepare one or two questions to ask the class at the close of his talk. If you are not willing to do the extra work which committees and special reports require, then do not have them. You will do more harm than good if you allow committees to work and pupils to prepare reports without showing them how these things are done properly. Pupils lose interest quickly when a report is dull or poorly delivered, and behavior problems arise. In fact, the pupils do not even hear the report, time is wasted all around, and they develop a distaste for the subject matter. On the other hand, if a pupil has a short, well-prepared, interesting topic, and gives it in his own words in a voice which can be heard, his report will add to the understanding of the unit and he will gain experience.

You must be sure that your pupils are achieving what you want them to achieve. You want them, eventually, to become intelligent adults, with an accumulation of knowledge and an increased ability to think. These outcomes are accomplished through the learning experiences which your pupils have. Each of the experiences should be evaluated by you. It is through regular evaluation that you are able to see whether or not your teaching has been effective.

To make your plans for the development part of the unit more complete, draw a three column chart and label the columns DESIRED OUTCOMES, ACTIVITIES, and EVALUATION. These column headings have been suggested by other authors; however, few teachers actually use them. Each of us is likely to think that he does not need to bother to write out lesson or unit plans in such complete form. "After all," we say, "experienced teachers don't write lesson plans." Nonsense! Experienced teachers, and excellent teachers, do write plans. They know where they are going as they teach, how they are going to get there, how they will take their pupils along with them, and how to determine whether or not their work has been effective. Don't you, as a beginning teacher—or as an experienced teacher who wishes to do an even better job—slip into the habit of neglecting to develop your lessons step by step, and failing to write down how the steps are to be carried out. The triple-column plan which has been suggested here, and which is illustrated in the pages which follow, is the best one that we have discovered. Unfortunately, we have no idea with whom it originated, but its inventor has given teachers a simple, logical method for developing a unit theme. It is even effective where the unit method of teaching is not used. If you are insecure and feel that you need to follow the textbook closely, or if your curriculum director insists that teachers must slavishly follow the text, your teaching methods will still be improved by using this plan.

The first column, DESIRED OUTCOMES, lists what your pupils will be able to do after they have completed the unit. Each desired outcome is a contributing factor in the solution of the major problem. It is important that you write each of these objectives in terms of some definite achievement which your pupils will make. They are not to be stated in terms of what you are going to do; neither should they describe learning activities. As you write each one, think, "When my pupils have finished this unit, they will all be able to . . ." and then complete the thought with the specific behavior changes which you wish to bring about. Avoid completing the thought with such words as "to understand" or "to appreciate" because the depth of these values cannot be measured. Instead, tell what your pupils will be able to do if they understand or appreciate.

The ACTIVITIES column is a list of the learning experiences which will help your pupils achieve the outcomes. These learning experiences might include making dioramas and posters, writing descriptive paragraphs, making distribution maps, graphs, and sketches, preparing reports, doing research, taking part in panel discussions, and so on. Too many times we have delusions about how effective our activities have been in helping pupils to learn. Frequently the activity is simply an activity, unrelated to goals and pursued merely because it is something to do. You must remember that activities, too, contribute to the solution of the major problem; they must never be busy work.

The third column, EVALUATION, is a list of ways in which to evaluate each desired outcome. Some of them may be evaluated by the activities; others require that answers to questions be written, or that discussions take place between you and your pupils.

The chart which follows is not intended to be complete. It indicates how the planning for the development part of the unit might be done.

Desired Outcomes, Activities, and Evaluation for the Study of India

DESIRED OUTCOMES	ACTIVITIES	EVALUATION
From the pupil's viewpoint he should be able to:		
1. Locate India and Pakistan.	1. On an outline map locate the two parts of Pakistan, and India.	1. (1)[a] Give one advantage and one disadvantage connected with Pakistan's separation.
2. Compare the size and population of India with the United States.	2. Check the statistics in the textbook. 3. Make a simple bar graph comparing the areas of the two countries. 4. Make a simple bar graph comparing the population of the two countries.	2. (2) About what fractional part of the area of the U.S. is the area of India? 3. (2) How does the population of the U.S. compare with that of India?

[a] The figure in parentheses refers to the number of the desired outcome in the first column.

DESIRED OUTCOMES	ACTIVITIES	EVALUATION
3. Describe the topography of India and to explain the land use of each type of surface.	5. On an outline map of India, locate the Himalayas, Western Ghats, Eastern Ghats, the Malabar and Coromandel coasts, the Deccan, and Ganges Plain. 6. Study the physical-political map to see what effect the mountains have upon the distribution of the rainfall. 7. Study a physical-political map and a population map of India to learn on which type of surface most of the people live.	4. (3) Identify the numbers of the land forms and water bodies shown on the outline map. 5. (3) Explain the effect of mountains in India. 6. (3) Where is the most densely populated area in India? Account for this.
4. Account for the monsoons and to note their effect upon the country and its people.	8. Study the seasonal maps of India. 9. Explain what is meant by high and low pressure areas. Account for the monsoons blowing from different directions during different seasons. 10. Try to find a story which will describe the coming of the monsoons and how they affect the people. 11. Make a climatic graph showing the rainfall of Calcutta. What does it show you about the amount of rain that Calcutta receives, and its distribution throughout the year?	7. (4) What are monsoons? What direction do they blow from in summer? In winter? 8. (4) Pretend that you are a Hindu child. Describe the coming of the monsoon. Write one paragraph.

D. *SUMMARY*   Summarizing pulls together the various concepts, facts, and relationships which your pupils have learned in a lesson or unit. The necessity for taking time at the end of each work period to summarize what your pupils have learned cannot be overemphasized. As you develop relationships and concepts, you may sometimes introduce extraneous material, all of which may be interesting to your pupils, but which makes it difficult for them to determine what it is that is most important. If they know the goal at the beginning of the unit or lesson, they should be made aware of how much has been achieved toward reaching that goal. As you have your pupils summarize the lesson, point out those things which it is important for them to understand. Sometimes a few quick questions and answers at the close of the lesson will be a sufficient summary. Another very good way to summarize is to give your pupils part of the relationship which you have taught and have them complete it:

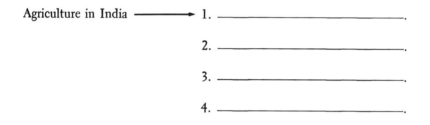

A "quiz kid" panel with a master of ceremonies will also meet the requirements of a good summary, as will contests which make use of questions relating to the lesson or unit. The relationship matching exercise (see page 26) is also an excellent way to summarize. The thing which you must remember is never to conclude a lesson or unit without a summary.

E. *APPLICATION*   Using information which has been gained in one situation in a similar but new setting helps to assure that learning takes place. Your pupils should have regular opportunities to apply their knowledge, since application requires them to do critical thinking. Each geography lesson should have application work for the pupils to do because it helps to assure that the facts they have learned will be retained longer.

There are many ways in which you can have your pupils apply geographic relationships, concepts, and facts. Some of the suggestions given below can be used at the close of geography lessons; others, which require more time, may be used at the completion of a unit.

GIVE the geographic background concerning a current event which occurred in the region under study.

SELECT geographic relationships and concepts which appear in a story about the country under study. The story may be one which the pupils are reading or which you have read to them.

MAKE a class book about the country, having each pupil contribute a page. (See page 244.)

MAKE posters advertising the products which the country has for sale.

DISCUSS whether or not you would advise an American corporation which manufactures _____ to establish a subsidiary company in the country under study.

BUILD a layout. This is an excellent way to apply most of the geographic relationships learned by the pupils during their unit work.

III. Testing

See Chapter 11.

IV. Evaluation

In evaluating the work of your pupils, check behavioral changes as well as scholastic achievement. Evaluation should be a continuous, encompassing, and integrated process, carried on cooperatively by you and your pupils throughout the entire unit. Evaluation can be used as a teaching device since it brings to light the purpose of their work and makes your pupils aware of where they have succeeded or failed. At the close of the daily work period it is wise to have them discuss how much they have accomplished and how this lesson has contributed to the realization of their problem solving goal. Good work should be commended. If they have not accomplished as much as they should have, ways of improving their work habits should be suggested by them, as well as by you, who are the guide and teacher. This kind of pupil participation helps them to develop a feeling of responsibility toward their work and its purposes.

You must evaluate your own work as well as that of your pupils. A frank analysis of your work, including both its strong and its weak points, will do much to assure the success of the next unit which you plan and teach. Refer to the objectives which you wrote at the beginning of your present unit to determine how many have been achieved. Conscientiously ask yourself these questions:

✓ Have I introduced and developed geographic concepts?

✓ Have geographic problem solving experiences increased the ability of the pupils to think?

✓ Has more interest in geography been created through the study of this unit?

✓ Have I increased their understanding of other peoples of the world?

✓ Have I taught relationship geography?

If your answers to these questions are affirmative, you have taught!

Improving the Quality of the Daily Geography Lesson

The development of the geography unit requires that many lessons be taught. The success of your teaching depends upon the quality of each of those lessons. Every teacher has had the experience of having made a good lesson plan and yet, in executing it, discovered that the lesson missed its mark because of the quality of the teaching. When one of your daily lessons fails in its purpose, do you ask yourself why? Quality in teaching depends upon many things. How can you improve the quality of your daily geography lessons?

BY BEING AN ENTHUSIASTIC TEACHER, WHO KNOWS GEOGRAPHY   We have heard many times that nothing can be accomplished without enthusiasm. This is especially true in the field of geography. If the teacher is enthusiastic about geography, his teaching will be interesting and it will bring excitement to the lesson. Pupils are eager to listen to, and work with, such a teacher. Let the tone of your voice indicate your eagerness and your positive attitude toward the lesson. Convey to your pupils the feeling that you have something very special that you want them to know. Enthusiasm is contagious and there is little learning without it. Geography is a live subject and every lesson deserves to be taught with enthusiasm.

BY PLANNING YOUR LESSON IN DETAIL   Good teaching does not just happen; it requires careful planning. Regardless of how long he has taught, the teacher should always have a plan for any lesson he expects to teach. The geographic concepts to be introduced and strengthened, and the relationships to be developed and taught, should be clear in his mind. A definite plan prevents him from using material which does not pertain to the major understanding being developed. Every geography lesson has several distinct parts—objectives, motivation, development, summary, and application—each of which has a function to perform. While objectives deal with changes which the teacher wishes to bring about in pupil behavior, the crucial part of teaching any lesson effectively is properly motivating it.

BY PLANNING AN EFFECTIVE MOTIVATION How many lessons have been ruined by a dull motivation, or because the teacher tells the pupils what they are to do instead of building interest in the topic and eagerness to learn about it! We learn when we are motivated to learn. Take time to motivate your pupils well. There are several steps to be followed in motivating a geography lesson. First, arouse the interest of the class in the topic. Second, give background for the lesson in order to orient them and to intensify the interest of the class. Third, set up problems which will give purpose to the development which is to come. Fourth, plan with the children how to do the work. Finally, let the pupils know why the lesson is being taught. If the purpose seems to be worthwhile to them, they will be interested and enthusiastic about it.

Many teachers fail to follow through with these steps. They hurry the motivation, devoting only a sentence or two to it. They fail to think through what to do to motivate. Having hastily gone through a motivation, they expect that all of the pupils have heard what they have said and that they are ready for the development. They are unrealistic if they believe this. Their pupils may be looking directly at them as they speak, not seeing them or hearing a word that is said. The motivation will be over before they sense what their teacher is talking about. Only confusion can result.

Each daily lesson needs its own motivation as well as some reference to the motivation for the entire unit. The pupils must be able to see how the day's lesson contributes to the progression of the unit. The daily motivation may be based upon the pupil-teacher evaluation of the work of the previous day. Part of the motivation will include finishing incomplete work, doing additional research, or completing the study of a relationship. If the lesson is to be a new step in the development of the unit or the teaching of a new relationship, background material must be provided for in the motivation. Try to end your motivation with a problem to be worked out, or a challenging statement which will need research for proof. The solution of the problem, or the explanation of the statement, require that concepts and relationships be developed. This is done in the development or working part of the lesson.

BY CAREFULLY DEVELOPING RELATIONSHIPS AND CONCEPTS The principal part of the lesson is the development or work portion. Here geographic relationships are taught and concepts are developed. Select the relationship which you plan to teach in a particular lesson from the list of relationships which you have previously made. Decide upon a method with which to present it. The method which you select may take the form of a teacher-pupil discussion in which the teacher will try to bring out the main points of the relationship through a study of physical-political, rainfall, population, and land use maps, pictures, charts, and textbooks. Certain points of the relationship might be assigned to individuals or to committees, depending upon the topic and the time available for the work. Various activities, such as the making of climatic and bar graphs, and charts may be necessary to illustrate important facets of the relationship. If your method has been to divide the group into committees to do this work, then call the pupils together near the close of the lesson to discuss the points which they have found to verify various aspects of the relationship. As you review these points, write the relationship on the board in the form of an arrow statement. You will have to develop many relationships with the class as a whole before the pupils are able to work out relationships by themselves or in committees. Give the pupils time to think as you discuss the relationship. Inexperienced teachers are inclined to provide the pupils with the information rather than to develop the relationship by means of questions. The result is that the material is covered too rapidly to be assimilated by them. This initial, slow development of relationships may seem to be tedious work, but you will be doing much more for the pupils by doing it than by simply teaching them facts which may change before the end of the year.

Why do relationships improve the quality of a lesson? If you are not teaching relationships, you simply are not teaching geography. Your pupils cannot work out relationships unless they do some thinking of their own and apply facts which they know. The quality and depth of your lesson are improved when your pupils are actively engaged in thinking through relationships.

New geographic concepts are not introduced in every lesson that you teach, but there are always opportunities to enrich and enlarge other concepts which the pupils have already begun to develop. You cannot teach concepts; they must be developed out of the child's own experiences, but you can plan the concept-building experiences by which the pupils come to know concepts. The concepts of the pupils change as their knowledge increases. No one can be certain just when a given concept becomes meaningful to each pupil, nor how much of the pupil's background of information has been integrated with the concept. These things depend upon the maturity and previous learning experiences of the pupil. As a result, a large amount of redevelopment of concepts has to be done, not by simply repeating the original work, but by providing new ways to apply it. What does this mean in terms of the quality of the daily lesson? It means that when you introduce a new concept you must give the pupils several examples which illustrate it, or you must explain it in several ways. A single explanation will reach some of the pupils, but not all of them. We must have patience and employ ingenuity as we try to present concepts in a variety of ways in order to help all of our pupils achieve some understanding.

We must constantly check their understanding of concepts concerning the subject matter, the geographic terms—even the wording of their textbooks—to see if they have correct ideas about geographic concepts which we take for granted. Keep in mind the fact that each term you are teaching a group of pupils who are not acquainted with the material of your sequence. Remember that you must begin to teach them at the level on which they understand. Keep the number of concepts to be introduced to a minimum. It is better for the pupils to understand a few concepts well than to confuse them. Those amusing answers which we find on the test papers of our pupils are not so amusing when we realize that somewhere in the sequences a teacher failed to develop a concept to the extent where it had meaning for the pupil.

BY PROCEEDING FROM THE KNOWN TO THE UNKNOWN
Do you remember the adage, "Hang new knowledge on old pegs of experience"? Association is the key to learning and understanding and the adage is especially true in teaching geography lessons. There are new terms to add to the geography vocabulary of the pupils, physical phenomena which must be explained, and many unfamiliar countries whose cultures and environments must be understood. Try to bring about understanding by having the pupils recall circumstances which they have experienced and which are somewhat similar to the new material. Then apply these concepts to the new situation being discussed. We should talk about the hot, humid days and the convectional storms of our own summers to fourth sequence pupils, for instance, when we want them to understand the discomfort of the climate in almost all of the equatorial countries, and of how annoying the insects are and how difficult it is for man to keep food fresh without refrigeration, or his leather shoes free from the mold which quickly gathers on almost everything. Such a discussion makes the country seem real, and it becomes easier for the pupils to appreciate its problems because they have experienced somewhat similar living conditions for a short period of time. Your daily lessons will be much improved if you try always to move from the old to the new, the known to the unknown, as you teach.

BY DEVELOPING THE PUPILS' POWERS OF IMAGINATION
A vivid imagination is essential for the enjoyment of life and learning. There would be no progress or beauty in the world without imaginative people to produce them. Modern life, with its television, movies, and picture magazines, has tended to limit the development of our power of imagination and we find that many of our pupils also lack it. They need a sense of imagination to understand and enjoy geography. We want them to "see" the grandeur of the Andes and Rockies when they read about them. We want them to be able to place themselves in any landscape which they are studying so that it becomes real to them. Use every oppor-

tunity to develop their ability to form mental images, always carefully distinguishing between the fanciful imagery of the primary pupil and the intermediate pupil's ability to visualize real scenes and objects not actually present. Read vivid descriptions about interesting parts of the country which the class is studying. Have them close their eyes as you read and try to visualize the scenes you are describing. After discussing what they saw—in mind's eye—reread the description slowly, sentence by sentence, as they try to sketch the scene on paper. If there are pictures of the region available, have them check their sketches with them. A waste of time? No; rather, a very real way to help them sharpen their perception. Occasionally, have the pupils imagine that they are visiting certain interesting areas of the world. Have them write a description of what they might see there. The descriptions may take the form of a newspaper or magazine article, a letter home, or a diary. There are many other ways to increase their ability to visualize, but remember that the power of imagination will serve our pupils well all through their lives. We especially need adults who can think clearly, but who have not lost their ability to imagine, to think creatively. Our task is to help develop such people through our teaching. Remember, "Only he who can see the invisible can do the impossible."

BY IMPROVING YOUR QUESTIONING TECHNIQUES   As we have indicated so often, our chief function as teachers is to help our pupils develop their ability to reason. This is a difficult task because elementary school pupils do not yet understand how they initiate thought patterns, organize them, and accept or reject them as they solve problems or consider facts. They must be taught how to use the limited background of thought patterns which they have accumulated, and how to proceed, step by step, through analysis and synthesis, to a conclusion. In this regard, our teaching must be done through the use of skillfully planned questioning. It takes time and patience to develop a pupil's ability to reason, but the teacher is repaid for his efforts, over and over again, as he watches the growth of this skill in his pupils. In class he cannot go hastily from one student to another, searching for the "correct" answer to a question which he has asked. He must proceed through the steps involved in the thinking process required to answer the question, or solve the problem, with his pupils, asking simple questions which will advance their reasoning, gradually and logically, to the correct answer. It may be necessary to repeat this process several times during a lesson, but each time it is done, the pupils will benefit from it.

The teacher who is interested in improving his teaching techniques will be question conscious. He will plan his questions so that they will be developmental, not hit-and-miss. There will be purpose behind each question. Will the question require only a factual response, or will it require reasoning? The rote memory question requires no thought and places emphasis on facts rather than the use of them. Too many teachers use this type of question. As a result their pupils seldom know how to use what they have learned. If we want to develop the ability to reason, we must ask "how" and "why" questions. Reasoning takes place when explanation is required. That is what geography is all about—explaining why things are as they are in different parts of the world. Every relationship in geography requires logical thinking, and reasoning questions are necessary to explain relationships.

We can improve our questioning techniques by using the suggestions which follow.

RARELY use questions which can be answered with "Yes" or "No." They are "dead-end" questions and lead nowhere. They are a waste of time because a second question nearly always has to be asked. They also encourage guessing on the part of the pupil.

Do NOT ask questions which suggest an answer, such as, "Do you think that the people living here would carry on grazing?" Instead, ask the pupils for three reasons why the chief industry *is* grazing.

BE PARTICULAR about the way you phrase questions. The wording can have a psychological effect. "Who can tell me . . . ?" may not have any effect upon the uninhibited pupil, but you will receive a much better response if you ask, "How many can tell me . . . ?"

Do NOT attempt to clarify one question with another, especially when the question requires time to think. Give your pupils time to think! When about half of the pupils have an answer, call for it; do not wait for the entire class. Avoid ambiguous or indefinite questions. Your question is poor if you have to make two or three attempts to obtain the response you seek.

MAKE it a matter of policy not to repeat a question, unless there is an unusual disturbance which prevents the class from hearing. Repetition encourages pupils to be inattentive. If it is necessary to have a question repeated, have a pupil repeat it. In giving a page number, let the pupils have a warning, such as, "Are you ready to find the place?" "Now, turn to page (pause) sixty-one."

Do NOT repeat the answers given by the pupils. You will be tempted to do this many times because you wish to emphasize the answer. However, it wastes time and slows the pace of the lesson.

[NOTE: In the model lessons provided in this text, the teacher does seemingly repeat the answers given by the pupils. This device has been used, however, to avoid setting down a complete dialogue which would include the pupil's response.]

Let us improve our lessons with better questioning techniques. Good teaching is largely a matter of drawing out, not of putting in.

BY USING ATTENTION GETTERS   A geography lesson is often ineffective because the teacher begins the lesson before he has the attention of every pupil in the class. Remember that you are teaching all of them and that you are responsible for every pupil knowing what you teach. Do not proceed with the lesson until you see that you have everyone's attention, but take steps to obtain their attention. Why don't pupils pay attention? Some are not interested in geography. The teacher may have failed to motivate them. The work may be too difficult for some. Some pupils have short attention spans. For others, the work may be too simple and they may be bored by it all. Try some of the following suggestions on your inattentive pupils. They work!

HELP get your pupils into a working mood with such remarks as, "Are we all ready?" and "Are you thinking with me?"

PAUSE in the middle of a statement. This will bring them back with a snap because they want to find out why you stopped. "Why do you think (pause) that there is so much corn grown in the middle west?"

CALL for an opinion or a vote on some answer. Have the pupils raise their hands. It stimulates circulation! "How many think that this is true? How many do not? How many don't know?" All of the pupils have had a chance to respond by raising their hands.

CHANGE the pace and the pitch of your voice. Be conscious of voice quality. Never let your voice become monotonous; it lulls pupils to sleep. If your voice has raucous quality, they will tune you out. Keep your voice alive, full of animation. As you speak, think of your voice quality in terms of fast, slow, high, low.

USE the name of the inattentive pupil at the end, rather than at the beginning of your question. "Why did New York become such a large city, Jim?" If the name is used at the beginning of the question the rest of the class knows that they will not be expected to answer.

CALL on people in all parts of the room for the answer. It keeps them alert because they will not know where lightning is going to strike next!

BY PROVIDING FOR INDIVIDUAL DIFFERENCES   If you want to improve the quality of your lessons, provide for individual differences. Much has been written on the subject, but the important thing to remember is that eagerness to do things is not restricted to the most capable pupils. Plan some work within the scope of the slower pupil's ability so that he may achieve some success. Plan some work which will challenge the most able pupils. In either case, the work should be planned in such a way that the pupil is not set apart from the other pupils in an undesirable way. The able pupil should not feel that he is having extra work piled upon him because he can do more, and the slower pupil should not feel that he is not being permitted to participate in the regular work of the class. Sometimes teachers provide maximum-minimum assignments which provide for most of the pupils and helps them to work according to their ability and at their own rate of learning. In this type of work, all of the pupils are expected to complete the minimum assignment, while those who are able to do so, may attempt to complete the maximum assignment for which additional credit is allowed. The new teacher is urged to consult some of the many textbooks and articles which deal with meeting individual differences in the classroom, where he will find additional suggestions. Such additional reading should be approached with the thought that you are teaching individual youngsters, each of whom is a unique being and has unique experiences apart from those which you provide for him in the classroom. Let him, somehow, have an opportunity to make use of his out-of-school experiences in the setting of the classroom.

BY INCLUDING ACTIVITIES IN THE DAILY LESSON   Pupil planning and pupil activity should be part of every lesson. Pupils need to be active if they are to learn, but the activities must not be ends in themselves. They must contribute to the major understanding if they are to be of value. When studying the climate of a place, the making of a rainfall or temperature graph will picture climatic conditions much more clearly for the pupils than will many paragraphs of descriptive material. One of the natural drives of children is to be active. Capitalize on it and include some pertinent activity in every lesson. The pupils are much more interested in the rest of the lesson because of the activity. Let us heed the implied suggestion when our pupils ask, "What are we going to *do* today?"

BY SUMMARIZING YOUR LESSON   Too many teachers neglect to summarize their geography lessons. The lesson loses its impact and amounts to little if the teacher fails to draw the loose ends together. The lesson may have included many irrelevant parts which have led the pupils away from the topic. It is difficult for pupils to know what the teacher thinks is important; therefore, he might ask a few questions about the important points covered in the lesson to summarize it. A relationship in arrow-statement form is also a good way to summarize the work. Another quick way to summarize the lesson is to ask several pupils to state one thing which they have learned from the lesson which they did not previously know about the subject. Never fail to summarize your daily lesson since the summary helps to create a feeling of accomplishment on the part of the pupil.

BY PROVIDING OPPORTUNITY FOR APPLICATION WITH YOUR LESSON   There is little learning by the pupil unless he uses what he has learned in a new situation. After the lesson has been summarized, have him use his learning in a different way. If your lesson were about some part of Mexico, you might ask the pupils what they would mention about this part of Mexico, if they were travel agents, to interest prospective tourists. Suggest that they think about the different interests of tourists and write a short paragraph about the region which would appear in the agency's travel folder on Mexico. To do this, the pupils would have to apply what they had learned in a lifelike situation. It is the use of facts which really counts; otherwise, they are quickly forgotten.

BY SHOWING YOUR PERSONAL INTEREST IN EACH PUPIL   Circulate among the pupils during the class period as they work to give help and to show them that you are really interested in their improvement. To leave them at work while you perform your clerical duties gives the pupils the feeling that their work is simply busy work and unimportant. You will achieve better rapport—and better results from your teaching—by being genuinely interested in the pupils' progress, and by praising even the slightest improvements appropriately, as well as sincerely. Always give praise where praise is due. Your interest is also shown when you refuse to accept work which is not the best of which the pupil is capable. Your pupils must know and understand that the work which they do must be accurate. You will receive the kind of work upon which you insist. It is seldom necessary to ask a child to do work over if you tell him that you assume that it *is* his best work. He will have to make the decision as to whether or not he can do a better job, and decision making is one of the skills which we attempt to teach. Place the decision squarely on his shoulders.

10

Teach a readiness program in the primary sequences

Primary pupils are eager to learn whatever helps to clarify their understanding of their own world. Their immediate environment is their world, and to gain an understanding of it they frequently ask how and why questions. The answers to these questions often involve geographic concepts and relationships. A geography readiness program is supposed to build a foundation for the geography which will be taught in later sequences. It should introduce many geographic concepts and expand others for the young "explorer." Too often new geographic concepts and relationships are introduced to primary children in an incidental manner, or else they are completely ignored. As previous chapters have indicated, the geography program must not be left to chance in the primary sequences since it is the one subject which requires children to do critical thinking from the very beginning. To leave it to chance is to sacrifice the most valuable years for learning in the children's lives and thrust them into the intermediate sequences totally unprepared for the geography program, and forced to acquire geographic concepts for which they have no background. The result is that some children never acquire the concepts which will help them live effectively as adults and their depth of understanding is limited because they have never learned to think in terms of relationships.

The young child, although he may not be aware of it, is interested in relationships. He wants to know why things in his environment are as they are. Telling him, or compelling him to memorize subject matter will not help him to really answer his why and how questions, nor satisfy him intellectually. Answering his questions requires that he be able to make accurate observations of the world about him. This act of observing makes him a participant in the search for answers to his questions, but you, as the teacher, must help him to interpret what he sees. It is your accurate and helpful interpretation which constitutes his initial contact with geographic concepts and relationships.

In the primary sequences he is introduced to globes, simple maps, weather, seasonal changes, sun position, and direction. You must plan carefully to make his first observations and experiences with them meaningful so that the understandings which he gains will be retained and still be of real use to him when he begins formal work in geography in the fourth sequence. Therefore, the primary readiness program must also be instructive.

Thralls' four topics—weather, direction, sun position, and seasonal change—are an excellent classification of the basic concepts with which primary pupils work.[1] There are many opportunities to show children the relationship of man's activities to these topics every day in the classroom. The relationships are there if you will only try to see them, and the explanation of them makes geography, and all learning, more enjoyable.

The work in the primary sequences which deals with relationship geography, sun position, seasonal change, and direction, has previously been discussed and may be found in Chapters 3, 4, and 5, respectively. This chapter is devoted to additional, related topics and activities which should be a part of the primary sequence readiness program.

Weather

Weather observations should be carried on throughout the year. This is necessary in order to show the children how weather affects all of their activities. Be sure to plan to have a large calendar (at least twenty-four inches by thirty-six inches), on the board or on a large piece of oak tag, on which to record the weather each day. If the day is sunny, a yellow disk might be placed over the date; if it is rainy, a few diagonal lines might be used as a symbol. Have the children use the correct terminology when they speak about weather conditions. To describe temperature conditions, use the words hot, mild, warm, cool, and cold. To describe rainy day conditions,

[1] Zoe A. Thralls, *The Teaching of Geography* (New York, Appleton-Century-Crofts, 1958), p. 275 ff.

use the terms light rain, heavy rain, steady rain, drizzle, or showers. Summarize the weather chart at the end of the month by recording the number of days on which each kind of weather has been experienced. Write the summary at the bottom of the calendar and keep it for purposes of comparison with that of the following month, or with the same month of the following year.

In your informal talks with your children each morning, when you discuss the weather, you will be able to make use of the Weather Clock (Figure 39), having the children set the hands at the terms which will appropriately describe the day.

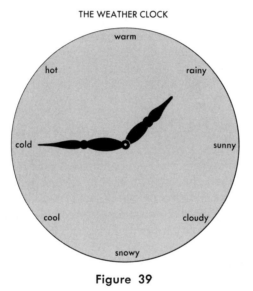

THE WEATHER CLOCK

Figure 39

Take time to discuss with the children what weather means, the different kinds of weather, and how each kind affects us. They should know that weather affects the way they dress, the food they eat, their activities, and indirectly, even the construction of their homes. To develop these concepts, have them list the activities in which they engage on rainy days, on sunny days, and on cool days. Have them compare them and account for the differences. Then discuss with them how the activities of workers, such as the baker, the grocer, the farmer, and the truck driver, will be affected by the weather. The baker will not make the same kinds of baked goods on a hot or rainy day that he makes on a cool day. Different kinds of baked goods will appeal more to his customers on a cool day than on a warm day. The farmer is very much concerned with weather conditions. If it is too dry, his crops will not grow well; if it is too wet, insects and plant diseases will flourish and bring ruin to his crops. A hail or wind storm could destroy all of his crops in a few minutes. If the weather has not been favorable to plant growth, crops will be small, food will cost more, and deliveries made by trucks to the markets will be delayed. The kinds of food we eat are related to the weather conditions of the area in which they grow.

Point out to the children that weather determines the kind of clothing we choose to wear. Have them discuss the clothing that is suitable for each of the many kinds of weather. Cut enlarged figures of a boy and a girl from heavy cardboard. Attach easels to the backs of the figures so that they will stand. Each morning have one of the children dress the figures in clothing suitable for the weather conditions that day. This will help to make them weather conscious. Have the children make articles of clothing from paper for the dolls. The wardrobes should include clothing for all kinds of weather. The children should also make a collection of materials from which clothing is made and observe the differences in the weaves of the materials and explain why some seem to be much warmer to wear than others. Help the children make a collection of pictures to illustrate the way to dress properly for different kinds of weather. All of this work is correlated with that on seasonal changes.

Have the children record the temperature at the same time each day and illustrate for them how the thermometer works by constructing one from cardboard and using a piece of sliding red tape for the mercury column. Summarize the temperature at the end of each week.

See to it that the children observe the effects of the wind. When they see smoke rising vertically from chimneys, teach them that the wind is blowing less than one mile per hour and that we say that it is calm. When they can feel the wind on their faces and hear the leaves rustle lightly, teach them to recognize this as a slight breeze and that the wind is blowing from four to seven miles an hour. A strong breeze will keep large branches in motion, cause the telegraph wires to whistle, make it difficult to use an umbrella, and be blowing at from twenty-five to thirty-one miles per hour. We say that we have high winds when whole trees are in motion and it is difficult to walk against the wind. The wind then is probably blowing from thirty-two to thirty-eight miles per hour. They should also be made aware that these interpretations are part of the Beaufort Scale for determining wind velocity.

Children in the third sequence would be able to keep a chart showing the direction from which the winds come and, with some assistance, arrive at a conclusion about the weather conditions which result from prevailing winds.

Acquaint the children with the work of the wind. Winds carry moisture; they drive windmills to pump water; they furnish power for sail boats; they carry seeds, soil, and insects long distances; and they assist migratory birds in their long flights. Winds can cause harm, too. Wind storms—tornadoes, hurricanes, and typhoons—cause much damage and often loss of life. In places where high winds are likely to occur with regularity, guy wires must be used to hold towers in place, and a special kind of building construction is often used.

You begin to teach the concept of rainfall in the primary sequences. On a rainy day, ask the children why they cannot see the sun. This question should lead into a discussion of different kinds of clouds: the dark rain clouds; the gray wind clouds; and the fluffy white clouds which are associated with mild, sunny days. Then ask, "What is a cloud?" and "What causes moisture in the air to condense and fall as rain?" Give several examples which are within the experience range of the children. Call attention to the beads of moisture which collect on a cold bottle of milk on a warm day, the dew which settles on the lawn at night, and the fog which sometimes obscures the landscape.

The young child usually thinks only in terms of the inconvenience which rain will cause him. You must teach him a bit of appreciation. Talk about the beauty of the rain: the sounds we hear on a rainy day, such as the *staccato* sound of rain against the window; the *dripping* of water from the leaves of the trees; the *splash* of the water as an automobile goes by; and the *slosh* of a person wearing rainboots. (It is best to wait until you have a rainy school day to do this; then, ask the children to be very still and see how many different kinds of rain sounds they can hear.)

Have the children watch the rain and decide from which direction the rain is coming. Keep a rainy day record which tells the direction from which the rain came, the date, and the length of time that it continued to rain. Speak of the work of the rain in making plants grow, in putting more water into rivers, and in carrying soil away. Speak of the rain, also, as a cleansing force in nature. Point out that heavy rains often bring floods. In winter, freezing water often causes trouble. It makes walking and driving very difficult and sometimes causes us to be uncomfortable. But it can be helpful, too. As water freezes in the crevices of rocks, it causes them to crack and break. When the process has gone on for a long enough period of time, the rocks are reduced to soil. Through the story of a drop of water, teach them about the water cycle.

The work which you do to develop the concept of rainfall in the primary sequences prepares the children for further development of it in the intermediate sequences. (See Appendix D.)

Your primary children will enjoy having a weather clothes line in their classroom because with it they will be able to predict the weather by noting the changes which occur in the color of the "clothes" which you will hang on the line. From white cotton cloth, cut pieces which are shaped like a dress, a shirt, and a pair of trousers. These need to be about three inches in length and width. Mix the solution described in the recipe below, place it in a flat bowl or tray, and dip each of the pieces of cloth into it, allowing them to soak thoroughly. Remove the fabric from the solution and allow it to dry without squeezing or wringing it. Press the three pieces with a steam iron and fasten them to a clothes line made of light string. If the weather is going to be clear, the clothes will turn blue; if it is going to rain, they will turn pink. Lavender indicates a change in the weather.

SOLUTION[2]

2 oz. water

½ oz. salt

¼ oz. gum arabic

75 grains calcium chloride

1 oz. chloride cobalt

[2] These ingredients can be obtained from a druggist.

Concepts Related to Weather

Listed below are some of the concepts related to weather which you must introduce to your primary children. There are many others, but your class should have a clear understanding of these, at least.

◇ Weather is different in each season of the year.
◇ Plants need both sunshine and rain.
◇ Weather affects what we do.
◇ Weather helps to determine what we wear.
◇ Weather helps to determine the foods we eat.
◇ Wind is air in motion.
◇ The wind works for us in many ways.
◇ A light wind moves the leaves on the trees.
◇ Winds scatter seeds.
◇ Winds can cause damage.
◇ Water is necessary for all forms of life.
◇ Water is always somewhere, even though it cannot always be seen.
◇ Water falls from the clouds as rain.
◇ Freezing water helps to break up rocks and create soil.
◇ Water changes to many different forms.

The geography program in the primary sequences is both a readiness program and a program of planned instruction. It creates the foundation for all future work in geography. Essential, initial relationships and concepts which deal with direction, sun position, weather, and seasonal change are introduced here. Children also have their first experiences with simple map and globe concepts in the primary sequences. Therefore, do not attempt to teach too much, but plan all that you teach, and teach it well.

11

Test with a purpose

The methods for teaching geography which have been suggested in this text have emphasized the understanding of relationships, the gradual development of geographic concepts, and the need to know how to use all geographic tools. Examples of tests to be used to determine the pupil's knowledge of certain relationships and skills have been given in some of the chapters, but nothing has been said about the construction of tests. This chapter is intended to be a brief guide for all of you who wish to prepare better geography examinations for your pupils.

Every college course in evaluation and educational psychology discusses the criteria for a good test. These criteria—validity, reliability, usability, practicality, appropriateness, and so on—are familiar to every teacher and teacher trainee. It is not our purpose to review them here. Instead, we want to make some practical suggestions about test construction and introduce some new ideas which work.

As a geography teacher you will want to test your pupils' ability to reason (think logically) and to visualize landscapes. You will also want to test to determine the amount of geographic information which they have accumulated and their ability to use geographic skills. Before constructing your test, decide which of these it is that you want to measure, and then select the kind of test which is most appropriate. Essay tests are good for testing your pupils' ability to organize information, to visualize, and to reason. They also help you to discover the geographic misconceptions which they may have, and the concepts which they have not yet completely developed. Objective tests are used to measure their ability to recall geographic facts, to recognize geographic relationships, to use geographic skills, and to apply geographic knowledge.

As you read about each type of test, keep in mind that teacher-made tests should not be used over and over. You will never have the same group of pupils again that you have this year, and you will never teach exactly the same things twice in the same way. Therefore, last year's tests will seldom, if ever, be suitable for this year's class.

Essay Tests

Essay tests deserve more than occasional use. The questions are difficult to construct because, to be of value, they must first direct the pupil's thoughts toward the recall of specific geographic information, then cause him to associate this information with other knowledge he may have and relate it to the question you have asked, and finally, to organize his answer and write a short paragraph. They are difficult to mark because each pupil possesses a unique background of information about geography, and geographic concepts are interpreted differently by every pupil. Children vary in their ability to use the vocabulary of geography, and in the extent of the other usable vocabulary which they possess. On the other hand, the teacher's estimation of the quality of a pupil's work might change slightly from day to day. Fatigue, the lapse of time between marking the first and the last essay paper, and the quality of each paper successively marked are also factors in making essays difficult to evaluate. Nevertheless, essay questions help you to determine how well your pupils can think geographically and whether they understand geographic concepts. They also indicate their ability to organize the material which they know, and they will often reveal where a pupil needs remedial instruction.

It will be necessary for you to teach your pupils how to write an essay examination; that is, to "take" one. Teach them to look for key words in your questions. The key words tell precisely how the answer is to be written. Some of these words are define, compare, contrast, and outline. Teach them the meaning of each key word and caution them to be alert for them as they read essay questions. It will also be helpful to them if they jot down the several points which they wish to include in the answer by making a short, simple outline. Allow them to use a dictionary as they write their answer in order to avoid misspelling words. Teach them that when they write answers to essay questions, they must always begin by restating, in slightly altered form, the question which has been asked. Take time to teach them how to write essay examinations. The more frequently you use the essay test, the more adept your pupils will become at expressing themselves in writing. Make the tests short; two or three essay questions on an examination are sufficient. Before giving the test, review with your pupils how essay answers are to be written, and discuss how you will grade their papers.

When you mark the essay examinations, scan all of the papers to determine the general quality of your pupils' writing. Then read the answer for the first question on all of the papers, then the second answer on every paper, and so on. As you read, arrange the papers in groups which will indicate their quality. Three such groups will do. Don't attempt to assign letter grades or percentages. Instead, use good, fair, and poor. Know exactly what each of these terms means in your own mind and keep their meaning as nearly constant as you can. Write some comment on each paper before returning it, always pointing out the good things about the pupil's work before you note those things which need improvement.

Objective Tests

While the essay question is the best method for determining how well your pupils think and understand, there are many times when you will want to test their knowledge of facts. The acquisition of geographic facts is important because facts are the raw material of geographic relationships and concepts; consequently, we must frequently test our pupils to see if they have the facts in mind. While it is necessary that your pupils learn certain geographic facts, they should not be compelled to commit to memory long lists of imports, exports, principal cities, or rivers. When geography is taught with relationships, your pupils come to know and remember facts because they learn to associate cause with effect. When you teach facts by means of arrow statements coupled with experiences, you are helping your pupils to retain what they learn because of associations which are inherent in relationships. If you have taught geographic relationships well, you are justified in using objective tests to assess how well your pupils know geographic facts. If you have not taught relationships, your objective tests will test only the ability of your pupils to memorize.

Objective tests are those in which the answers are short and fixed. Generally, not more than one answer is correct for each question and, therefore, anyone can mark them. There are several kinds of objective tests, but only the three which are most frequently used will be discussed here. These are the multiple-choice test, the matching test, and the completion test. True-false tests have been omitted entirely since they tend to encourage pupils to guess rather than to think, and therefore have little value in a geography testing program. False statements might be accepted by the slow learner as being true.

When you construct multiple-choice tests, be certain that each answer from which your pupils must choose is a plausible one. Make certain, too, that the question is based upon some relationship with which the pupils have worked. Provide at least four plausible answers for each question to help keep your pupils from guessing, and be certain that all four answers are homogeneous. Phrase each multiple-choice item as a question; avoid using sentences which are to be completed with the answer the pupil selects. The direct-question form helps to eliminate errors in grammatical construction which you might make as you prepare the test, and which might serve as clues for your pupils.

If you wish to test your pupils' knowledge of terms, ask "What is latitude?" and follow it with four definitions. Do not give a definition for latitude and then list four possible terms as answers. The former style requires that the pupils reason; the latter style permits them to guess.

If you prefer, have your pupils record the letters which correspond with their answer choices on a separate answer sheet. The page of test questions should be as attractive as you can possibly make it. Leave wide margins, type or write carefully, and double space between each question-answer group. Five to ten questions, based upon the geographic relationships studied in a unit, should be sufficient for the multiple-choice part of a test for intermediate sequence pupils.

In constructing a matching test, be certain that each column contains only items which are related. One column could contain only a list of terms, alphabetically arranged; the other column, in this case, would contain only definitions or descriptive phrases, also in some systematic order. The alphabetical arrangement saves time for your pupils when they look for an answer, and it also saves your time when you construct the test since you will not have to worry about having answer items opposite question items. Matching tests may include sentences, parts of relationships, or phrases which are to be matched. When items of dissimilar nature are included in the same column, they make the matching test confusing and tempt the pupil to guess. Confine the matching test to a single page; your pupils should not have to turn pages to look for matching test answers. The test may be constructed with the same number of items in each of the two columns or with one or two additional items in the response column.

Completion tests—"fill in the blanks"—are the most difficult of all tests to construct. They are more frequently used by elementary school teachers than any other kind of test. It is not easy to phrase a statement in such a way that one word, and one only, will complete it with meaning. If the completion test is of the direct question type, it is more likely to be fair to the pupil and encourage him to reason. Do be specific in indicating what you want for an answer when you write completion questions. Write, "Mount Rainier is in the state of _____," not "Mount Rainier is in _____." *Don't* provide so many blanks that the statement can be completed in several ways, as in this example: "Mount Rainier is in the _____ of _____." "Mount Rainier is in the_ middle _of _ nowhere _." Do not quote directly from the pupils' textbook, omitting a few words here and there, and feel that you have constructed a completion test. Don't provide the pupils with unnecessary clues, either with words or by the length of the blanks which you provide for the answers. It is better, too, to provide for one word responses rather than phrases. As you prepare the test consider the fact that more than one response might be plausible and correct. Make a list of them and give the pupils credit for them, or avoid the situation by rewording the question or statement. You may wish to prepare an answer sheet on which the pupils will write. Doing so will help you to avoid having to glance here and there on each paper as you mark it.

Testing Geographic Skills

The geographic skills which you help your pupils to acquire include the ability to (1) make, read, interpret, and enlarge or reduce many kinds of maps; (2) read globes and interpret lines of longitude in terms of time; (3) draw profiles of regions of the countries which they are studying and make inferences from them; (4) read and interpret statistics; (5) use statistics to make graphs; (6) interpret graphs; (7) identify natural and cultural features of the landscape and their interconnecting relationships; (8) identify specific relationships that belong to a country or region; (9) read pictures; and (10) use lines of latitude and longitude to determine location. The following questions illustrate how to test some of these skills.

TESTING KNOWLEDGE OF CULTURAL AND NATURAL FEATURES

In the blank opposite each feature of the landscape, place a C if the feature is cultural, and an N if it is natural.

a. Trees	_____		e. Bay	_____
b. Waterfall	_____		f. Roads	_____
c. Automobile	_____		g. River	_____
d. Coal mines	_____		h. Wheat fields	_____

TESTING ABILITY TO USE LINES OF LONGITUDE

This question tests your knowledge about time belts.

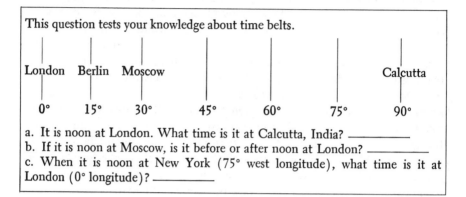

a. It is noon at London. What time is it at Calcutta, India? _____
b. If it is noon at Moscow, is it before or after noon at London? _____
c. When it is noon at New York (75° west longitude), what time is it at London (0° longitude)? _____

TESTING ABILITY TO USE STATISTICS AND MAKE MAPS

Can you make a distribution map? Use these statistics and the outline map below to make one here.
What important points must you consider when you make a distribution map? (See Figure 40 for map.) _____

TESTING ABILITY TO USE THE SCALE OF MILES

What are the straight line distances between each pair of cities listed below? Use the edge of a piece of paper to make measurements on the map in your testbook.

a. Boston to Philadelphia   _____ miles
b. Pittsburgh to New York   _____ miles
c. New Orleans to Chicago   _____ miles

USING LINES OF LATITUDE AND LONGITUDE TO DETERMINE LOCATION

Turn to page 70 in your atlas. Find the cities which are located at the intersection of the lines of latitude and longitude given below.

Latitude	Longitude	City
a. 40° north	75° west	_____
b. 42° north	88° west	_____
c. 30° north	90° west	_____

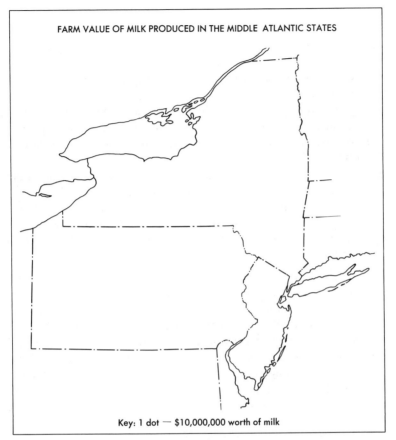

FARM VALUE OF MILK PRODUCED IN THE MIDDLE ATLANTIC STATES

Key: 1 dot — $10,000,000 worth of milk

New York $411,000,000
Pennsylvania 267,000,000
New Jersey 70,000,000

Figure 40

TESTING ABILITY TO READ AND INTERPRET MAPS

You are being tested on how well you can read relationships from a map. This means how well you see facts, and how able you are to draw conclusions about a country from the facts. Turn to page 126 in your atlas. List <u>at least</u> three things which you think must be true about Greece after you study the map. Note the latitude to obtain a clue regarding climate. The surface conditions will tell you what some of the people will do to earn their living. Be sure to give the reason why you think each fact is true.

TESTING GEOGRAPHIC THINKING　　The ability to think geographically means that your pupils must be able to pull together many widely divergent geographical concepts and relationships to solve problems. The following examples illustrate the type of question which requires geographic thinking.

✔ a. If you were a jeweler, in what part of Australia would you be especially interested and why? A wool manufacturer? A meat packer?

✔ b. If you suffered from hay fever, where might you go to escape its effects? Why?

✔ c. If you were a contractor building a highway from Rio de Janiero to Brazilia, what difficulties might you encounter?

✔ d. For what reasons might you move your factory from one of the northern states to one in the southern part of the United States?

✔ e. If you wish to become a manufacturer of boys' bicycles, what factors must you consider?

TESTING GEOGRAPHIC IMAGERY　　Geographic imagery is the ability to obtain mental pictures of topography and living conditions from written descriptions. Your pupils should be able to make simple sketches of scenes after they have been given such descriptions. They should also be able to identify specific localities, or a number of related localities, which are described to them. The imagery test may involve either sketching or identifying, or both. You may read a paragraph to your pupils which describes a location or an activity and have them quickly sketch what they "see," or you may use the type of test which is illustrated below.

In what part of the United States would you see

a. straight highways stretching over flat plains, and fields of corn on all sides?
b. snow-capped mountains in July?
c. acres of oil storage tanks and derricks on one side of the highway and the Pacific Ocean on the other?
d. a mighty industrial city built among the hills on the triangle formed where two rivers meet?
e. a wide valley, where winters are usually severe, with acres of cheesecloth-covered tobacco fields in summer?

Open Book Tests

The open book test is another way to test skills and understanding. It should never simply involve searching through the textbook for words or statements which fill in a blank. The test given below illustrates how text-books, maps, and other aids may be used in such a test.

For this test you may use your textbook, the wall maps, the globe, and other reference books if you wish.

a. Make a list of the imports of Chile. Opposite each import, suggest a country from which it might be sent to Chile. State why each item must be imported.
b. Give the straight line distances between Santiago and Antofagasta; Santiago and Puenta Arenas; Santiago and Buenos Aires.
c. From the statistics available in your textbook, figure out what Chile's population density is. Why isn't this figure a correct picture of Chile's population distribution?
d. Read pp. 64–66 in your textbook. Select and complete three relationships about the agricultural region of Central Chile.
e. Study the map on page 73. Explain why Concepción is the best location in Chile for steel mills.

12

Make your program active

The Necessity for Activities

In a classroom where the teacher does most of the talking, or where the only activity is reading from the geography textbook, the pupils learn little. They need to experiment, to make things which explain what they are learning, to voice their thoughts, and to learn through discovery. Allowing the pupils to take an active part in their lessons helps to satisfy this basic need. In addition, they learn best when they are actively involved in the lesson. As we plan our work in geography, we should capitalize on their need to be active by including some kind of activity in each lesson. This activity may be the making of a sketch of a scene they can "see" in a descriptive paragraph in their texbook, the drawing of a rainfall graph to show the distribution of rainfall during the year and how it affects the agriculture of a region, the making of a crop distribution map which will help pupils to understand food problems, or the filling in of an arrow statement with words or sketches to show relationships. All of these activities will be a welcome change for the pupils from the excessive verbalism of the teacher, and will provide them with an opportunity to learn by doing. Activities or learning experiences are not limited to those which require construction, drawing, or experimentation. Equally important are activities which involve the pupils in research, listening, discussing, reading, writing, and observing. They may be engaged in by whole groups or by individuals, but they must be related to the topic under study. They should be used to contribute to the understanding of geographic relationships and concepts undergoing consideration in the lesson or unit.

What are some of the activities which can help to bring about an understanding of a country? Since all activities should promote thinking and additional research, they should not be used by the pupils as a means for escaping mental exercise. In teaching a unit about Brazil, activities which would help to make the study meaningful might include drawing maps to show topography, the distribution of such crops as coffee and cotton, the coffee-producing countries of the world, and sources of imports. A profile of Brazil, drawn at a given latitude, would be useful to show land use. Bar graphs showing the value of the exports of Brazil (including the total value of all exports), and the value or amount of coffee produced by the chief coffee producing countries of the world would make relationships more apparent and statements in the textbook much more meaningful. Climatic graphs showing the rainfall and temperature of widely separated Brazilian cities would explain climatic conditions in different parts of Brazil. If a model of a coffee *fazenda* is built, the textbook would probably become one much sought after source of information. A plan of a coffee *fazenda* showing the location of the drying field, the warehouses, the homes of the owner and workers, the portion of the *fazenda* devoted to coffee trees and the other field crops would have to be made and discussed before the actual construction of the model began. The construction of the homes of the workers and the other buildings would probably lead to a discussion of the lives of the people on the *fazenda*. The music of such artists as Hector Villa-Lobos and Camargo Guarnieri could be enjoyed as the pupils work. The pupils will suggest many other activities as work progresses because their interest is stimulated by involvement in the learning. Active interest could lead to the study of other topics related to Brazil since learning and interest do not cease when activities are completed.

What is the value of activities to the teaching of geography? Interest and motivation are at a high level and learning is easier when activities are used to clarify some geographic concept. Activities help slow learners and poor readers to cope with meaning, something they frequently cannot do when only the printed pages of the texbook are available to them. Activities are begun and completed in order to summarize geographic understandings, to illustrate relationships, and to contribute to the overall development of concepts. They provide practice for the pupil in the geographic skills he has learned, and they allow advanced students to test their knowledge and understanding at some length and in greater depth than the regular classroom work. They provide the manually-oriented pupil with an opportunity to compete with his academically-oriented peers and to make a contribution to the development of the lesson or unit. Activities can also do much to create and enhance good teacher-pupil relationships. The attitude of the pupil toward the teacher changes as he sees the teacher working as a member of a team helping him to reach his goal. The concomitant learnings resulting from activities, such as learning to cooperate and to accept responsibility, often prove to be just as valuable to the pupils as their acquisition of subject matter.

Activities can be a waste of time. Simply because a pupil suggests an activity is no indication that it should be carried out by the class. Activities should be selected because they help the pupils to achieve the objective of the lesson or the unit. If the value of the completed activity does not promise to be commensurate with the amount of time spent on it, it is wasteful. Never be guilty of using activities just to keep the pupils busy. There must be a purpose for every activity.

When activities include layouts, dioramas, murals, or shoebox scenes, be certain that they are authentic. If an activity fails to picture the country it portrays or the lives of the people accurately, the pupils will build incorrect concepts and their thinking will have no validity. Some teachers, as we have written, picture the Netherlands as a land of wooden shoes and lace caps. In the primary grades, paper tepees are often made to represent the homes of the Indians. These are incorrect concepts. (The study of different tribes of Indians can be a real adventure in geography if the children are shown how the Indians' activities and culture in different parts of the United States were related to the environment in which they lived, an environment which they were unable, or unwilling, to change.) Miniature dairy cattle are often used in layouts where beef cattle should be used. Pupils should learn to recognize the differences in animals and in the conditions under which they are raised. It requires a long time and much reteaching to erase an incorrect concept from a pupil's mind, so be very particular about the accuracy of the concepts you teach and the activities which you employ.

A teacher must have definite goals which he hopes to achieve through the use of the activity. His objectives should be (1) to stimulate pupil interest in the unit; (2) to aid in developing a better understanding of geographic concepts and relationships found in the work on the unit; (3) to apply geographic concepts already acquired; (4) to encourage creativity among the pupils; (5) to encourage further research; (6) to provide the slow learner with an opportunity to taste success, and to give the able child a chance to try his wings; and (7) to develop geographic skills through the use of geographic tools, such as maps, pictures, graphs, and the textbook.

Ask yourself these questions before you initiate any activity in connection with the work of a unit:

- Does this activity contribute to the objectives which I have set up?
- In what way will this activity add to the major understanding?

✓ Will this activity appeal to most of the pupils? Is it suited to the nature and needs of the pupils?
✓ Can the pupils do the work involved?
✓ Can it be completed in the time available?
✓ Are the materials needed for this activity readily available?
✓ Will it use all of the pupils most of the time?
✓ What will the pupils learn by doing this activity?
✓ Is it important enough to justify the time and effort which it will require?

The success or failure of the activities carried out by your class depends upon your ability to organize them. Every step in the procedure must be carefully planned and problems must be anticipated. Consider the following points as you plan group activities in which a large part of the class will participate. They will help to ensure success.

1. Have the activity jointly planned by teacher and pupils. Discuss the purpose of the activity so that the class will understand how it will contribute to the geographic understandings of the lesson or unit on which they are at work. Then discuss with the pupils how the activity is to be carried out. Make an over-all plan and list the methods of procedure. If the activity takes more than a single work period, daily plans and revisions will be needed as it progresses.

2. Plan for individual differences. Teach success instead of failure by seeing to it that each pupil has work assigned to him at which he can succeed. The slow learner will find meaning in activities and will be able to make a contribution if the work he is asked to do is within his ability range. The more able pupil, on the other hand, needs to be provided with opportunities to plan his own work and to carry on independent study.

3. Plan for a definite amount of work to be done by each pupil or group. The secret of success in using activities is contained in this step. Do not leave anything to chance or to spur-of-the-moment planning. If you do, you are headed for failure. If you plan for a definite amount of work to be done by each child or committee, the work will go smoothly. It may be necessary to meet with the chairmen of the committees before school begins in the morning to see that plans are made and tasks assigned to each member of the various committees.

Plan to use the various abilities of the pupils in each activity, but be careful that the most capable pupils do not always have the same type of work assigned to them in every committee. It is a temptation to have the pupil who is gifted in art do the art work, but he needs to have experiences which challenge him and in which he is not yet skilled, and learn how to meet them. The chairman of a committee can help you to select the right pupil for a specific task. He knows his classmates' ability better than you think he does!

Plan some method for checking the amount of work done by each pupil or group. From the fifth sequence onward, the pupils may keep individual work sheets. Have the pupils record the date and then list the work they have done on that day. The work done may consist of a list of books in which a pupil has done research and the number of pages he has read in each one, or the handwork completed, such as the number of trees or houses he has made. It will take only a minute or two at the close of the class period each day to record the work done, but the effect of seeing his accomplishments listed will spur him to want to do more work, if for no other reason than to see the list of accomplishments grow. At the end of the week, the chairmen hand in the work sheets of their committees. The teacher checks them and writes some comment, or a grade, on each before they are returned. The comments range from, "I am sorry that you were not able to accomplish more; shall we try harder next week?", to "You have certainly made excellent progress during the past week. Keep up the good work!" Such comments let the pupils know that you are interested in their work, and have a good psychological effect on the pupil who may not have worked up to his capacity.

4. Establish time limits for certain stages of the work on the activity. Establishing time limits helps to eliminate aimless work habits. Do not relent, even though the work is not finished. Here is where guidance by the teacher is most effective. Emphasize the importance of accepting responsibility, meeting the terms of a contract, and acquiring a sense of duty, not only as preparation for adult life, but also as obligations to one's classmates.

5. Teach good work habits. Try to impress the pupils with the importance of good work habits in carrying out activities. Make them feel that you are working for them in trying to improve their geographic skills, in order to increase their reasoning ability and to help them gain more knowledge about the world. Explain the value of the work which they are doing and how it fits in with their total education. Commend them often as they try to improve their power of concentration. However, do not hesitate to stop the work of the class if it becomes too noisy. Unless you take a definite stand, and mean it, their self-discipline will become worse instead of better. If the conduct of the children doing the activity work is deteriorating, go back to formal work for a day or two and put it squarely up to the pupils as to whether or not they will continue with the activity. Pupils are interested in doing activity work and it will not take long for them to reach a conclusion. Never lose your control of your class. Occasionally, children need to be made aware of "an iron hand in a velvet glove."

6. Have materials readily available. Keep colored pencils, rulers, scissors, and so on, in a definite place so that the pupils will know where to find them when they need them. This saves them from having to stand around waiting to ask you for them and it is less wearing on you. Have a place reserved for their uncompleted work. A suitbox will do for putting away unfinished parts of houses, animals, trees, and so on. Putting their

work away carefully and quickly at the close of each work period helps to train them in responsibility and the proper care of materials.

7. Have continuing evaluation as the activity progresses. Evaluation is the process of determining how well you have accomplished what you set out to do, and it is a continuing process when teaching with activities. We want our pupils to see that evaluation is part of learning. By means of evaluation pupils can determine their own growth, spot some of their weaknesses, and take steps to bring about improvement. During the daily evaluation have the committees report on what they have accomplished during the work period. Then, ask for suggestions for the improvement of the class work, or for comments about things which have been especially well done. Do not fail to call attention to work well done. Children strengthen self-discipline through self-evaluation.

Unless you have had a great amount of teaching experience, keep the first few activities simple in scope. Use activities such as map and graph making, sketching, or making a desk mural which will keep the pupils in their seats and yet allow a little freedom, each pupil doing his own work. When you know your pupils well and can depend on them, try having a few of them working together in groups of two while you are teaching the others. Be sure that each group knows exactly what it is supposed to do. Discuss with the class, later, why these committees worked well, or how their work could be improved. In doing so, you are laying the groundwork for other small committees and for activities which will require the work of the entire class, later.

In any event, when you decide to do group work, begin with a small group of pupils and include yourself as a part of the group. Act as group chairman, explaining that as the work progresses, the pupils should observe how you carry out the duties of chairman. Add that, later, they will become group chairmen and will be able to use what they have learned through their observation. Having carried through an activity with your own small group, you are ready to allow several groups to work, each with a chairman who was formerly a member of your own group. When these chairmen are assigned to other groups, advise the remainder of the pupils to observe how they conduct the groups in order that they, too, may learn how to act as chairmen. Finally, attempt to provide opportunities for every member of the class to act as chairman of a small group in some purposeful activity.

Worthwhile Activities in Geography

SKETCHING   Sketching should be one of the most used activities. Having pupils make sketches is an excellent way to check their geographic concepts because the teacher can see at a glance if a concept needs reteaching. The pupil must visualize a landscape, scene, or relationship before he can sketch it. At first he may be a little reluctant to sketch because he may possess little artistic ability, but when the teacher explains that good geography sketches picture ideas rather than artistic skill, and that stick figures are acceptable in sketches, he will soon become accustomed to using sketches to express himself.

Sketches may be used in several parts of the lesson. In developing the lesson, the teacher may ask the pupils to sketch what they see as they read several paragraphs in the textbook. This helps to encourage careful reading. The lesson may be summarized by having the children make a sketch which will include several points in the lesson. In summarizing the lesson on the agriculture of Norway, for example, the pupil would make a sketch showing a fiord, that narrow inlet of the sea between high precipitous mountain sides. At the head of the fiord, the small delta of alluvial soil which is used for farming would be shown. The small fields around the farm buildings, the hay drying on racks, the saeter (highland pasture) above the tree line, and the wooded mountain slopes which surround the little farm would indicate some of the problems of the Norwegian farmer. Sketching may be used as an application exercise and also in testing.

DESK MURALS[1]   A desk mural is an excellent summary, or application exercise, to be made at the close of the study of a unit. It provides motivation for review and promotes further research.

The materials needed for each pupil are a piece of wrapping paper approximately twenty-four inches by seven inches, crayons or colored pencils, a sheet of unlined manila paper nine inches by twelve inches and as many pictures of the country as are available.

Discuss the meaning of the word mural (on the wall) and the composition of murals the pupils may have seen. Teacher and pupils list topics about which a mural of a country might be made. The list might include historical events connected with the country just studied, products of the country, its industries, cities, places of scenic beauty, plant and animal life, or a combination of several of these topics.

After each pupil has decided on the subject for his mural, he is ready to plan it on paper. Have him fold the nine-by-twelve-inch piece of manila or newsprint in thirds, lengthwise. This represents, roughly, the shape of the piece of wrapping paper which he will use for his desk mural and provides him with extra practice paper. Have him plan his mural on this paper, sketching quickly and somewhat roughly. He will be tempted to draw carefully on the plan, but this will be too time consuming. Ovals or circles will do to show the amount of space each sketch will occupy on the completed mural. Attention must be paid to the relative importance of each item to be pictured. Place the most important concept concerning the country in the center and have it occupy more space than other items.

[1] This activity was devised by Linnie B. James.

A "binder"—a border made up of a series of small sketches—across the bottom and/or top will tie the main sketches together and will add to the beauty of the mural. The "binder" might be a series of sketches showing the technological advances made in the industry, agriculture, or transportation of the country. After the plan is made, the pupil is ready to do research and look for pictures which will help him to make finished sketches on his mural. Tie the sketches together by coloring the spaces between them with a color which will suggest either cloud formations or foliage. Color very lightly, using a circular motion. Place a title across the top or bottom of the mural.

THE DAILY GEOGRAPHIC NEWS[2]   The *Daily Geographic News*, a pupil newspaper, is an activity which will give pupils an opportunity to plan and direct work, help to increase their number of geographic concepts, enable them to apply learned information and do research, and permit them to practice cooperation with others and assume responsibility. This learning experience can be adapted to several classroom situations, depending upon the amount of time you wish to devote to it, the number of students who will work on it, and whether it will be a daily or biweekly publication. It can be a simple, individual project for the more able child in the upper primary sequence who would be capable of compiling a daily sheet giving the weather report and any news items which might be classified as geographic. On the other hand, it can be a class activity which will occupy the full time allotted to geography every day for a number of weeks. It can be used to meet individual differences by providing activity for a small group of more able pupils who work on it after their regularly assigned work has been completed. The activity described would be suitable for pupils of the sixth or junior high school sequences. If a small group of younger pupils were handling it, fewer sections of the paper would be included. Probably the weather report, news item, and geography behind the news would be all that could be handled daily by them. If the newspaper cannot be duplicated, a single copy can be made and displayed on the bulletin board.

"Have any of you visited the newsroom of one of our daily papers? Have you seen one portrayed on television? What takes place in a newsroom? How do the reporters feel about their work? Why is the deadline so important to them? Since our newspaper will be called the *Daily Geographic News* we will have to emphasize the geographic side of the news articles and pick out features which show how we are influenced by geography. What sections can we have in our paper?" Suggestions such as the following would be given.

NEWS ITEMS   Pupils appointed to be news readers select two or three interesting news items daily from the daily newspaper, radio, or television.

[2] The *Daily Geographic News* was devised by Linnie B. James.

GEOGRAPHY BEHIND THE NEWS   Geography of the country mentioned in the news item for the day is discussed. It should include a map and a brief description of the country. Tell about the location, surface, climate, natural resources, industries, and something about the people. If possible, tell how the news item may have been influenced by the geography of the country. Graphs and charts related to the geographical aspects of the news item add interest, too.

WEATHER REPORT   Includes today's weather and a portion of the predicted weather conditions given in the news.

GEOGRAPHY QUIZ   Crisscross puzzles, missing word puzzles, unnamed maps, riddles, and questions about unusual facts may be included here.

FEATURE ARTICLES

1. *Scientific reports.* These are short articles about volcanoes, tidal waves, hurricanes, earthquakes, and other phenomena.

2. *Travel news.* This should feature places to visit. Descriptions of the attractions of some of the popular resorts, something about the climate of the regions and their scenery will make interesting articles. Plans for trips may be written which tell what to see en route, the type of clothing to be taken, and so forth.

3. *Strange as it may seem.* Unusual facts collected about places.

4. *Architecture.* Sketches of the homes of people living in the lands mentioned in the news item, with a short account telling in what way the style of architecture may have been influenced by geographic conditions.

WOMEN'S PAGES

1. Articles about the dress of the people. Explain how the type and style of clothing is affected by the geography of the country. Select countries mentioned in the news item of the day.

2. Tell about the handicrafts of the country. Sketch designs used on the handicrafts, or in creating them.

3. Design material for ladies' print dresses. Designs often originate from ideas prompted by the study of the geography of countries such as the grapes of France or the palm trees of tropical lands.

4. Geography of cookery includes recipes which are popular in the country mentioned in the news item or in the travel section. Discuss ingredients which are indigenous to the region.

ADVERTISEMENTS   Advertise products exported by the country mentioned in the news item.

ART SECTION   Use sketches made by the pupils to illustrate the articles.

After listing the sections of the paper, the pupils will have to decide how the work is to be done. An editorial staff will have to be organized and its duties listed. This staff should include an editor-in-chief and his assistant, a cartographer, proof readers, typists, and the editor of each department.

The editor makes the master plan of what the daily issue will contain. This plan should be made out two days before the date of issue so that the teacher will have a chance to check it with the editor. The editor and his assistant should meet twice a week with the teacher before school to plan two or three issues in advance. This will give the teacher an opportunity to make suggestions so that the pupils will receive assignments suited to their abilities and by which they will increase their own geographic knowledge. It is helpful to have a large piece of paper marked off in two inch squares with the names of the pupils at the left and the dates listed at the top of the columns. Opposite the pupils' names, write in the assignments for which they are responsible. In this way the list of articles which are to appear in any one issue can be seen and assignments checked off by the editor as they are completed. It also provides a complete picture of the daily issue, each pupil feeling that he has a responsibility for making the issue complete.

The class as a whole should be called together once a week to summarize and check their learnings. The geography behind the news should be reviewed and discussed. Feature articles should be reported, also. Maps should be studied and relationships noted. Every pupil must be responsible for the geography in the week's issues of their *Daily Geographic News*. The work of the class should then be evaluated by the pupils and the teacher.

This activity is worthwhile only if it is conscientiously carried out. It teaches the pupils how to accept responsibilities and it makes them conscious of world affairs and the part that geography plays in them.

LAYOUTS   Layouts are models showing the geographic personalities of countries, regions, or smaller areas. They provide excellent opportunities to apply facts and relationships, and to demonstrate geographic skills learned while studying a country or region. This activity motivates further research and gives pupils a chance to exchange ideas while working with others as they develop manual skills. Here are instructions for planning and making the layout.

1. After the study of the country or region is completed, the teacher and pupils discuss what could be shown on a layout which would create a true picture. List the facts and relationships which will be shown in the layout.

2. Cut a piece of wrapping paper a little larger than the bottom of the carton in which the layout will be made. On the paper make a plan of what will appear. Show where each detail of the setting will be placed by outlining the space which it will occupy. This will help to keep the parts of the layout in proportion to each other. If a pupil is planning a layout of a scene in Switzerland, show where the mountains, river, falls, powerhouse, chalet, summer pastures, tree line, village, valley farms, and

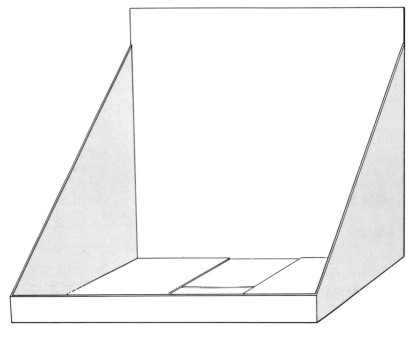

Figure 41

hotels will be. Then plan with the pupils what things, such as trees, houses, or animals, need to be made, what size they will have to be, and who will make them. On the side of the carton to be used (the carton should be at least eighteen inches by twenty-two inches) draw a diagonal line from the top at the back of the carton, to within an inch of the lower corner at its front. Cut along the line. Do the same thing with the other side of the carton. This removes part of the sides so that more of the layout is visible. (See Figure 41.)

3. To make the surface features, use a piece of pliable, one-inch mesh chicken wire a little larger than the paper on which the plan was made to show the surface. Bend the wire into shape to show mountains, valleys, lakes, and a river bed. Sew the edge of the wire to one *side* only of the carton, using heavy string and a large needle. A curved upholsterer's needle is best. (See Figure 42.) The wire can be raised to one side while crushed newspaper is packed into the box under the wire to hold it in place. The paper must be packed tightly so that the wire and paper together form a solid surface. The plaster covering, which will be added next, will crack unless the surface is firm. After the paper is in place, fasten the wire to the other three sides.

4. You may now make the covering which is needed to prevent the

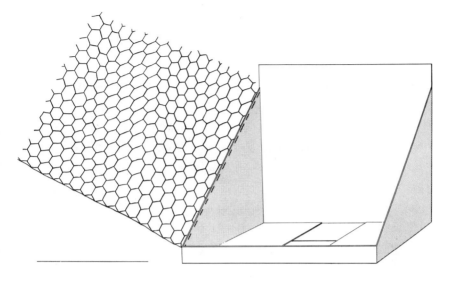

Figure 42

plaster from falling through the holes of the wire. Tear a newspaper into strips about an inch wide. Dip the strips into diluted paste which has the consistency of thick cream. Then place the strips in all directions over the wire, pressing them down to fit the contour of the layout. Do this until three layers have been made. Allow the layout to dry overnight. If the surface is broken in the process, or bits of wire stick through, mend it with a piece of masking tape or another piece of paper which is firmly pressed down.

5. To make the landscape, mix one part of patching plaster with two parts of vermiculite. Add enough water so that the mixture will spread over the paper cover of the layout. The vermiculite gives a texture which resembles earth. If a small amount of brown and black paint is added to the water, it will be easier to cover the plaster-vermiculite mixture with paint later. Particles of white show through uncolored mixtures, making them difficult to paint later. If the brown color should show through, it will resemble earth. Cover the entire layout with a layer one-fourth to one-half inch thick. Work rapidly because the plaster sets in a few minutes. If "flock" is available, spray it onto the plaster while it is still damp, although it can be put on later if the surface is brushed with paste. Gray flock will help mountains and stones look real; green flock will make grasslands look natural; tan flock may be used for a wheat field. If you are unable to obtain flock, paint the surfaces with poster paint, which serves just as well. Put in the roads, trees, and buildings which help to picture the relationships previously planned by the class. Lichen, which can be purchased at a hobby

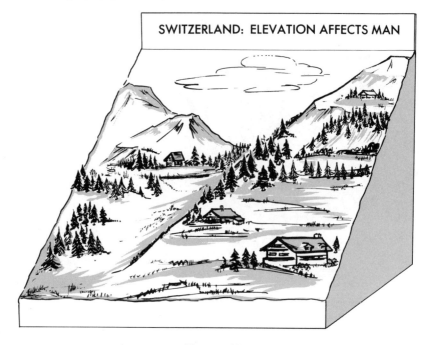

Figure 43

shop, makes lifelike trees when it is put on tiny forked twigs. The small "houses" from Monopoly games, or half-inch cubes of wood will provide the buildings needed. Sketch a simple background on art paper or cardboard to give the layout depth and place it at the back of the layout. A title gives the layout a finished look. In the case of Switzerland the title might read, "Switzerland: Elevation Affects Man." (See Figure 43).

THE PARADE OF COUNTRIES OR STATES—MAKING FLOATS   Make floats out of the covers and boxes in which school pencils are packed. In planning the floats remember that the two sides of a float ought to be nearly alike so that people on both sides of them see their meaning. This project will require a review of the most outstanding facts about countries. The discussion might begin with having pupils recall the Tournament of Roses. Then have them assume that they have been appointed to plan floats for a Parade of Countries, each of which will correctly portray a country which they have studied during the school term. List the things which the pupils associate with each country. After the pupils select the plans which they like best, they are ready to design the floats and build them in the boxes. Wheels made from cardboard might be mounted beneath the boxes to give them the appearance of mobility.

SHADOW BOXES   Shadow boxes may be made in the cover of a box or in a ground-meat container. Have the pupils plan a landscape which would be typical of the country they are studying. Cut the parts of the scene out of colored paper. Paint the outside and the back of the shadow box with black paint. When the paint is dry, paste the parts of the landscape to the inside of the cover. If the cover is deep enough, pipe-cleaner figures may be put along the front edge. This gives the scene a three-dimensional look. Keep the scene simple.

THE SAND PAN OR SAND TABLE   No other audio-visual aid can substitute for a sand pan or sand table. Geographic concepts are easily understood when this teaching device is used. A carton with the sides cut to a height of four inches and lined with clear plastic wrapping paper will make a good sand pan. Large cake tins may also be used. Have several such pans in your room. In them you can quickly construct land forms, show the personality of a country, or a scene.

THE TASTING PARTY AND MENU   This activity has great appeal. At the conclusion of a unit, the pupils or the teacher might plan to bring in some of the foods in which the country, or a region in the country, specializes. When the dairy industry of the Netherlands is studied, the pupils might try a piece of Gouda or Edam cheese on a cracker. In offering the cheese on a cracker, consider that some pupils may not like cheese. Say, "If any of you do not care for cheese, I have placed crackers here without cheese which you may take." This activity adds realism to geography and is very popular. It takes very little effort to prepare, yet offers additional experience which pupils might not otherwise have.

A related activity is that of menu making. Pupils may write menus which are characteristic of the region or country which they are studying, in which they will include foods that can be produced there. The menu might be for a single meal or for an entire day. A typical American menu may be prepared to show the contrast. The menu form may be altered and the foods used in a meal listed in one column while the source of each is listed in an adjacent column. Sketches pertaining to the production of each food might also be made and the relationships noted. An activity such as this will help to make the pupils conscious that the dietary habits of people of other countries are directly related to the foods which are raised in their countries. It will make them eager to try new foods when they travel, instead of always asking for typical American foods regardless of where they are.

TELEVISION OR RADIO COMMERCIALS   Have the pupils write and deliver convincing radio or television commercials which advertise the products mentioned in the unit. Have them emphasize the reasons for the top quality of the products.

TRAVEL FOLDERS   Discuss with the pupils the purpose of travel folders. Have them pretend that they work for a travel bureau and that they are to design a travel folder which will make people want to visit a certain city or country.

A CLASS PROJECT: THE REGION BOOK   As a summary to the study of a country, or group of countries, have each child contribute a page, twelve by eighteen inches in size, to a book about the country or region. The teacher and pupils should list all of the possible topics about which a page might be written, including sketches, maps, and graphs which might be made to illustrate each page. For a book on Brazil, topics such as surface, climate, climatic graphs, Amazonia, coffee production, life on a *fazenda*, Rio de Janeiro, and Sao Paulo might be included. When the pages have been completed, bind or tie them together. Each pupil has had an opportunity to contribute something that is original and a part of himself to a group project of which all will be proud.

THE CURIOSITY TRAY   On the teacher's desk, or on a table near the door of the classroom, place an attractive tray, or a simple box lid or paper plate. On it the teacher can place any item with which the pupils are probably not familiar. Such items as a piece of coral, jute, or petrified wood might be included. Place only a single item on the tray each day. Have an agreement with the pupils that they are not to tell what it is if they know, since every pupil should have an opportunity to try to discover what the item for the day happens to be. The teacher should show the class where the item came from, locating it on a map, and provide other helpful data. If it is a plant, the teacher might list the climatic require ments of it and discuss its use. The pupils are thus provided with enough clues to enable them to discover what the item is.

13

Factors to which some of man's activities are related

Most elementary school teachers have reasonably adequate knowledge about each of the many subjects which they must teach, but the requirements which they must meet for certification are, in most cases, so rigid that there is little time for thorough study in any field. The liberal arts courses which the teacher trainee takes are usually introductory courses that are intended to help him develop basic concepts rather than accumulate a mass of details peculiar to each discipline. This is true of the student's geography courses at the undergraduate level—if, indeed, he has been required to take an introductory course in geography,—and he has probably not taken any courses beyond the introductory one.

This chapter is intended to acquaint the teacher who lacks an adequate background in geography with some of the factors to which man's activities are related. No attempt has been made to discuss each of the factors in its entirety. Space does not permit doing so. Only essential factors, which are most likely to be needed by the elementary school teacher to write out geographic relationships, have been given. There are many factors related to man's activities besides those which we have selected. Man's culture must also be considered by the geography teacher as he writes the relationships for his lessons. Natural conditions in two widely separated areas may be nearly identical, yet the people might make different kinds of adjustment to them, using their resources differently due to the distinctive characteristics of their cultural backgrounds. This contributing factor, as well as many others, must be kept in mind as the student considers each of the topics listed.

The material included in each topic could have been written in a much more formal style; however, it has been written purposely in the simplest language possible so that the teacher may use the material as it is in his classes. The simplicity of its form will make it easier for the pupils to learn it, and the teacher will have the least possible difficulty in extracting arrow statements from it.

Climate

Climate is a summary of weather conditions occurring over an extended period of time. It is the most important factor of the natural environment. It depends upon many things, a few of which are temperature, precipitation, humidity, the number of days of sunlight, and the recurring cycles of winds and storms. Climate, as a factor in man's activities, is really born when radiation is received by the earth from the sun. Climatologists refer to this radiation as *insolation*. The radiation, in the form of heat, creates temperature variations, depending upon the amount of sunlight which penetrates the earth's atmosphere. Penetration of the atmosphere is dependent upon the angle at which the sun's rays strike the earth, the intensity and duration of sunlight at any point on the earth, and the density and clarity of the atmosphere during sunlight hours. (The density and clarity of the atmosphere also help to determine how much of the heat received by the earth is retained during hours of darkness.) The temperature variations, in turn, create air pressures which vary from place to place on the surface of the earth. Changes in barometric pressure (air pressure) produce winds; winds, carrying moisture, eventually return their accumulated moisture to the land in some form of precipitation.

Man's activities and his health are affected by climate. He has had to adjust his mode of life and his activities to the climate of the region in which he makes his home. The length of the growing season and its mean temperature, the total number of days of sunshine during the growing season, and the amount of rainfall and its distribution throughout the year all help to determine the kinds of crops which he can grow. (Some crops, such as hay and oats, will grow where the skies are rather frequently cloudy, but corn and wheat both need sunshine.) Elementary school pupils need to learn some of the factors which affect climate so that they can

GENERAL ARRANGEMENT OF PLANETARY WINDS

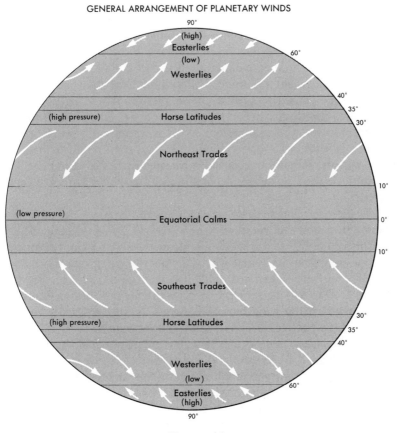

Figure 44

account for the climates of the specific places which they study. The factors affecting local areas include (1) latitude, (2) position relative to large land masses, (3) nearness to large bodies of water, (4) altitude, (5) mountain barriers, (6) prevalence of cyclonic storms, (7) prevailing winds, and (8) ocean currents.

A general understanding of the wind system is essential if geography relationships are to be taught successfully.[1] The system of calms and winds does not extend around the earth in the definite bands shown in Figure 44. Topography, ocean currents, frontal systems, and the uneven heating and cooling of large land masses cause exceptions in the wind pattern. However,

[1] There is some disagreement concerning the value of teaching a theorized or generalized system of wind belts, and the authors are well aware that frontal systems are found in all of the so-called "wind belts." They are also aware that frontal systems influence climate. Nevertheless, they feel that some general knowledge about planetary winds will help the young geographer to understand the major types of climates.

a knowledge of the chief wind belts will help the geography teacher to account for the presence of such things as the marine west coast climate, the rainy winters in countries having Mediterranean climate, for many of the deserts of the world, and for other facts about the earth which are related to climate. The latitudinal boundaries of the wind and calm belts are relative. In some places they are much wider or narrower than in others.

Winds are caused by changes in air pressure which are produced by temperature variations. High temperatures on the land warm the atmosphere by radiation and conduction. As air is warmed it expands, becomes less dense, is better able to absorb moisture, and rises, producing centers of low air pressure. When air is cooled, it becomes more dense and heavy, and tends to settle toward the surface of the earth, producing areas of high air pressure.

The direction and strength of winds are also largely determined by air pressure. In a low air pressure region, the air moves counterclockwise toward its center where it rises. In a high air pressure region, the air moves clockwise away from its center where the air is moving downward toward the earth's surface. When the cold, heavy air of a high pressure region rushes in to take the place of the rising warm air in a low air pressure region, we say that the wind blows. If there is a great difference in the air pressures of the two regions, there will be strong winds.

At the equator there is a belt of low pressure which is closely associated with high temperatures and the almost daily convectional storms. (As a result, rain forest vegetation occurs at the equator at low altitudes.) The air is heated by the almost vertical rays of the sun. Warm air absorbs moisture, and the warm, moist air rises to the upper atmosphere where it is cooled. The cooling causes the moisture to condense into droplets of water which fall to the surface of the earth as rain. The cooled air becomes more dense, heavy, and dry as it flows northward and southward from the equator. It begins to settle at a latitude of about 30° to 35° north and south of the equator, where it creates high pressure regions called the horse latitudes. This dry, heavy, settling air forces the air at the surface of the earth in these regions outward, toward the equator and the poles. Many of the world's poor grazing regions and deserts are located in the horse latitudes.

The winds which blow into the low air pressure belt near the equator are called trade winds. The northeast trade winds of the northern hemisphere and the southeast trade winds of the southern hemisphere are so named because of the direction from which they blow. The rotation of the earth, or coriolis force, gives them their easterly direction. They blow toward the equatorial calms, or doldrums, to take the place of the warm, rising air. The lowlands in these wind belts enjoy a frost-free, breezy climate. North and south of the horse latitudes, the westerlies blow. The rotation of the earth also causes the westerlies in the northern hemisphere to turn slightly to the north, and in the southern hemisphere to turn slightly toward the south.

Usually, the wind belts and calm belts north and south of latitude 60° are grouped together under the name of polar winds because so few people of the world are affected by them. There is little reason for elementary school pupils to know about them. However, elementary teachers should have an understanding of them so that they can account for conditions in the polar regions. At the far north and far south of the westerlies are the polar easterlies, which blow from the northeast in the northern hemisphere and from the southeast in the southern hemisphere. The slight northeast or southeast direction of these winds is due, again, to the rotation of the earth. Wherever the polar easterlies and westerlies meet, a front develops. One of the two winds must rise above the other. The westerlies rise because they are warmer and a low pressure region is created at about latitude 60° north or south of the equator. A small high air pressure area results at the poles.

The wind belts and air pressure belts of the northern hemisphere are farther north in the summer than in the winter. (The same condition exists in the southern hemisphere during the summer there.) This is because the vertical rays of the sun reach a point farther north on the globe during the summer in the northern hemisphere. In the winter, the opposite is true. Some parts of the earth have one prevailing wind in winter and comparative calm in the summer. The areas of the world where there is a Mediterranean type climate, for instance, have westerly winds in winter and a high pressure region (horse latitudes) in summer. This accounts for their mild, rainy winters and dry, hot summers.

Agriculture

The life of man and his activities both depend upon his food supply. The kinds of food produced, and the methods used in their production, are determined by climatic conditions. Food production also depends upon the cost of land, labor, equipment, transportation, fertilizer, and marketing; soil conditions; population density; and the cultural heritage of the people producing the food. Some of the methods used by man as he produces his food supply are discussed in the pages which follow.

MIXED OR GENERAL FARMING   The general or mixed farm produces some of the food required by its owner, as well as crops intended for use by farm animals. Any surplus is sold to produce cash income. Hay, grains, vegetables, and fruits are grown. Dairy cattle, some beef cattle, hogs, and poultry add to the farm income. The mixed farm must be located in an environment favorable to diversified crop production. Consequently, this type of farming is found in most of the world's temperate climates. It is economically more feasible that the farm be located near to an urban market center, or near means of cheap, rapid transportation. The operator of the farm must be a rather well educated individual with a diversity of skills since he must be, among other things, a veterinarian, soil chemist, electrician, mechanic, machinist, carpenter, and agronomist. The success of his farm depends not only upon the relative constancy of favorable environmental conditions (adequate rainfall, sunlight, length of growing season, freedom from early or late frosts), but also upon the skill with which he rotates the crops on his land for the purpose of rejuvenating the soil or allowing it to rest (lie fallow). For his efforts, the general farmer has a variety of sources of income, not all of which are likely to suffer from low prices or unfavorable growing conditions at the same time. The demand made upon his farm machinery is spread rather evenly throughout the year, and the animals which he raises help put his crops to their most profitable use. (Grains fed to animals bring more income in the form of milk, beef, butter, or eggs which can be sold.)

DRY FARMING   Dry farming is practiced in semiarid regions where there is only a limited amount of rainfall during the growing season. Fields are allowed to lie fallow for one season, during which time they store up enough moisture to produce a single crop the following season. The soil of the fallow fields is broken up after each rainfall in order to permit the moisture to penetrate deeply into it. During the season in which a crop is grown, the fields are harrowed frequently in order to produce a fine dust which settles over the surface and prevents the stored-up moisture from evaporating. The growing crop uses the stored moisture and the small amounts of rain which may fall during the growing season. Dry farming requires large acreage in order to have both fallow fields and producing fields. It illustrates how man is able to adapt his methods of crop production to limited amounts of rainfall, and make use of submarginal land at least every other year. It is widely used in the western wheat producing regions of the United States and other such semiarid regions of the world.

DAIRY FARMING   Dairy farming is a relatively small scale, intensive kind of agriculture. A successful dairy region is usually located in a cool, moist climate in which forage grasses, hay, and grains will grow well. A long grazing season is desirable. The most important factor is accessibility to markets because the main product, milk, is bulky and perishable. Therefore, dairy farms are located near large cities or near main arteries of transportation. Dairy products, such as cheese, butter, and preserved and powdered milk, can be brought from distant dairy regions because of the rapid means of transportation, refrigeration, and processing which are now available. (New Zealand, with its market for dairy products in England, is an example of this.) Dairy products furnish food for the families of dairy farmers as well as income. Dairying requires more skill, work, and expensive equipment that do most other types of farming. Dairy cows are expensive animals and must be attended to most carefully. They may be pastured on rough, or partially stony, ground which is unsuitable for purposes other than growing grasses. Level or rolling land is preferable, although other types of terrain are used. During the cold season of the year, the dairy cows must be kept in well-built dairy barns which usually have storage lofts for hay, and in most cases, an outside silo in which ensilage is stored. Ensilage, also called silage, is fodder which is stored for winter use in silos where it is allowed to ferment. Green corn stalks, one form of silage, are cut by machine into six or twelve inch lengths and then blown into the opening at the top of the silo. The fermented silage is removed from the bottom of the silo as it is needed.

Grasses grown on the dairy farm include alfalfa, timothy, and the various clovers. When they have been cut and allowed to dry in the sun, they are either stored in the barn in bulk, or more frequently in tightly packed bales, and are generally known as hay. (If hay is to be baled, it is usually not permitted to dry as long as when it is to be stored in bulk.) Straw for use as bedding for the animals is the dried portion of grain producing grasses from which the grains have been threshed or removed. It, too, is either stored in bulk or in bales. The more familiar are the oat, wheat, and rye straws. Grains fed to the dairy cattle are usually grown on the dairy farm.

The chief dairy breeds are Holstein-Friesian (commonly known as Holsteins), Guernsey, Jersey, Ayrshire, Danish Red, and Brown Swiss. Most of these breeds are named for the lands from which they originally came. Dairy cows prefer a cool, moist climate; consequently, the chief dairying regions are found in western Europe and in northern and northeastern United States.

TRUCK FARMING: COMMERCIAL VEGETABLE GROWING

Market garden areas are usually near the large cities, whereas truck gardening may be carried on quite a distance from the market, the vegetables being brought in by means of rapid transportation. The principal factors for the growing of commercial vegetables are nearness to markets, demand, suitable climate, availability of rapid transportation, and the proper amount of rainfall or irrigation waters. ("Suitable climate" and "proper amount" are words which have relative values and should be carefully used by the geography teacher. A "suitable" climate for the growing of bananas, for instance, would not be "suitable" for the growing of wheat.) The problem of soil is not so important as other factors since, with modern methods, the soil can be fertilized or otherwise conditioned to suit growing requirements. Much manual labor is needed for this type of farming even though an increasing amount of machinery is used. Improved methods of handling, packing, shipping, and marketing vegetables have made it possible to send vegetables and berries great distances to the consumers.

In the United States the outstanding vegetable regions are the Middle Atlantic Commericial vegetable region along the east coast; Florida; the Gulf Coast; and states bordering on the Great Lakes; and some irrigated areas of the far west. Thus, because of climatic variations, fresh vegetables are available during the entire year. One advantage which the vegetable region on the east coast enjoys is the porous, sandy soil which warms quickly in the spring. Here the vegetables grow quickly, mature earlier, and are marketed when the price of vegetables is high. Much fertilizer is needed for this sandy soil, but its cost is balanced by other favorable factors such as nearness to markets and the high prices paid for early vegetables.

In Europe one of the chief commercial vegetable areas is located in Belgium and the Netherlands. Of course, their markets are in England, West Germany, and their own lands because this is the most densely populated part of Europe. Many of their vegetables and fruits are grown outdoors, but thousands of acres are under greenhouses where growing conditions can be more easily controlled. The greenhouses of the Netherlands and Belgium make possible the production of out-of-season vegetables, as well as some vegetables and fruits which require different climatic conditions than those afforded by the natural environment.

Market gardening regions are found near the Mediterranean in southern France, in parts of Italy, Greece, Spain, and on several of the islands in the Mediterranean Sea.

IRRIGATED FARMING   Irrigated farming is a way of making profitable use of lands having too little rainfall. Methods of irrigation vary from one region to another throughout the world, depending upon the source of water and the culture of the people. Irrigation requires a source of water and an efficient method of distribution. The source may be surface waters, such as lakes, rivers, or flowing wells, or it may be ground water from pumped wells. The manner of storage of irrigation waters may vary from the "tank" located behind a mud dam on a small stream in India, to a massive reservoir such as Lake Mead in the western United States. It may be distributed in ditches on the surface of the land, through systems of pipelines stretching many miles, or through underground tunnels similar to the *foggara*, or *kanat*, of the dry lands of the Middle East which convey water many miles from upland streams and springs to the fields. Subsurface distribution involves delivering the irrigation water to the roots of the plants, which helps considerably in avoiding loss through evaporation. One modern system of irrigation is by means of sprinklers. The development of lightweight aluminum pipe, and standards to hold the pipes above the ground, has made possible the irrigation of thousands of acres of land in the arid regions of the southwestern United States and in other, more humid areas where additional water will increase the size of the crops. Over ten per cent of the irrigated lands of the United States use this method. The entire system is easily moved from field to field and is tapped into a main water supply pipe system from the storage basin which may be many miles away. It is also used to distribute water from wells, streams, and rivers.

Irrigation is necessary in most lands which have Mediterranean climate, in monsoon lands during the dry monsoon season, and in the arid regions of the western United States, the Middle East, and in the Sahara Desert. Minor irrigation systems are also in use wherever man wishes to carefully control the supply of water to his crops.

Since irrigation is expensive, especially where the water used must be purchased, it is used more frequently on fertile land for the growth of cash crops, or for the cultivation of specialty fruits and vegetables which bring high prices in urban markets. The Imperial Valley and Valley of California are known for their intensive cultivation of such crops. In Egypt, cotton is grown on irrigated land as an industrial cash crop. Irrigation waters are also used in some countries, such as Australia and Argentina, as well as in the western United States, for the production of forage crops for livestock. In the Middle East and the countries of Northern Africa, the waters are used for small farm grain agriculture. Thus, demand and latitude are determinants of the kind of crops to be grown in some parts of the world, while in many other parts, food crops peculiar to the region must be raised on irrigated lands as a matter of survival.

Topography plays an important part in an irrigation project. The source of water is often in mountainous land. A dam is usually built across a river valley between fault-free mountains. Thus, the reservoir formed back of the land is in mountainous country but the fields to be irrigated may be miles away where the land is level enough to be farmed and watered by irrigation water.

Drainage is particularly important in the use of irrigation waters since, unlike rain water, they contain salts in solution which, if allowed to remain long on the soil, sometimes make it unfit for cultivation. It has been estimated that a foot of irrigation water on an acre of soil would leave behind a ton of such salts. Therefore, the topography of the land must permit adequate drainage. Evaporation accounts for the loss of much of the water stored for irrigation and while the water is being distributed to the fields. In large storage dams, such as Lake Mead, evaporation is a serious problem. Care must be taken in applying the irrigation waters to the crops, also. In particularly hot climates the water must not be applied during the hottest part of the day because the plants would literally be cooked. It is generally thought that almost three-fourths of all irrigation water in use today is wasted in the process of applying it to the fields. Soil conditions must be such that the irrigation waters do not permeate the land too quickly. In sandy soils, for instance, much of the water would be lost before it reached the plants. Therefore, many irrigation ditches are lined.

Regardless of the care and expense involved in irrigating farm land, it has its advantages in that the farmer is able to deliver the right amount of water, at the right time, to the exact spot where plants need it. An abundance of sunlight in regions with little rainfall not only produces rapid plant growth but also helps to protect plants from disease. The quality of the crop and yield per acre are thus increased, offsetting the cost of irrigation, the expense of the labor necessary to operate the irrigation system, and the cost of transporting the crops to urban centers.

RAISING DECIDUOUS OR HARDY FRUITS   Apples, peaches, pears, plums, cherries, and apricots are deciduous fruits which are common in the United States and other middle latitude countries. More apples are grown than any other of the hardy fruits. Orchards of deciduous fruits are usually planted along sunny hillsides where cool night air will drain into the valley below, thus protecting the trees from late frosts which would kill the blossoms. They are planted in well-drained soil and require a considerable amount of moisture. The growing season of from five to six months should be free from frost. Most species are susceptible to disease and, in commercial orchards, require frequent spraying. The orchards are usually located near to the markets since most of the hardy fruits are perishable, the term "hardy" merely indicating that the trees can withstand the winter temperatures of the middle latitude region without damage. They require a rest period between producing seasons. Europe produces almost two-thirds of the world's apple crop, while the United States produces about half of the world's peach crop. World production of peaches, plums, and pears is under 5,000 tons each yearly. World production of cherries and apricots is much less, being under 1,500 tons yearly for each fruit.

VINICULTURE   Grapevines require well-drained soil, but because they have deep tap roots they can be grown where there is very little precipitation and can survive long periods of drought. In mountainous countries which have a climate favorable to grape production and where crop land is limited, vineyards frequently occupy the southern slopes of the mountains. The sun's rays strike these slopes at a nearly right angle, thus providing the vines with the maximum amount of warmth and sunlight. The vines are planted in rows which run in the direction of the slope so that the grapes on both sides of vines receive sunlight. The slopes provide good drainage for the vines, there is little danger from killing frosts, and the fertile bottom lands are freed for the production of food crops. The vines require a frost-free growing season one hundred fifty days in length. The temperature during the month in which the grapes reach maturity

(September in the northern hemisphere, March in the southern hemisphere) must be above 60°F. Following the bearing season, the vines must have a period in which they can lie dormant. Grapes are grown for table use as fresh fruit, for raisins, and for wine. Four-fifths of the world's annual crop of grapes are used for the fermentation of wines. Grapes used for raisin production require long, sunny summers and mild winters. They also require mild, rain-free autumns during which the harvested grapes can be dried in the sun. Regions having the climatic requirements for the production of raisin grapes frequently require irrigation. Such is the case near Fresno, California, where irrigation waters are drawn from mountain streams. In the Great Lakes region of the United States, a climate which would otherwise be inhospitable to the grape is tempered by westerly winds blowing over the lakes during the ripening season. Large bodies of water, such as the Great Lakes, heat and cool slowly. Therefore, winds blowing across them toward the land are warmed and help to lengthen the growing seasons of the vineyards planted on their shores, such as in western Michigan.

Commercial Fishing

Commercial fishing is carried on in the shallower waters above the continental shelves, usually where a warm and a cold current meet. The waters range in depth from two hundred to six hundred feet; however, most of the catch is taken from the shallower depths. Some varieties of fish—herring and salmon in cold waters, tuna in warm waters—live and feed near the surface. Others, such as cod, haddock, flounder, and halibut, occupy the bottom waters. Surface feeding fish migrate periodically and must, therefore, be fished for on a seasonal basis. The beds where the bottom fish live and feed remain almost constant and fishermen are able to return to the same grounds repeatedly. Various devices are employed to obtain a catch, including the trawl, the drift net, and the fishing hook and line which is used for the larger fish, such as tuna. Shellfish, generally found in shallow waters near the shoreline, require special fixed nets or pots, or digging and dredging for the catch which may lie in the muddy bottom waters. The catch is extremely perishable and must either be rushed to market or preserved at once on board ship. Only a few hundred of the more than twenty-thousand varieties of fish are consumed by man. More varieties of cold water fish than warm water fish are edible. Exhaustion of the fishing grounds is a continuing possibility and world treaties are necessary to maintain the sovereignty of nations over those near to their shores. The treaties are frequently violated.

Manufacturing

There are six major factors which help to determine whether or not a country or region will engage in manufacturing. They are (1) capital for investment, (2) the availability of raw materials, (3) a source of cheap power to operate machinery, (4) cheap, rapid transportation, (5) skilled workmen, and (6) markets for the manufactured products.

Some form of capital is absolutely essential to the founding of all industries and to continuing them. Capital is obtained from people who have saved money and wish to invest it. For the use of their money to operate the industry—and help found it—they receive a form of interest called dividends. The investors are known as stockholders, or shareholders, since they actually own a part of the industry which they have helped to found. Raw materials are also essential to manufacturing. They must either be available at the site of the industry or easily transported there at reasonable cost. There is very little iron ore in Pennsylvania, for instance, but Pennsylvania has large supplies of coal. It is easier and cheaper to transport iron ore from the western tip of Lake Superior to Pittsburgh, than it is to transport coal from Pennsylvania to the site of the iron ore deposits. Some source of power must either be available near the site of the industry, or available from a distance at a reasonable rate. It is possible, for instance, to transport both electrical power and supplies of natural gas over great distances at very reasonable cost. Electrical power is produced in many ways, chief of which are water-driven turbines (from waters impounded in dams), and steam-driven turbines (run either on steam produced by the burning of coal or gas, or the heat from atomic reaction). Industry depends upon inexpensive, safe, rapid transportation, both to bring raw materials to it and to carry its finished products away. Heavy carriers are most commonly used by industry. These include railroads, highways (for truck transport), and waterways. Some heavy transport is done by air. Transportation is also a factor in bringing workmen to the industrial site to work. Industry cannot function efficiently without skilled, well-educated workmen. In countries where the standard of living is very low and the illiteracy rate is very high, it is difficult to engage in manufacturing until workers can be trained. The low wages which unskilled, uneducated workers obtain do not necessarily guarantee efficient production. Finally, manufactured products must be sold, and there must be a demand for them before the industrial plant is built.

There are other, minor factors which help to determine the success of any manufacturing endeavor. One is an adequate supply of water, to be used either directly or indirectly in producing the product; another is a means whereby wastes can be disposed of without harm to the natural environment. Climate may also be a factor in determining where a manufacturing plant will be located, or how efficiently it will operate. Similarly, the cost of land on which to build the factory is important. Large, flat areas are best for manufacturing plants, but in mountainous countries such land is frequently unavailable or too costly; therefore, adjustments must be made.

COTTAGE MANUFACTURING   All over the world there are millions of people who manufacture in their homes or tiny shops. Their skills have been handed down from generation to generation. Many of the fine products which we can use and admire come from these cottage manufacturers. Carved ivory from India, cloisonné enamel from China, cotton batik from Indonesia, fine linen and embroidery from Ireland and Switzerland, objects of silver and tin from Mexico, lacquer ware and hand-thrown pottery from Japan, and thousands of other kinds of goods originate from home industry. All of the factors relating to cottage manufacturing cannot be enumerated. They may include a cheap supply of labor, the uniqueness of the raw material which is available, the skill passed on from generation to generation, a secret process, or a combination of these and other factors.

APPENDIX A

Types of Climate

A. Tropical Rain forest (Range 0°–10° north and south of the equator)

Hot, humid; dark, gloomy; luxuriant vegetation; insects. Trees, vines, undergrowth form mass of vegetation difficult to penetrate. Has continuous high temperature and heavy rainfall. Rainfall around 100 inches annually. Products: Rubber, cacao, copra, bananas.

B. Savanna Climate (Range 5°–15° north and south of the equator)

Less rainfall than tropical rain forest; has distinct wet and dry seasons. Lies on sides of tropical rain forest nearer the poles. Has tall grass, open forest. Tree growth heavier on equatorial side. Some grasslands devoted to grazing suffer during the dry season because the grass becomes coarse. Tropical diseases and insects also bother the cattle. Man earns his living chiefly through agriculture and grazing.

C. Dry Climates (Range 15°–30° north and south of the equator)

1. *Low latitude deserts.* Occupy center and leeward sides of continents in tradewind and horse latitude areas. East coasts of lands in trades are humid; west coasts are relatively dry because the moisture is dropped on the east side. Annual rainfall in hot deserts: 5" to 10".

2. *Low latitude steppes.* Semiarid lands at edges of low latitude deserts. Rainfall meager and undependable. Sparse population. Irrigation must be practiced. During good years, grazing may provide occupation for people.

3. *Middle latitude deserts.* Mainly in deep interiors of larger continents, far from oceans. Asia has greatest area of dry climate. Dryness due mostly to location of large land masses. Rain-bearing winds have lost almost all their moisture before reaching the area.

4. *Middle latitude steppes.* Semiarid regions between middle latitude deserts and adjacent humid regions. Temperatures quite like those of the desert. Receive more rainfall than desert, better suited to habitation.

D. Mediterranean climate. Few rainy days, blue skies, much sunshine, mild winters. Rainfall moderate to low, most falling during winter; summers have little rain. Borders Mediterranean Sea, central and southern California, central Chile, southern tip of Africa, and parts of southern Australia.

E.   Humid Climate.

1. *Humid subtropical climate.* On eastern sides of continents. Semiannual rainfall from 30″ to 65″. Rain throughout most of year; generally heavier in summer. Growing season: from seven months to twelve months.

2. *Humid continental climate.* North America and Eurasia. Land controlled; carried to the east by westerly winds. Warm to hot summers; cold winters. Maximum rainfall during summer months. Regions with long summers have growing season of from five to seven months and moderately severe winters. "Corn belt" climate. Short summer regions known for spring wheat growing. Summers usually warm for only a few months; growing season of only three to five months. Long, summer days of these high latitude regions offset this disadvantage.

3. *Marine west-coast climate.* On westward, or windward sides of middle latitude continents, poleward from about 40°. Summers moderately cool; too cool for the best growth of most cereal crops. Cloudy, rainy regions, with small daily temperature range. Seattle, highest average daily July temperature is only 73°. Winters are abnormally mild for the latitude. Rainfall varies with surface type; adequate for plant growth.

4. *Subarctic climate-forested lands.* Greatest temperature extremes on earth found here. Growing season only fifty to seventy-five days. Freezing temperatures sometimes occur even during July and August. Siberia: record for low temperatures, Verkhoyansk having average for January of minus fifty-nine degrees F. Subarctic Eurasia and North America largely covered by taiga, softwood forests.

APPENDIX B

Climatic Regions

The following maps portray simplifications of dynamic world climatic patterns. Divisions appearing on the maps as sharp lines represent what are, in fact, transition zones between the definite, so-called cores of the regions shown. In Africa, for example, the climate of the tropical savanna region (B) is like that of the rain forest in that it is hot all year because the sun is never far from being directly overhead; however, the amount of seasonal rainfall is responsible for the difference between the two regions. In the rain forest region (A) it rains every day, but there is little or no rainfall for six months in the savanna region (B). At the boundary line between A and B the forests would be less dense, but if one traveled north or south from the rain forest region, more grassland would be evident and the trees would be scattered. Farther north and south the grasslands would have shorter grass, finally becoming a semiarid grazing land (C), and eventually a desert region.

Remember that as you study the countries and regions of the world with your pupils, you must make it clear that there is a blending of one climatic region into another. The reason for the gradual change and the effect which it will have upon man's activities and culture must also be pointed out to them, since we often find that identical climatic conditions do not produce identical cultures.

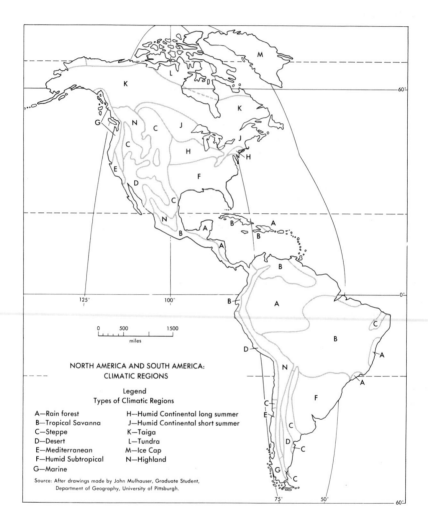

NORTH AMERICA AND SOUTH AMERICA:
CLIMATIC REGIONS

Legend
Types of Climatic Regions

A—Rain forest   H—Humid Continental long summer
B—Tropical Savanna   J—Humid Continental short summer
C—Steppe   K—Taiga
D—Desert   L—Tundra
E—Mediterranean   M—Ice Cap
F—Humid Subtropical   N—Highland
G—Marine

Source: After drawings made by John Mulhauser, Graduate Student,
        Department of Geography, University of Pittsburgh.

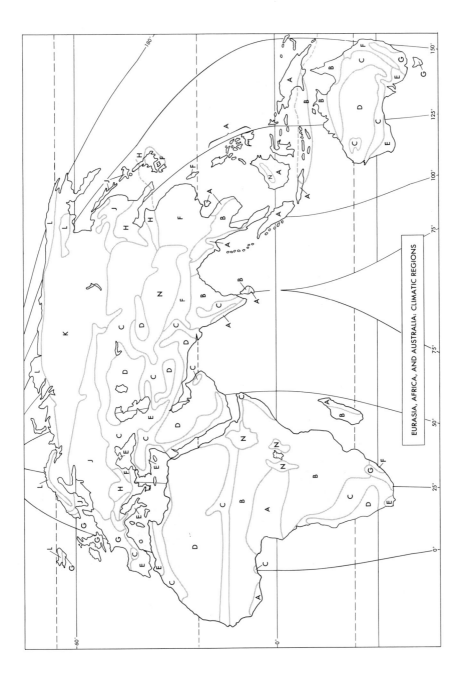

EURASIA, AFRICA, AND AUSTRALIA: CLIMATIC REGIONS

APPENDIX C

Climatic Data

Climatic Data for Selected Cities Located in Certain Climatic Regions, Including Average Monthly Rainfall Expressed in Inches and Average Monthly Temperature Expressed in Degrees Fahrenheit

TYPE OF CLIMATE	CITY	ELEVATION IN FEET	MONTH												
			J	F	M	A	M	J	J	A	S	O	N	D	
Tropical rain forest	Belem, Brazil	42	78	77	78	78	79	79	78	79	79	79	80	79	Temp.
			12.5	14.1	14.1	12.6	10.2	6.7	5.9	4.4	3.5	3.3	2.6	6.1	Rain.
	Leopoldville, Republic of the Congo	1,066	79	79	80	80	79	75	73	74	77	79	79	78	Temp.
			5.3	5.7	7.7	7.7	6.2	.3	.1	.1	1.2	4.7	8.7	5.6	Rain.
Tropical savanna	Sao Paulo, Brazil	2,690	69	69	68	65	60	59	58	59	61	63	65	68	Temp.
			8.8	7.5	5.8	2.5	2.5	2.0	1.1	2.0	3.0	4.4	5.4	7.1	Rain.
	Calcutta, India	211	67	71	80	85	87	85	84	83	83	81	73	67	Temp.
			.3	1.1	1.4	1.9	5.7	11.9	12.5	12.7	9.9	4.2	.7	.2	Rain.
Steppe	Tashkent, U.S.S.R.	1,610	30	35	46	58	68	77	80	76	66	54	45	37	Temp.
			1.8	1.4	2.6	2.6	1.1	.5	.1	.1	.2	1.1	1.4	1.7	Rain.
	Bahia Blanca, Argentina	95	75	72	68	61	54	48	48	50	54	59	66	72	Temp.
			1.9	2.5	2.3	2.2	1.4	.6	1.0	.6	1.7	2.8	1.9	2.2	Rain.

Climate	Station	Elev.												
Taiga	Archangel, U.S.S.R.	50	8	10	17	30	41	53	59	55	46	34	21	12	Temp.
			.9	.7	.8	.7	1.2	1.8	2.4	2.4	2.2	1.6	1.2	.9	Rain.
Desert	Yuma, Arizona	141	54	59	64	70	76	85	91	90	84	73	62	55	Temp.
			.3	.4	.3	.1	.1	.1	.2	.5	.5	.3	.2	.5	Rain.
	Touggourt, Algeria	226	51	60	61	70	77	87	92	90	84	72	61	53	Temp.
			.2	.4	.6	.1	.2	.1	.0	.0	.0	.2	.6	.4	Rain.
Mediterranean	Rome, Italy	208	45	47	51	57	64	71	76	75	69	62	53	47	Temp.
			3.3	2.6	2.9	2.6	2.2	1.5	.7	1.0	2.5	5.0	4.5	3.9	Rain.
	San Diego, California	93	55	55	57	59	61	64	67	69	67	61	57	51	Temp.
			2.0	2.2	1.6	.7	.3	.1	.1	.1	.1	.5	.7	1.8	Rain.
Marine west coast	London, England	18	41	41	43	47	55	59	63	62	57	51	44	41	Temp.
			1.8	1.5	1.7	1.5	1.7	2.1	2.2	2.2	1.9	2.7	2.2	2.3	Rain.
Humid subtropical	Buenos Aires, Argentina	89	74	73	69	62	55	50	49	51	55	60	66	71	Temp.
			3.1	2.8	4.3	3.5	3.0	2.4	2.2	2.4	3.1	3.4	3.3	3.9	Rain.
Humid continental, warm summer	Chicago, Illinois	824	24	26	36	47	57	67	73	71	65	54	40	29	Temp.
			1.7	1.6	2.7	2.6	3.4	3.4	3.1	3.3	3.5	2.4	2.1	1.9	Rain.
Humid continental, cool summer	Moscow, U.S.S.R.	480	14	17	25	39	55	61	66	62	51	40	28	19	Temp.
			1.1	.9	1.2	1.5	1.9	2.0	2.8	2.9	2.2	1.4	1.6	1.5	Rain.
Tundra (Polar)	Barrow, Alaska	13	−17	−17	−15	0	20	35	40	38	31	17	0	−12	Temp.
			.2	.2	.1	.1	.1	.3	.9	.7	.5	.6	.3	.3	Rain.

SOURCE: W. G. Kendrew, *The Climates of the Continents*, 4th ed., 1953, by permission of Clarendon Press, Oxford.

APPENDIX D

Teaching the Concept of Rainfall—
Intermediate Sequences

In the fourth sequence the children should learn the meaning and the effect of heavy, light, and moderate rainfall. In the study of Australia, for instance, there will be an opportunity to teach the effect of too little rainfall upon the activities of men. In describing desert conditions, make it clear that a desert is an area of dryness and not a surface feature. Deserts may be found on plains, plateaus, or mountains. Ofter deserts receive a small amount of rainfall. The dry desert air and clear skies permit rapid radiation. Plants adjust to dryness by developing characteristics which retard evaporation, store water, or keep grazing animals away from them by having hard, shiny leaves, thick fibers, woody stems, tough outer coverings, spikes, or thorns.

When studying the equatorial region, show the pupils the effect of heavy rainfall in the dense rain forest growth, the effect of leaching upon the soil, and the many tributaries of rivers which are needed to carry the large amounts of water. The heavy rainfall influences the type of houses built by the people. As there is little or no wind in the equatorial calm belt, the rain falls vertically. Consequently, no deserts are possible.

In the Amazon region, the land is nearly flat. The heavy rains cause large areas of swampland. In Africa and Indonesia, the higher lands cause the water to drain off.

In the study of Eurasia, speak of the westerly winds which flow over most of Eurasia. These winds bring rain to western Europe and then proceed on their way over the rest of the continent as dry winds. As a result of this, much of China is too dry for successful agriculture.

Early in the fifth sequence, before the pupils are introduced to the annual rainfall map, explain the meaning of inches of rainfall.

Sometimes after an unusually heavy rainstorm, the weather report will include the number of inches of rainfall. Discuss how rainfall is measured. How does the meteorologist measure rain? Could we measure rainfall? (It could be measured if any straight-sided container having a flat bottom were used.) Next, study a rainfall map. Find the number of inches of rain which several regions receive. From this point on, the children should give rainfall in the definite

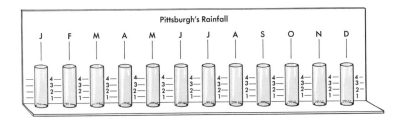

Pittsburgh's Rainfall

number of inches of rainfall which a given place receives. To further strengthen the understanding of rainfall, make a cumulative rainfall chart for a city near your school.

Draw vertical lines, one for each month. At the bottom of the chart mark off inches along each vertical line. This is to show actual inches of rainfall. In front of the lines, place glass bottles which are of equal size. Small olive bottles about one and one-half inch in diameter will do. It will be easier to keep the bottles in place if they are wired to the chart.

At the end of September, put colored water, or a piece of colored paper, in the bottles to show the correct amount of rainfall for the month of September. Because fifth sequence pupils are just beginning to study decimals, the figures are rounded off into fractional parts. Continue showing the amount of rainfall in the bottles for the entire year. It is necessary to have the first line be the January line because this work will lead into the making of rainfall and temperature graphs in the sixth sequence. Keeping this chart will give more meaning to "inches of rainfall" and to the rainfall map.

In the study of North America, it will be interesting to note the differences in the amount and distribution of rainfall from one region to another and to account for the variations and the effect on man's activities.

In the sixth sequence, rainfall graphs are introduced. It is an easy step from the rainfall chart to the rainfall graph. (See page 164 for the development of climatic graphs.)

The pupils should be able to associate the type of vegetation they might expect to find with a definite number of inches of rainfall: desert areas, 0"–5"; semiarid, 5"–10"; grazing lands, 10"–20"; agricultural lands, 30"–40"; and tropical lands, 60"–80".

The pupils should have access to seasonal rainfall maps during the sixth sequence. The annual rainfall does not present a true picture of the distribution of the rainfall because it indicates that the rainfall has taken place at regular intervals. Some areas in South America have a wet and a dry season. It is necessary that the pupils understand the problems involved in this distribution of rainfall.

The effect of mountain barriers upon the amount and distribution of rainfall has been introduced in the study of the Pacific States in the fifth sequence. There are several places in South America and Europe which will provide additional opportunities for strengthening this concept when they are studied.

APPENDIX E

Growing Conditions, Special Requirements, and Production Figures for Selected Crops

PRODUCT[a]	LENGTH OF GROWING SEASON REQUIRED (IN DAYS)[a]	RAINFALL[a] REQUIRED (IN INCHES) (MINIMUM)	SPECIAL REQUIREMENTS AND NOTES[a]	CHIEF PRODUCERS (IN METRIC TONS)	
					1962–63
Wheat	90	9	Growing season must be frost free. Temperatures must average above 50° F. Germination period should be cool and moist. Ripening period should be warm and dry. "Wheat is adaptable to a wider range of climate and soil conditions than any other major food plant."[b]	World Total	263,100,000[c]
				U.S.S.R.	70,778,000
				United States	29,765,000
				Canada	15,392,000
				France	14,054,000
				India	12,039,000
				Italy	9,497,000

Potatoes	100[d]	10	Average temperatures of warmest month around 65° F. Low night temperatures. Needs considerable moisture. Generally cool growing season is required.[e]	1963–64	
				World Total	276,500,000[c]
				U.S.S.R.	67,499,000
				Poland	44,868,000
				West Germany	25,812,000
				France	15,974,000
				East Germany	12,886,000
				United States	12,331,000
				Switzerland	6,692,000
Oats	120	10	Grows best in short summer, humid continental and marine west coast regions. Has least demanding soil requirements of the cereals.[f]	1963–64	
				World Total	48,300,000[c]
				United States	14,217,000
				Canada	6,988,000
				France	2,876,000
				Poland	2,830,000
				West Germany	2,321,000
				United Kingdom	1,471,000
				Australia	1,238,000
				Sweden	1,179,000
Rye	90	9	A winter-hardy cereal. Requires cool climate. Can stand more moisture than wheat. Does not require rich soil.[g]	1962–63	
				World Total	35,010,000[c]
				U.S.S.R.	17,000,000
				Poland	6,685,000
				West Germany	2,965,000
				East Germany	1,726,000
				United States	1,036,000

PRODUCT[a]	LENGTH OF GROWING SEASON REQUIRED (IN DAYS)[a]	RAINFALL REQUIRED (IN INCHES) (MINIMUM)[a]	SPECIAL REQUIREMENTS AND NOTES[a]	CHIEF PRODUCERS (IN METRIC TONS)
Maize	140	25–50	Growing season must be frost free. Average summer temperature of 75° F. Night temperatures must exceed 58° F. Needs 7" or more rainfall during silking and tasseling stage. Needs good drainage but not extra rich soil.[h]	1962–63 World Total 219,000,000[c] United States 92,375,000 U.S.S.R. 23,461,000 Brazil 10,418,000 Mexico 6,015,000 Republic of South Africa 5,809,000
Rice	130 (4 to 6 months)	15–35 per month	Temperatures above 68° F. Annual rainfall not less than 40". No excessive rainfall during harvest season. "Rich, heavy alluvial soils with impervious subsoils . . ." "Two to six" of water cover fields from planting until harvest.[1]	1960–61 World Total 239,800,000[c] China 85,000,000 India 51,297,000 Japan 16,073,000 Pakistan 16,053,000 Indonesia 13,151,000 Thailand 7,789,000 Burma 6,789,000 Brazil 5,392,000

Cane Sugar	12 to 24 months	50 to 65 inches annually	Gives heavier yield per acre than beet sugar. Stalks become 15' or more high. Each joint of the stalk has "eye" which creates new stalk when planted. High temperatures are required. Must have dry season for harvest. Good soil, deep, well-drained.[j]	1963–64	
				World Total	54,380,000[e]
				U.S.S.R.	6,016,000
				United States	3,882,000
				Cuba	3,500,000
				Brazil	3,333,000
				India	2,776,000
				France	2,009,000

[a] Information in these columns, unless otherwise noted, is taken from *Geography of Commodity Production* by Richard M. Highsmith, Jr. and Granville Jensen (New York, J. B. Lippincott Company, copyright 1958, 1963).

[b] *Ibid.*, pp. 14–25.

[c] Statistics, unless otherwise indicated, are taken from *The Statesman's Year-Book, 1965–1966*, London, Macmillan & Co. Ltd.

[d] Dupuy, William Atherton, *Our Plant Friends and Foes* (Philadelphia, John C. Winston Company, 1930), p. 42.

[e] *Geography of Commodity Production, loc. cit.*, p. 53.

[f] *Ibid.*, p. 47.

[g] *Ibid.*, p. 47.

[h] *Geography of Commodity Production, loc. cit.*, p. 41.

[i] *Ibid.*, p. 36.

[j] *Ibid.*, p. 89.

271

APPENDIX F

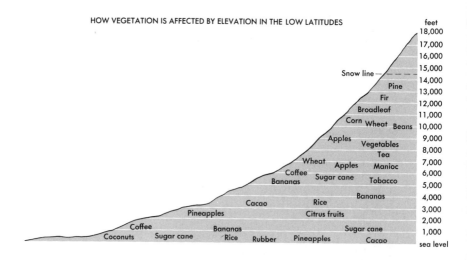

HOW VEGETATION IS AFFECTED BY ELEVATION IN THE LOW LATITUDES

APPENDIX G

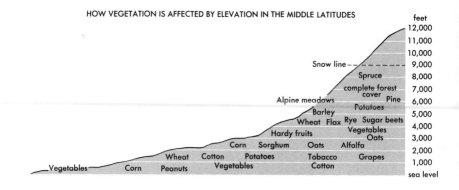

HOW VEGETATION IS AFFECTED BY ELEVATION IN THE MIDDLE LATITUDES

APPENDIX H

Crops are Determined by Latitude, Elevation, and Rainfall

	PLAINS	PLATEAUS	MOUNTAIN SLOPES
Equatorial Calms 0°–10° north and south	rice cacao rubber bananas	rice cacao coffee oil palm	cinchona kapok spices nutmeg

	PLAINS	PLATEAUS	MOUNTAIN SLOPES
	babassu nuts	sugar cane	pepper
	oil palm	kola nuts	cloves
	oiticica	peanuts	hardwoods
	coconut	(ground nuts)	rattan
	mahogany	rubber	
	manios	mahogany	
Trade Winds 15°–25° north and south	citrus fruits	peanuts	wheat
	pineapples	citrus fruits	chicle
	bananas	sugar cane	barley
	coffee	cacao	hardwoods
	corn	tobacco	a few cattle
	henequin	pineapples	and sheep,
	sugar cane	winter vegetables	although
	cotton	tea	this is not
	coconuts	corn	a very good
	sisal		climate for
	jute		domestic
			animals
Horse Latitudes 30°–35° north and south	poor grazing lands nomadic herding	if irrigation waters are available: winter vegetables, cotton, melons, alfalfa, citrus fruits, sugar cane	
Westerlies 40°–60° north and south	vegetables	tobacco	softwoods
	hemp	dairy products	sheep
	corn	sugar beets	cattle
	oats	corn	
	sorghum	grapes	
	grapes	oats	
	wheat	wheat	
	sugar beets	cattle	
	wool	hogs	
	potatoes	flax	
	rye	wheat	
	barley	hardy fruits	
	alfalfa	rye	
	hay	softwoods	
		barley	
		sheep	
Westerlies 50°–60° north and south	softwood trees, vegetables which require a short growing season, wheat, barley		

APPENDIX I

Leading Producers of Essential Products

CACAO (in metric tons)	World Total, 1963	1,250,000
	Ghana	427,000
	Nigeria	220,300
	Brazil	143,500
	Ivory Coast	97,200
	Cameroun	85,000
	Dominican Republic	38,000
	Ecuador	36,000
	Mexico	30,000
	Colombia	17,000
COFFEE (in metric tons)	World Total, 1963	3,980,000
	Brazil	1,560,000
	Colombia	468,000
	Ivory Coast	254,500
	Angola	168,000
	Mexico	129,200
	El Salvador	113,400
	Guatemala	105,000
	Ethiopia	91,500
	India	67,400
COTTON[a] (in bales)	World Total, 1964	50,919,000
	United States	15,340,000
	U.S.S.R.	8,000,000
	China	5,500,000
	India	5,250,000
	Brazil	2,200,000
	Mexico	2,110,000
	Egypt	2,037,000
FISH (in metric tons)	World Total, 1963	46,400,000
	Uruguay	6,901,300
	Japan	6,697,800
	U.S.S.R.	3,977,000
	United States	2,711,900
	Norway	1,331,700
	Canada	1,191,300
	Spain	1,097,900

[a] *The Statesman's Year-Book 1965–1966* (London, Macmillan & Co. Ltd., 1965).

LINSEED (FLAXSEED) (in metric tons)	World Total, 1963	3,400,000
	United States	800,000
	Argentina	771,000
	Canada	536,000
	India	385,000
	Uruguay	62,000
	Brazil	20,000
MILK (COW) (in metric tons)	World Total, 1963	323,100,000
	U.S.S.R.	61,200,000
	United States	56,601,000
	France	24,147,000
	West Germany	20,858,000
	Poland	12,641,000
	United Kingdom	12,591,000
	Italy	8,552,000
	Canada	8,354,000
NATURAL RUBBER (in metric tons)	World Total, 1963	2,205,000
	Malaysia	801,200
	Indonesia	697,300
	Thailand	187,800
	Ceylon	104,800
	Vietnam	71,800
	Nigeria	63,900
	Cambodia	40,800
	Liberia	40,200
	Dem. Rep. of the Congo	37,600
OIL PALM (in metric tons)	World Total, 1963	1,180,000
	Nigeria	405,000
	Dem. Rep. of the Congo	223,500
	Indonesia	148,300
	Malaysia	125,600
	Ivory Coast	25,400
	Angola	16,700
	Dahomey	12,200
SOY BEANS (in metric tons)	World Total, 1963	31,400,000
	United States	18,091,000
	China (1962)	10,210,000
	Indonesia	373,000
	Brazil	325,000
	Japan	318,000
	U.S.S.R.	300,000
	Korea	156,000
	Canada	136,000
	Thailand	28,000

SUGAR[b] (CENTRIFUGAL[c]) (in short tons)	World Total, 1963	59,491,000
	U.S.S.R.	6,500,000
	Cuba	4,000,000
	Brazil	3,564,000
	India	3,452,000
	United States, continental, beet	3,100,000
	France	2,248,000
	West Germany	2,235,000
	Mexico	2,070,000
	Philippines	1,971,000
	Australia	1,925,000
	United States, continental, cane	1,185,000
	Hawaii, cane	1,150,000
TEA (in metric tons)	World Total, 1963	828,000
	India	344,800
	Ceylon	219,800
	Japan	81,100
	Indonesia	38,500
	Pakistan	24,600
	China (Taiwan)	19,500
	Kenya	18,100
TOBACCO (in metric tons)	World Total, 1963	4,140,000
	United States	1,059,800
	India	366,800
	Brazil	206,800
	Japan	158,000
	U.S.S.R.	154,200
	Turkey	126,900
WOOL (in metric tons)	World Total, 1963	2,620,000
	Australia	809,000
	U.S.S.R.	371,000
	New Zealand	279,000
	Argentina	179,000
	South Africa, including Basutoland and S. West Africa	146,000
	United States	130,000

[b] *The World Almanac* (New York, The New York World-Telegram and Sun, 1965).

[c] Centrifugal sugar includes both cane and beet sugars produced by the centrifugal process.

SOURCE: Unless otherwise noted, *1964 Statistical Yearbook* (New York, The United Nations). Copyright, United Nations, 1965. Reproduced by permission.

Leading Producers of Essential Minerals

ASBESTOS (in metric tons)	World Total,[a] 1963	2,395,000
	Canada	1,153,900
	South Africa	186,600
	Southern Rhodesia	129,100
	United States	60,400
	Italy	57,200
BAUXITE (in metric tons)	World Total, 1963	26,720,000
	Jamaica	7,078,000
	U.S.S.R.	4,300,000
	Surinam	3,508,000
	British Guiana	2,861,000
	France	2,005,000
	United States	1,860,000
COAL (in metric tons)	World Total, 1963	1,929,000,000
	United States	430,450,000
	U.S.S.R.	395,129,000
	United Kingdom	198,936,000
	West Germany	142,786,000
	Poland	113,150,000
	India	65,956,000
COPPER (in metric tons)	World Total,[a] 1963	4,050,000
	United States	1,100,600
	Chile	724,900
	U.S.S.R.	700,000
	Zambia	588,100
	Canada	410,600
CRUDE STEEL (in metric tons)	World Total, 1963	386,600,000
	United States	99,120,000
	U.S.S.R.	80,198,000
	West Germany	31,597,000
	Japan	31,501,000
	United Kingdom	22,881,000
	France	17,557,000
IRON ORE (in metric tons)	World Total,[b] 1963	250,600,000
	U.S.S.R.	79,460,000
	United States	41,542,000
	Mainland China	35,000,000[c]
	France	18,812,000
	Canada	15,036,000
	Sweden	14,182,000

LEAD (in metric tons)	World Total,[d] 1963	2,040,000
	Australia	416,900
	U.S.S.R.	360,000[c]
	United States	229,900
	Mexico	190,000
	Canada	180,500

MANGANESE (in metric tons)	World Total,[e] 1963	6,000,000
	U.S.S.R.	3,000,000[c]
	South Africa	567,600
	India	510,000
	Mainland China	300,000[c]
	Ghana	195,600
	Morocco	144,400
	United States	47,800

MOLYBDENUM (in metric tons)	World Total,[f] 1963	34,000,000
	United States	29,488,000
	U.S.S.R.	5,700,000
	Chile	2,906,000
	Mainland China	1,500,000[c]
	Peru	480,000

NICKEL (in metric tons)	World Total,[g] 1963	280,000
	Canada	196,886
	U.S.S.R.	80,000[c]
	New Caledonia	45,000
	Cuba	16,700
	United States	12,792

PETROLEUM (in metric tons)	World Total, 1963	1,303,500,000
	United States	372,001,000
	U.S.S.R.	206,070,000
	Venezuela	169,671,000
	Kuwait	97,202,000
	Saudi Arabia	81,049,000
	Iran	73,029,000

TIN (in metric tons)	World Total, 1963	168,500
	Malaya	60,909
	Mainland China	24,400
	Bolivia	22,603[c]
	Thailand	15,835
	Indonesia	13,155

TUNGSTEN
(in metric tons)

World Total,[h] 1963	12,830
Mainland China	13,560[c]
U.S.S.R.	6,600[c]
Rep. of Korea	3,655
United States	3,079
North Korea	2,400[c]

[a] excluding U.S.S.R. and Mainland China
[b] excluding Mainland China and North Korea
[c] estimated
[d] excluding Mainland China and U.S.S.R.
[e] excluding Mainland China
[f] excluding Mainland China and U.S.S.R.
[g] excluding U.S.S.R.
[h] excluding Mainland China, U.S.S.R., and North Korea

Source: *1964 Statistical Yearbook* (New York, The United Nations). Copyright, United Nations, 1965.

APPENDIX J

Land Use Data for Selected Countries[a]

	CULTI-VATED	PERMA-NENT MEADOW AND PAS-TURE	FORESTS	BUILT-ON OR WASTE
Western Hemisphere				
United States	20%	27%	33%	20%
Argentina	11%	40%	35%	14%
Brazil	2%	12%	61%	25%
Canada	5%	2.5%	45%	47.5%
Chile	8%	.6%	22%	69.4%
Mexico	10%	32%	17%	41%
Eastern Hemisphere				
United Kingdom	30%	50%	8%	12%
Australia	4%	58%	4%	34%
Belgium	30%	23%	20%	27%
France	38%	24%	22%	16%
India	49%	4%	17%	30%
Italy	52%	17%	20%	11%
Japan	16%	2%	69%	13%
Netherlands	29%	38%	8%	25%
Nigeria	23.5%	0%	34.5%	42%
Norway	3%	.3%	23%	73.7%
Switzerland	10%	43%	25%	22%
West Germany	35%	23%	29%	13%
U.S.S.R.	10%	20%	40%	30%

[a] Compiled from *Production Yearbook 1964*, vol. 18 (Rome, Food and Agriculture Organization of the United Nations, 1965). Reproduced by permission.

APPENDIX K

Population and Area of Twenty Selected Countries

COUNTRY	AREA IN SQUARE MILES	POPULATION
Mainland China	2,279,134	686,400,000
India	1,221,880	449,381,000
U.S.S.R.	8,655,890	226,253,000
United States	3,628,150	183,285,009
Pakistan	364,737	98,612,000
Japan	142,688	96,160,000
Brazil	3,286,270	77,521,000
Nigeria	339,169	55,653,821
West Germany	95,931	55,430,000
United Kingdom (England, Scotland, Wales, Northern Ireland)	94,511	53,500,708
Italy	116,372	51,507,000
France	212,659	48,133,000
Mexico	758,259	38,416,000
Vietnam (North and South)	127,000	31,517,000
Argentina	1,072,700	21,762,000
Canada	3,851,809	18,238,247
East Germany	41,645	16,044,000
China (Taiwan)	13,886	11,884,000
Australia	2,971,081	10,965,100
Belgium	11,775	9,221,000
World (Continental Area)	56,500,000	3,218,000,000

SOURCE: *The World Almanac* (New York, The New York World-Telegram and Sun, 1965).

bibliography

The following bibliography is selective rather than exhaustive. Comments have been included about some of the works, but all of them are excellent. Once the study of geography has begun, the student will find that there is a wealth of material available, both in books and in periodicals. The breadth and scope of his reading will be limited only by the time which he has available for study.

General Works

Broek, Jan O. M., *Geography: Its Scope and Spirit* (Columbus, Charles E. Merrill Books, Inc., 1965).

Dohrs, Fred E., Lawrence M. Sommers, and Donald R. Petterson, *Outside Readings in Geography* (New York, Thomas Y. Crowell Company, 1955).

Freeman, T. W., *A Hundred Years of Geography* (Chicago, Aldine Publishing Company, 1961).

Gross, Herbert H., Ed., *The Journal of Geography* (River Forest, Illinois). Periodical.

James, Preston E., and Clarence F. Jones, eds., *American Geography: Inventory and Prospect* (Syracuse, N.Y., Syracuse University Press, 1954).

National Geographic Society, *The National Geographic Magazine* (Washington, D.C.). Periodical.

Kendall, Henry M., Robert M. Glendenning, and Clifford H. MacFadden, *Introduction to Geography* (New York, Harcourt, Brace & World, Inc., 1951).

Peattie, Roderick, *Geography in Human Destiny* (South Norwalk, Conn., George W. Stewart, Publisher, Inc., 1940).

Semple, Ellen Churchill, and Clarence Fielden Jones, *American History and Its Geographic Conditions* (Syracuse, N.Y., Syracuse University Press, 1954).

Whipple, Guy M., Ed., *The Teaching of Geography* (Bloomington, Illinois, National Society for the Study of Education, 32nd Yearbook, 1933).

Brown, Ralph H., *Historical Geography of the United States* (New York, Harcourt, Brace & World, Inc., 1948).

Geography and the Social Studies

Kohn, Clyde F., Ed., *Geographic Approaches to Social Education* (Washington, D.C., National Council for the Social Studies, 1948).

Jarolimek, John, *Social Studies in Elementary Education*, 2nd ed. (New York, The Macmillan Company, 1959, 1963).

Price, Roy A., Ed., *New Viewpoints in the Social Studies* (Washington, D.C., National Council for the Social Studies, 1958).

Teaching of Geography

Logan, Marguerite, *Geography Techniques* (Ann Arbor, Edwards Brothers, Inc., 1958).

Peattie, Roderick, *The Teaching of Geography* (New York, Appleton-Century-Crofts, 1950).

Thralls, Zoe A., *The Teaching of Geography* (New York, Appleton-Century-Crofts, 1958).

Maps and Globes

Greenhood, David, *Mapping* (Chicago, University of Chicago Press, 1964).

Harris, R. M., *Rand McNally Handbook of Map and Globe Usage* (Chicago, Rand McNally & Company, 1960).

Harrison, Lucia C., *Daylight, Twilight, Darkness and Time* (Morristown, N.J., Silver Burdette Company, 1935).

Odell, C. B., *Successful Teaching with the Globe* (Chicago, Denoyer-Geppert Co.).

Robertson, D., "The Globe as a Geographic Tool," *Journal of Geography*, Vol. 55, 1956.

Starkey, O. P., "Maps are Liars . . . ," *Science Digest*, Vol. 13, 1943.

The Education Index lists numerous magazine articles which have been written about maps, globes, and teaching with them.

Climate

Kendrew, W. G., *The Climates of the Continents*, 4th ed. (Oxford, Clarendon Press, 1953). (This work is authoritative and a necessary tool for every teacher of geography.)

Blair, Thomas A., *Climatology* (Englewood Cliffs, N.J., Prentice-Hall, Inc., 1951).

Economy and Production

Highsmith, Richard M., Jr., and J. Granville Jensen, *Geography of Commodity Production* (Philadelphia, J. B. Lippincott Company, 1958, 1963). (This is an excellent work. Again, the teacher of geography cannot afford to be without it. It is also excellent reading material for general information.)

Statistics

Steinberg, S. H., Ed., *The Stateman's Year-Book* (London, Macmillan & Co. Ltd., 1965). (This excellent statistical work, published annually, deserves a place on every geographer's bookshelf, and certainly in the library of elementary schools.)

United Nations Publishing Service, *Production Yearbook*, and *Statistical Yearbook* (New York, United Nations Publishing Service, A. Mazaud, Secretary). (Both of these statistical works belong in school libraries.)

The World Almanac (New York, The New York World-Telegram and Sun, Luman H. Long, Ed.). (An inexpensive and reliable statistical work which the geography teacher can certainly afford to keep in his classroom, and in his home library.)

There are many other statistical works; however, this list is selective. The geography teacher should not overlook the yearbooks published by individual countries. The *Commodity Yearbook, Agricultural Yearbook, Statistical Abstract of the United States,* and the *South American Handbook* are also valuable sources for statistics and general information.

index

Activities, 230–245
  Brazil, 231
  commercials, 243
  country, understanding of, 231
  curiosity tray, 244
  desk mural, 236
  evaluation, 235
  floats, 242
  globes, 52–53
  goals, 232–233
  graphs, bar, 231
  graphs, climatic, 231
  layouts, 239–242
  maps, 231
  materials, 234, 235
  menu making, 243
  models, 231
  necessity for, 230–235
  newspaper, pupil, 237–239
  planning, 233–235
  profiles, 231
  region book, 244
  sand pan, 243
  sand table, 243
  shadow boxes, 243
  sketching, 235–236
  tasting party, 243
  time limits, 234
  travel folders, 244
  value of, 231–232
  see also Lesson plan: application exercises
Africa:
  climate, 101–102
  climatic regions (map), 263
  Congo Basin, 102
  drainage, 266

Africa (*Cont.*)
  elevation, 101
  Ghana, 102
  location, 102
  lesson plan, development, 101–103
  lesson plan, summary, 103
  maps, 101–103
  Nigeria, 102
  rainfall, 102
  Republic of the Congo, climate, 102
  rivers, 102
  Ruwenzori Mountains, 101
  topography, 101–102
  see also various countries
Agricultural Statistics, 86
Agriculture, 249–255
  factors influencing, 249
  Japan, 147
  types of, 249–255
  see also Dairy farming, Dry farming, Fruit farming, General farming, Irrigated farming, Truck farming, Viniculture
Agriculture Yearbook, The, 169
Air pressure, 246, 248
Air pressure belts, 249
Alaska:
  Anchorage, 56
  Arctic, 51
  canning, 61
  climate, 44, 61
  day, length, 60, 61
  Eskimos, 61
  Fairbanks, 60, 61
  Fort Yukon, temperature, 52
  growing season, 61
  housing, 61

Alaska (*Cont.*)
  Indians, 61
  industries, 61
  latitude, effects of, 60–62
  manufacturing, 61
  Point Barrows, 60
  rainfall, 61
  Sitka, 61
"Alaska Proudly Joins the Union" (Gruening), 61n
Alaskan time belt, 68, 69
Almanacs, statistics, 103
Alps, Switzerland, 13, 90, 92
Amazon region, rainfall, 266
Amazonia *see* Brazil: Amazonia
American Geography: Inventory and Prospect (James and Jones), 6n
American History and Its Geographic Conditions (Semple and Jones), 11n
Analemma:
  defined, 73
  illustrated (fig.), 74
  lesson plan, 73–75
Anchorage, Alaska, 56
Antarctic Circle, 52, 53
  drawing, 48, (fig.), 49, (fig.), 50
Antarctica, Kohler Range, 34
Application, need for, 104
Application exercise:
  desk mural used as, 236–237
  sketching used as, 236
Application exercises:
  lesson plan, 104–105
  see also Activities
Application work, 24, 25, 26–27, 204–205
  dioramas, 186
  latitude, 59–63
  layouts, 186
  lesson plan, pictures used in, 137
  maps, outline used in, 104
  maps, physical-political, 117
  pictures, used in lesson plan, 137
  time belts, 70
  travel folder, 122
Application work, in daily lesson, 213–214
Applications, development of, 194
Arctic, 51
  temperature, 51, 52
Arctic Circle, 52, 53
  drawing of, 48–50, (fig.), 49, (fig.), 50
Arctic Ocean, 46
Area:
  countries, selected, 281
  New Zealand (tab.), 148

Area (*Cont.*)
  World, 281
Argentina, 106
  area, 281
  land use data, 280
  population, 281
Arrow statements, 213
  advantages, 31
  arrangement, 18, 19, 20
  summary, 25, 26, 30
  symbol, 18
  test questions, 26, 27, 28
  writing, method, 18, 20
Asbestos:
  producers, 277
  production by countries, 277
Association, and teaching, 209
Association test *see* Tests, association
Aswan High Dam, Egypt, 67
Atacama Desert *see* Chile, Atacama Desert
Atlantic Ocean, 46
Atlas, *Goode's World Atlas*, 102n
Atmosphere, 246
  dispersion of the sun's rays (fig.), 38
  refraction, 60
Attention getters, 212
Attitudes, development, 194
Audio-visual aids, 181–186
  dioramas, 186
  film strip projector, 183
  films, 183–185
  layouts, 186
  models, 186
  opaque projector, 185
  overhead projector, 185
  phonograph, 182
  slide projector, 183
  slides, 182
  tape recorders, 182–183
Audio-Visual Materials (Wittich and Schuller), 186
Auguries of Innocence (Blake), 33
Australia:
  area, 281
  climatic regions (map), 263
  land use data, 280
  population, 281
Autumnal Equinox *see* Equinox, Autumnal
Axis, 41, 43
  day, length, 45
  teaching, 41

Bar graphs *see* Graphs, bar

Barometric pressure, 246
    see also Air pressure
Bauxite:
    producers, 277
    production by countries, 277
Beaufort Scale, wind velocity, 218
Belgium:
    area, 281
    land use data, 280
    miners, 13
    population, 281
Belloc, Hilaire, 37
Bering Standard Time Belt, 68, 69
Berlin, Germany, 70
Bibliography, 283–285
Biogeography, 6
Blake, William, 33, 34
Boston, Mass., population (tab.), 141
Brahmaputra Valley, 190
Brazil, 14, 106, 107
    activities, 231
    aid to, 21
    Amazonia, 44
    Amazonia rain forest, relationships, 18,
        19, 21, 26, 27
    area, 281
    Buenos Aires, 56
    coffee, 22–27
    coffee, harvest, 23
    coffee, relationships, 22–27
    East Central Plateau, 22, 23, 24
    land use, 14
    land use data, 280
    land use graph (fig.), 163
    population, 281
    project, 21
    Sao Paulo, rainfall graph, 24
    Sao Paulo, temperature graph, 24
Bridgeport, Conn., population (tab.),
    141
Broken bar graphs *see* Graphs, broken bar
Buenos Aires, Brazil, 56
Business and geography, 8
    application work, 205
    see also Industry

Cacao:
    producers, 274
    production by countries, 274
Calcutta, India, 197
California:
    canning, 61
    climate, 61

California (*Cont.*)
    day, length, 60, 61
    growing season, 61
    industries, 61
    latitude, effects of, 60–62
    Los Angeles, smog, 62
    manufacturing, 61
    oranges, 56
    San Diego, 60
Calm belts, 247–249
    see also Wind belts
Canada:
    area, 281
    fifth sequence, 55
    Great Bear Lake, 52
    land use data, 280
    population, 281
    wheat, 56
    Yukon Territory, 51
Cane sugar *see* Sugar, cane
Canning:
    Alaska, 61
    California, 61
    Norway, 100
Cape Farewell, Greenland, 67
Capes, defined, 117
Captions, pictures, 135
Cartography, 6
Census, statistics, 86
Central Time Belt, 68, 69
Centrifugal sugar:
    defined, 276n
    see also Sugar
Charts, 170–172
    criteria for, 171
    relationships shown by, 171
    summary, 171
    types, 171
    value, 170–171
Charts, cumulative global, 52–53
Charts, weather, primary sequences (fig.),
    156
Child-centered Curriculum *see* Curricu-
    lums
Chile, 106, 175, 177
    Atacama Desert, 17
    land use data, 280
    latitude, 175, 177
    latitude, effect, 187
China:
    agriculture, 266
    area, 281
    population, 281
    rainfall, 266

Christensen, D. E., 186
Circle graphs *see* Graphs, circle
Circle of illumination, 48, 49
Cities, Norway, 100
Cities, growth, reasons for, 121
City, map symbol, 79–80
Class book, 205, 244
Class tree, 37
Clay model (fig.), 94
Climate, 246–249
 Alaska, 61, 101–102
 bibliography, 284
 California, 61
 defined, 246
 effects, 246
 effects on man's activities, 246–249
 frost free, 17, 18, 22, 23, 26, 27
 influenced by, 246–249
 Norway, 100
 statistics, distribution shown by, 140
 temperate, 52
 types of, 259–260
Climate, Continental, 260, 265
Climate, dry, 259–260
Climate, Marine West-Coast, 260, 265
Climate, Mediterranean, 259–260, 265
Climate, Savanna, 259, 264
Climate, Subarctic, 260
Climate, Subtropical, 260, 265
Climate *see also* Climatic data
Climates of the Continents, The (Kendrew), 265n
Climatic data, selected cities, 264–265
Climatic graphs *see* Graphs, climatic
Climatic regions:
 Africa (map), 263
 Australia (map), 263
 Climatic data for selected cities, 264–265
 Eurasia (map), 263
 North America (map), 262
 South America (map), 262
Climatic zones *see* Latitudes, and Polar regions
Climatology, 6
Cloth and crayon maps *see* Maps, cloth and crayon
Clouds, primary sequences, 219
Coal:
 producers, 277
 production by countries, 277
Cocoa, 22
Coffee, 22–27
 producers, 274
 production by countries, 274

Colombia, coffee, 22
Colors, maps, 111
Columbia Records, 182n
Columbia Records, Panorama Colorslide Travel and Nature Series, 182n
Columbus, 46
Combination graphs *see* Graphs, combination
Commercials, 243
Committee work, 200–201, 233–234, 235
Committees, chairman of, 235
Commodity Yearbook, The, 86, 169
Completion tests, 224–225
Concepts, development in daily lesson, 207–209
Concepts, geographic, India, 193
Concepts, readiness, 28
Concepts, weather, 220
Congo Basin, Africa, 102
Congo region, 44
Connecticut:
 area, (tab.), 141
 Bridgeport, population (tab.), 141
 Hartford, population (tab.), 141
 New Haven, population (tab.), 141
 population, 84, (tab.), 141
 Waterbury, population (tab.), 141
Consumption of goods, 18
Continental climate *see* Climate, continental
Copper:
 producers, 277
 production by countries, 277
Corcovado (Mt.), Brazil, 14
Core Curriculum *see* Curriculums
Coriolis force, 248
Corn, 7
 maps, distribution, 111
 see also Maize
Correlated Curriculum *see* Curriculums
Cottage manufacturing *see* Manufacturing, cottage
Cotton, 7, 18, 31, 32
 graphs, 155
 line graph, 163–164
 producers, 274
 production by countries, 274
 production by state (tab.), 142, (fig.), 159
 production, U.S. total, 142
 value of production by state (tab.), 158, (fig.), 159
"Creative Map-Making of Historical-Geographical Units" (Mapes), 110n

Crop map, 82
Crop production:
  elevation, crops determined by, 272–273
  graphs, 156
  latitude, crops determined by, 272–273
  statistics, distribution shown by, 140
Crops:
  New Zealand (tab.), 149
  production figures, for selected crops, 268–271
  rainfall, crops determined by, 272–273
  requirements, for selected crops, 268–271
  rotation, 250
Crude steel *see* Steel
Cuba, sugar cane, 18
Cultural elements (items), 17
Cultural features, testing, 225
Cultural geography, 6
Cultural items, maps, physical-political, 116
Cumulative global charts *see* Charts, Cumulative global
Curiosity tray, 244
Current events:
  globes used with, 35
  in application work, 205
  see also Geographic education: current events
Curriculum, organization, 44
Curriculums:
  child-centered, 9
  core, 9
  correlated, 9
  experience, 9

DEW Line *see* Defense Early Warning System
Daily Geographic News, The, 12, 237–239
Daily plans *see* Plans: daily
Dairy cattle, breeds, 251
Dairy farming, 250–251
  defined, 251
  location, 250, 251
  products, 250–251
  requirements, 251
Dairy products *see* Milk
Dairying:
  Switzerland, 20
  Wisconsin, 18, 20
Date Line, International *see* International Date Line
Day:
  length, 29, 35, 36, 37, 41, 43, 45, 47,

Day (*Cont.*)
  48, 49, (fig.), 49, (fig.), 50, 53, 54, 60, 61, 75
  length, chart, 41
  length, graphs, 156, (fig.), 157
  solar, 75
Deciduous fruits *see* Fruit farming
Defense Early Warning System (DEW Line), 67
Degree:
  distance, 59
  minutes, 60n
Degrees:
  defined, 59
  distance measured in, 59
Demography, 6
Denver, Colorado, 59
Deserts, 265, 266
  see also Low latitude deserts, Middle latitude deserts
Desk mural, 235, 236–237
  application exercise, desk mural used as, 236–237
  summary, desk mural used as, 236–237
Desmond, Alice Curtis, 25
Development:
  film strips used in, 183
  lesson plan of Africa, 101–103
  pictures used in, 136
  slides used in, 183
Dioramas, 186
  application work, 186
Direction, 28, 35, 36, 37
  primary sequences, 216
  primary sequences, game, 123–124
  testing, sample test, 105
Direction, concept of, first sequence, 123
Direction *see also* Up, Down
Distance:
  latitude, 59, 120
  meridians as measure, 65
Distribution maps *see* Maps, distribution
Dividends, 256
Doldrums, 248
Dots, size of on distribution maps, 103
"Dot" maps, 82–85, 103
  fifth sequence, 82
  see also Maps, distribution
"Down," concept of, 42, 43
Dry climate *see* Climate, dry
Dry farming, 250
  location, 250
  requirements, 250

Dupuy, William Atherton, 271n
Dutch, 12, 13

Ear for Uncle Emil, An (Gaggin), 93
Earth:
  atmosphere, 51
  curvature, 34, 38, 45
  inclination, 45
  insolation, 50, 51
  orbit, 47–49
  photographs, 33, 34
  shape, 45
East Germany *see* Germany, East
Eastern Time Belt, 68, 69
Economic geography, 6
Economics:
  bibliography, 285
  defined, 121
  land use map, hypothetical maps, 115
  maps, hypothetical, land use map, 115
Ecuador:
  cacao, 108
  coffee, 22
Egypt, Aswan High Dam, 67
Eighth sequence, 32
  globe study, 66–75
  lesson plan, maps, hypothetical, 115–123
  maps, hypothetical, lesson plan, 115–123
  see also Junior high school
Elektra Records, 182n
Elevation:
  (figs.), 89
  Africa, 101
  as it affects people, 90–93
  concept, 88–93
  concept, fourth sequence, 88–93, 112
  concept, profiles, 93–97
  crops determined by, 272–273
  effect, 187
  fourth sequence, 88
  lesson plan, 88–93
  maps, relief, 112
  models, 90
  surface, 88–93
  third sequence, 88
Encyclopaedia Britannica, 52n
England, Greenwich, 64, 65
  Herstmonceux Castle, 65
  see also United Kingdom
Environment:
  elements of, 17
  man's activities as related to, 18

Equator, 41, 42, 43
  as Great Circle Route, 56
  distance from, 58
  teaching, 41
Equatorial calms, 121, 248
  crops determined by elevation, latitude, and rainfall, 272–273
Equatorial region, rainfall, 266
Equinox:
  autumnal, 47, 48
  vernal, 47, 48
Escarpment, 23, 27
Eskimos, Alaska, 61
Essay tests, 222–223
  use, 221–222
Ethiopia, coffee, 22
Eurasia:
  climatic regions (map), 263
  rainfall, 266
Evaluation, 221–229
  activities, 235
  teacher, 206
  teacher-pupil, 26
"Evening at the Farm" (Trowbridge), 37
Experience curriculum *see* Curriculums
"Experimenting with Geography Teaching by Television" (Christensen), 186
Explorers, 46
Explorers' Club, 46
Exports:
  graphs, 156
  New Zealand (tab.), 149

Fairbanks, Alaska, 60, 61
Fall equinox *see* Equinox, autumnal
Farming:
  Norway, 100
  see also Dairy farming, Dry farming, General farming, Irrigated farming, Truck farming
Faulkner, William, 13
Fazenda, 14, 22, 24, 25
  model, 231
Field, Rachel, 28, 29
Field trip, 124–127, 127–128
Fifth sequence, 30, 31
  Canada, 55
  foundation work on latitude, 53
  globe study, 55–66
  Great Circle Route, concept, 56–57
  latitude, 58–63, 111
  latitude, teaching, 58–59
  map, outline of the U.S., 100–101

Fifth sequence (*Cont.*)
  maps, distribution, 111
  maps, "dot" maps, 82
  maps, hypothetical, 117
  maps, motivation through, 100–101
  Mexico, 55
  motivation through maps, 100–101
  North America, 55
  picture reading skills, 139
  profiles, 93
  rainfall, amount, 266–267
  rainfall, distribution, 266–267
  rainfall chart, 267
  rainfall map, 266–267
  statistics, 140–143
  winds, westerlies, 117
  work sheets, individual, 234
  see also Intermediate sequences
Film strip projector, 183
Film strips, used in development, 183
Films, 183–185
  use, 184–185
Fine arts *see* Geographic education: fine
  arts
First sequence:
  direction, concept, 123
  field trip, 124–127
  globe, preferred type, 35
  globes, 35, 36
  maps, 123–127
  sun concepts, 36
  see also Primary sequences
Fish:
  catch by countries (tab.), 161
  producers, 274
  production by countries, 274
  United States, 154
  see also Fishing and Fishing, commercial
Fishing:
  Alaska, 61
  California, 61
  methods, 255
  Norway, 100, 160–161
Fishing, commercial, 255
  graphs, broken bar (fig.), 162
  influenced by, 255
  pictograph (fig.), 160
  treaties, 255
Fishing treaties, 255
Flaxseed *see* Linseed
Floats, 242
Florida, 52
Flow charts, 171

Foggara, 252
"For a Sundial" (Belloc), 37
Foreign Agriculture Circular, 86
Format, of unit, 189–190
Fort Yukon, Alaska *see* Alaska: Fort Yukon
Fourth sequence, 18, 29, 30
  elevation, 88
  elevation, concept, 88–93, 112
  globe concepts, 44–47
  globe skills, 53
  globe study, 43–54
  location, 58
  map reading readiness, 123
  picture reading skills, 138–139
  profiles, 93
  rainfall, concept, 266
  statistics, 140
  see also Intermediate sequences
France, 13
  area, 281
  land use data, 280
  population, 281
Frontal systems, 247, 249
Fruit farming:
  climate, 254
  location, 254
  production, 254
Fruit Isle:
  land use map (fig.), 119
  physical-political map (fig.), 118
  see also Hypothetical countries
Fruits *see* Fruit farming

Gaggin, Eva (Roe), 93
Ganges River, 190
General farming, 249–250
  defined, 249
  influenced by, 250
  location, 249–250
"Geo" *see* Geography, defined
Geographic concepts:
  correcting faulty, with hypothetical
    maps, 115
  introducing, with hypothetical maps, 115
Geographic education:
  bibliography, 283–284
  current events, 12, 237
  fine arts, 12, 13
  literature, 13
  music, 13, 231
  skills, geographic, 53, 188, 225
  skills, geographic, testing, 225–229

Geographic education (*Cont.*)
  social studies *see* Social studies
  statistics, 139–154
  thinking, geographic, testing, 228
  tool subject, 10–13
  tools, geographic, 14, 15, 188
  travel enriched by, 9
  value, 1–15
Geographic illiteracy, 6–9
Geographic imagery, testing, 228
Geographic personality:
  defined, 190
  of a region, 189–190
Geographic readiness, primary sequences, 28, 215–220
Geographic relationships *see* Relationships, geographic
Geographic shorthand, arrow statement, 31
Geographic skills *see* Geographic education: skills, geographic
Geographic tools *see* Geographic education: tools, geographic
Geographic vocabulary, 131
"Geographical Filmstrip—A Neglected Teaching Aid in Higher Education" (Grilzner), 186
Geography:
  branches, 6
  defined, 5
  distribution, story of, 76
  relationship centered, 5
Geography of Commodity Production (Highsmith, Jr. and Jensen), 86, 271n
Geography readiness, primary sequences, 126
Geography textbooks *see* Textbooks, geography
Germany, East
  area, 281
  population, 281
Germany, West
  area, 281
  land use data, 280
  population, 281
Gershwin, George, 13
Ghana, Africa, 102
Glacier, 92
Globe study:
  fifth sequence, 55–66
  Junior high school sequence, 66–75
  phonograph records used for motivation, 182
  primary sequences, 216

Globe study (*Cont.*)
  sixth sequence, 55–66
  subjects of interest, 66–67
Globes, 33–75
  activities, 45–46
  analemma, 73–75
  bibliography, 284
  concepts, 35–75
  concepts, fourth sequence, 44–47
  concepts, major, 43
  concepts, primary sequences, 35–53
  concepts, primary sequences, teaching suggestions, 41–43
  cradle, 35
  distance represented, 55
  Great Circle Route concept shown on, 56–57
  interpretation, need of correct, 34
  model of earth, 41–43
  physical-political, 67
  project, 35, 44, 67
  rotation, 39
  type, 35, 44, 47
  type, beginner's, 44
  type, slated, 44
Goode's World Atlas, 102n
Grapes, 56
  use, 255
  see also Viniculture
Grapevines *see* Viniculture
Graphs, 154–169
  cotton, 155
  crop production, 156
  criteria, 169
  day, length (fig.), 157
  exports, 156
  imports, 156
  intermediate sequences, 156–157
  interpretation of, 157
  natural resources, 156
  need for, 154–155
  population, 156
  primary sequences, 155–156
  products, 156
  sequential development, 155–157
  third sequence, 156–157
  types, 156–169
  value, 155
  weather calendar, monthly, 155–156
Graphs, bar, 162–163
  exports, 231
  illustrated (fig.), 163
  land use, 163

Graphs, bar (*Cont.*)
  production, 231
  sixth sequence, 163
Graphs, broken bar, 160–162
  fishing, commercial (fig.), 162
Graphs, circle, 164
Graphs, climatic, 23, 164–169
  climatic conditions, 231
  Mystery Cities (fig.), 167
  Mystery Country (fig.), 152
  Peru, 166–169
  Pittsburgh (fig.), 165
  reading of, sample lesson, 166–169
  see also Graphs, combination
Graphs, combination, 166
  illustrated (fig.), 166
Graphs, land use:
  Brazil (fig.), 163
  Japan (fig.), 141
Graphs, line, 163–164
  cotton, 163–164
Graphs, population, 156
Graphs, product, 156
Graphs, rainfall, 165
  Sao Paulo, Brazil, 24
  sixth sequence, 267
  see also Graphs, combination
Graphs, temperature, 23, 164–165
  Sao Paulo, Brazil, 24
  sixth sequence, 267
  weather calendar, monthly, 155–156
  see also Graphs, combination
"Graphy" *see* Geography: defined
Great Britain *see* United Kingdom
Great Circle Route (fig.), 57
  concept, 56–57
  concept, shown on globe, 56–57
  questions covering, 57
  teaching, 56–57
  travel, 56–57
Great Lakes, 99–100
Greenland, Cape Farewell, 67
Greenwich, England, 64, 65
Grieg, Edward, 13
Grilzner, C. F., 186
Growing conditions, 268–271
  see also Growing season
Growing season, 246
  Alaska, 61
  California, 61
  defined, 23
  maps, 82
  see also Growing conditions

Gruening, Ernest, 61n
Guatemala, coffee, 22

Hamilton, Anna E., 37
Hardy fruits *see* Fruit farming
Hark! The Years, 182n
Harte, Bret, 13
Hartford, Conn., population (tab.), 141
Hawaii, latitude effects, 62
Hawaiian Islands, 17
Hay, 251
Heidi (Spyri), 13, 93
Hemisphere, 41, 42, 43
  teaching meaning, 41, 42
Henry, Marguerite, 13
Herstmonceux Castle, 65
High latitudes, defined, 52
Highsmith, Jr., Richard M., 86, 271n
Himalaya Mountains, 190
History *see* Social studies
Home movies, 183–184
Homes *see* Housing
Horse latitudes, 118, 121, 248, 249
  crops determined by elevation, latitude,
    and rainfall, 273
Housing:
  Alaska, 61
  rain forest, 30
  Nigeria, 7
Huckleberry Finn, 13
Human geography, 6
Hydrology, 6
Hypothetical countries:
  description, 116
  travel folders, 116, 122
  see also Maps, hypothetical
Hypothetical map test (fig.), 108
Hypothetical maps *see* Maps, hypothetical

Illiteracy, geographic *see* Geographic
    illiteracy
Imagination, and learning, 209–210
Imports:
  graphs, 156
  New Zealand (tab.), 149–150
India:
  agriculture, 191, 192, 193
  area, 190, 202, 281
  Brahmaputra Valley, 190
  Calcutta, 197
  climate, 191, 192, 203–204
  climate relationships, 192
  crafts, 191

India (*Cont.*)
  development, unit plan, 194–205
  division of, 197–198, 202
  food, 198, 199
  Ganges plain, relationships, 193
  Ganges River and Valley, 190, 193
  geographic concepts, 193
  Himalaya Mountains, 190
  Indus Valley, 190
  land use data, 280
  location, 192, 197, 202
  location relationships, 192
  manufacturing, 191, 192–193
  manufacturing relationships, 192
  mineral resources, 191, 193
  monsoons, 191, 192, 193, 203–204
  motivation for unit plan, 197–199
  objectives for unit plan, 190–194
  population, 190, 191, 198, 202, 203, 281
  population compared with U.S. (fig.), 198
  population relationships, 193, 198
  rainfall, 191
  religion, 198
  topography, 190–191, 192, 203
  wage, average, 199
Indian Ocean, 46
Indians, Alaska, 61
Individual differences, 212, 214
  activities, 233
Indonesia, drainage, 266
Indus Valley, 190
Industries:
  Alaska, 61
  California, 61
  New Zealand (tab.), 150
  Norway, 100
Industry, 256–257
Industry, and geography, 8
"Influence" (Hamilton), 37
Insolation, 38, 50, 51, 246
  defined, 246
Intermediate sequences:
  graphs, 156–157
  maps, hypothetical, 115
  maps, relief, 112–113
  pictographs, 157–160
  rainfall, concept, 266–267
International Date Line:
  illustrated (fig.), 71, (fig.), 72
  lesson plan, 70–73
Ireland *see* United Kingdom

Iron ore, 17
  producers, 277
  production by countries, 277
  United States, 154
Irrigated farming, 252–254
  climate, 253
  cost, 254
  drainage, 253–254
  location, 252, 253
  topography, 253–254
  see also Irrigation
Irrigation:
  drainage, 253–254
  evaporation, 253
  means of, 252–253
  see also Irrigated farming
Italy, 7
  area, 7, 281
  distribution of land, 7
  income, average, 7
  land use data, 280
  population, 7, 281
  rainfall, 7
  topography, 7
Ives, Ronald L., 64n

James, Linnie B., 236n, 237n
James, Preston E., 6n
Japan, 145–147
  agriculture, 147
  area, 281
  crops (tab.), 147
  exports (tab.), 145
  imports (tab.), 145
  land use data, 280
  land use graph (fig.), 146
  phonograph record, 182
  population, 281
Java, 130–131
Jensen, J. Granville, 86, 271n
Jones, Clarence Fielden, 6n, 11n
Jorge's Journey, 25
Junior high school sequences:
  analemma, 73–75
  globe study, 66–75
  globe study, subjects of interest, 66–67
  graphs, climatic, reading of, sample lesson, 166–169
  International Date Line, 70–73
  maps, hypothetical, 115
  newspaper, pupil, 237–239
  statistics, 143–154
  time belts, 68–70

Jura Mountains, Switzerland, 90, 92
Jute, 196–197

Kanat, 252
Kendrew, W. G., 265n
Kenya, coffee, 22
Key words, testing, 222
Kohler Range, Antarctica, 34
Kontiki, 46

Land use:
  data for selected countries, 280
  New Zealand (tab.), 148
  Norway, 100
Land use graphs *see* Graphs, land use
Land use maps *see* Maps, land use
Landscape imagery:
  sample test, South America, 106–108
  testing, 105, 106–108
Latin America, motivating questions, 195
Latitude:
  application work, 59–63
  Chile, 175, 177
  climate affected by, 247
  concept, 58–63
  concept, application, 59–63
  concept, exercise, 63
  crops determined by, 272–273
  degrees, 59
  distance, 59, 120
  effects, 60–62, 187
  effects on Alaska, 60–62
  effects on California, 60–62
  fifth sequence, 111
  how to teach, 58–59
  living, problems, 61
  sixth sequence, 111
  teaching in fifth sequence, 58–59
  testing use of, 226
  textbook used to teach, 174–175
Latitude stick, 64n
Latitudes, high, 51, 52
Latitudes, horse *see* Horse latitudes
Latitudes, low, 51, 52
Latitudes, middle, 52
Latitudes *see also* High latitudes, Low
  latitudes, and Middle latitudes
Layouts, 186, 239–242
  application work, 186, 205
  illustration of construction (fig.), 240,
    (fig.), 241, (fig.), 242
  Switzerland, elevation (fig.), 242

Lead:
  producers, 278
  production by countries, 278
Lesson plan:
  activities *see* Activities
  Africa, development of unit on, 101–
    103
  Africa, summary, 103
  analemma, 73–75
  application, need for, 104
  application exercises, 104–105
  application exercise, desk mural used as,
    236–237
  application exercise, sketching used as,
    236
  application exercises *see also* Activities
  application work, pictures used in, 137
  association test, 104–105
  Brazil, 22–28
  development, maps used in, 101–103
  development, statistics used in, 146–147
  development of unit, pictures used in,
    136
  development of unit on Africa, 101–103
  eighth sequence, maps, hypothetical,
    115–123
  elevation, 88–93
  elevation, as it affects people, 90–93
  International Date Line, 70–73
  latitude, concept, 58–59
  latitude, effect, 60–63
  longitude, concept, 63–66
  maps, hypothetical, 115–123
  maps, motivation for unit on, 100–101
  maps used in, 98–105
  maps used in development, 101–103
  maps used in summary, 103–104
  motivation, maps used, 98–101
  motivation, pictures used, 135–136
  "Mystery Country," 148–154
  New Zealand, 148–154
  Norway, motivation for, 100
  pictures, application work, 137
  pictures, development of unit, 136
  pictures, motivation helped by, 135–136
  pictures, used in testing, 137–138
  profile, 94–97
  relationships, Brazil, 22
  statistics used, 144–148
  statistics used in development, 146–147
  statistics used in motivation, sample, 145
  statistics used in testing, 148
  summary, 193–104

Lesson plan (*Cont.*)
  summary, desk mural used as, 236–237
  summary, maps used, 103–104
  summary, United States, 103–104
  testing, pictures used, 137–138
  testing, sketching used as, 236
  testing, statistics used, 148
  testing *see also* Testing
  time belts, 68–70
  United States, summary, 103–104
  water resources, motivation, 99
Levels, 3
Lindbergh, Charles, 46
Line graphs *see* Graphs, line
Linseed:
  producers, 275
  production by countries, 275
Literature *see* Geographic education:
    literature
Location, 10, 11
  Africa, 102
  climate affected by, 55, 247
  day, length, 55
  seasonal change, 55
  testing ability to use longitude and
    latitude, 226
Location, as shown on physical-political
    map, 77
Location skills, testing, 105
London, England, 64, 65
  longitude, 65
Longitude:
  concept, 63–66
  need for, 64
  sixth sequence, 111
  testing, 226
Los Angeles, California, smog, 62
Low latitude deserts, 259
Low latitude steppes, 259
Low latitudes:
  defined, 52
  vegetation affected by elevation, 272
Low pressure, 248
Lumbering:
  Alaska, 61
  California, 61

Maine:
  area (tab.), 141
  population, 84, (tab.), 141
Maize:
  growing season, 270
  producers, 270

Maize (*Cont.*)
  production by countries, 270
  rainfall required, 270
Major understanding, 189
  defined, 190
  India, 190–191
  maps, 111
  writing, 188, 190
Manganese, 197
  producers, 278
  production by countries, 278
Manry, Robert, 46
Manufacturing, 256–257
  factors affecting, 256–257
Manufacturing, cottage, 257
  factors affecting, 257
  products, 257
Map game, primary sequences (fig.), 127
Map interpretation:
  prerequisite, 123
  skills, 100–101
  testing, 105
  used as a test, 227
Map making:
  criteria, 111–112
  testing, 226
  waste of time, 111
Map reading:
  ability, 111
  interpretation, 111
  prerequisite, 123
  readiness, 123
  skills, testing, 105–106
  skills, testing, construction of tests,
    105–109
  skills, testing with hypothetical map,
    108–109
  testing, 227
Map skills:
  enlarging maps, 109–110
  recording, 109
Map stencil, 115
Map symbols, second sequence, 128
Map test (fig.), 104, (fig.), 107
  hypothetical (fig.), 108
Mapes, Carl H., 110n
Maps, 76–128
  Africa, 101–103
  appearance of, 112
  bibliography, 284
  colors, 111
  crop, 82
  defects, 76

Maps (*Cont.*)
 development of lesson plan, 101–103
 distortion, 34
 distribution *see* Maps, distribution
 enlarging, 109–110, (fig.), 110
 errors, 33, 34
 fifth sequence, 82
 fifth sequence, motivation through,
  100–101
 first sequence, 123–127
 growing season, 82
 imports, source of, 231
 interpretation, 77–97
 interpretation and reading, objectives, 78
 interpretation, need for correct, 34
 key, 85
 kinds of, 83–87
 land use *see* Maps, land use
 lesson plan, development, 101–103
 lesson plan, motivation, 100–101
 lesson plan, summary, 103–104
 lesson plans, use in, 98–105
 mineral resources, 102–103
 motivation, fifth sequence, 100–101
 motivation, maps used in, 98–101
 mounting, 104
 need for, 76
 ornamental, 114
 pictorial, 87
 primary sequences, 125, 216
 primary sequences, relationships,
  124–128
 printing, 112
 products, special, 102–103
 pupil-made, creative, 110
 pupil-made, types, 112–114
 reading, 77–97
 reading and interpretation, objectives,
  78
 scale of miles, distance determined, 85
 scale of miles, teaching, 80–82
 second sequence, 127–128
 special products, 102–103
 summary of lesson plan, 103–104
 symbols, 78–82
 symbols, aids to comprehension, 78
 symbols, captions, 78–79
 symbols, city represented by, 79–80
 symbols, nonpictorial, 79
 symbols, pictures used in teaching
  meaning, 131
 symbols, semipictorial, 79
 symbols, teaching of, 79–82

Maps (*Cont.*)
 teacher-made, 115
 teaching of social studies, 11
 tempera paint, 114
 testing, maps used in, 105–109
 topography shown by, 231
 transportation facilities, 102–103
 types, 82
 use, 98–110
Maps, cloth and crayon, 114
Maps, distribution, 76–77, 82–85, (fig.),
  83, (fig.), 84
 construction, 114
 corn, 111
 criteria, 85
 crops, 82, 231
 "dot," 82–85, 103
 fifth sequence, 111
 growing season, 82
 land use, 82
 milk, farm value (fig.), 227
 rainfall, 82
Maps, hypothetical:
 description, 116, 122
 development, 115–123
 economics, land use map, 115
 eighth sequence, lesson plan, 115–123
 islands, names for, 116
 land use, economics, 115
 land use map, 115, (fig.), 119, 120–
  122
 lesson plan, eighth sequence, 115–123
 physical-political maps, 115–120, 122
 physical-political maps, cultural items,
  116
 physical-political maps, natural items,
  116
 purpose, 115
 sequence, any, 115
 teaching of, need for, 115
 testing map reading skills, 108–109
Maps, land use, 82
 hypothetical, 115, (fig.), 119, 120–122
Maps, outline, 85–86, 103
 used in application, 104
Maps, physical-political:
 colors, 90, 92, 95, 111
 distances shown on, 77
 hypothetical (fig.), 118
 location shown on, 77
 see also Maps, hypothetical: physical-
  political

Maps, population, 23, 83–85
  interpretation, 103–104
Maps, rainfall, 82
  fifth sequence, 266–267
  seasonal, sixth sequence, 267
Maps, relief, 112–114
  construction, 112–114
  intermediate sequences, 112–113
  materials, 113–114
Maps, road, primary sequence, 87
Maps, sketch, 86–87
Marine West-Coast climate *see* Climate,
  Marine West-Coast
Massachusetts:
  area (tab.), 141
  Boston, population (tab.), 141
  New Bedford, population (tab.), 141
  population, 84, (tab.), 141
  Worcester, population (tab.), 141
Matching tests, 224
Mediterranean Climate *see* Climate,
  Mediterranean
Memorization, 20
  primary sequences, 216
Menu making, 243
Meridian:
  International Date Line, 70–73
  measure of distance, 65
  Prime, *see* Prime Meridian
Meridians, 34
  as Great Circle Routes, 56
Mexico:
  area, 281
  coffee, 22
  fifth sequence, 55
  land use data, 280
  population, 281
Mica, 197
Middle latitude deserts, 259
Middle latitude steppes, 259
Middle latitudes:
  defined, 52
  vegetation affected by elevation, 272
Midnight sun *see* Sun, midnight
Milk:
  farm value, map, distribution (fig.), 227
  map, distribution (fig.), 227
  producers, 275
  production by countries, 275
Mineral deposits, 18
Mineral resources, maps, 102–103
Minerals, essential, producers, 277–279
Minerals, statistics, distribution shown by,
  140

Minutes, degree, 60n
Mississippi River, 13
Misty, 13
Mixed farming *see* General farming
Models, 186
  clay (fig.), 94
  elevation, 90
  fazenda, 231
  see also Layouts
Molybdenum:
  producers, 278
  production by countries, 278
Monsoons *see* India: monsoons
Morrisville, 17
Moscow, U.S.S.R., 70
Motion, relative, 39
Motivation:
  audio-visual aids *see* Audio-visual Aids
  daily lesson plans, 207
  fifth sequence, maps as motivation, 100–
    101
  globe study, recordings used in, 182
  India, 197–199
  lesson plan, maps, 100–101
  lesson plan, Norway, 100
  lesson plan, water resources, 99
  maps, fifth sequence, 100–101
  maps used in, 98–101
  phonograph records used for, 182
  pictures used in, 135–136
Motivation of unit plans, 194–205
Mount Siple, Antarctica, 34
Mountain Time Belt, 68, 69
Mounting, maps, 104
Movies *see* Films
Mulhauser, John, 262, 263
Multiple-choice tests, 224
Mural *see* Desk mural
Music *see* Geographic education: music
"My Shadow" (Stevenson), 37
Mystery cities, graphs, climatic (fig.), 167
"Mystery Country":
  graph, climatic (fig.), 152
  lesson plan, 148–154
  profile (fig.), 168

National Aeronautics and Space Admin-
  istration, satellite, 33, 34
National Council of Geography Teachers,
  194
National Geographic Magazine, 136
Natural elements (items), 17
Natural features, testing of, 225

Natural items, maps, physical-political, 116
Natural resources:
  graphs, 156
  Norway, 100
"Navigating with the Kamal" (Ives), 64n
Netherlands, 12, 13
  land use data, 280
New Bedford, Mass., population (tab.), 141
New Hampshire:
  area (tab.), 141
  population, 84, (tab.), 141
New Haven, Conn., population (tab.), 141
New Orleans, La., 59
New Zealand:
  area (tab.), 148
  crops (tab.), 149
  exports (tab.), 149
  imports (tab.), 149–150
  industries (tab.), 150
  land use (tab.), 148
  lesson plan, 148–154
  population (tab.), 148
  products (tab.), 150
Newspaper, pupil, 12, 237–239
Nickel:
  producers, 278
  production by countries, 278
Nigeria:
  Africa, 102
  area, 281
  climate, 7
  corn, 7
  cotton, 7
  Hausa village, 7
  housing, 7
  land use data, 280
  peanuts, 7
  population, 281
Nimbus I, 34
1964 *Statistical Yearbook*, 143, 276n, 279n
Ninth sequence *see* Junior high school sequence
North America:
  climatic regions (map), 262
  fifth sequence, studies in, 55
  location, 55
  rainfall, amount and distribution of, 267
North Atlantic Drift, 77
North Atlantic Drift, Norway, 100

North Pole, 41, 42, 43, 44, 45
Norway, 56
  canning, 100
  cities, 100
  climate, 44, 100
  farming, 100
  features shown on map, 77, 78
  fishing, 100, 160–161
  industries, 100
  interpretation of map features, 77–78
  land use, 100
  land use data, 280
  lesson plan, motivation for, 100
  motivation for study of, 100
  natural resources, 100
  North Atlantic Drift, 100
  population, 100
  rainfall, 100
  sketching, 236
  topography, 100

Oats, 143–144
  growing season, 269
  producers, 269
  production by countries (tab.), 143, 269
  rainfall required, 269
  total world production, 143
Objective tests, 223–225
  use, 222
Oceanography, 6
Oil *see* Petroleum
Oil palm:
  producers, 275
  production by countries, 275
One-step relationships *see* Relationships: one-step
Opaque projector, 185
Open book tests, 228–229
Oranges, California, 56
Orbit of the earth *see* Earth: orbit of
Orbits:
  measuring of, 67
  space vehicles, 66, 67
Orchards *see* Fruit farming
Oregon Trail, 11
Organization of American States (OAS), 14
Ornamental Maps *see* Maps, ornamental
Our Plant Friends and Foes (Dupuy), 271n
Outline maps *see* Maps, outline
Over-all plans *see* Plans: over-all

Overhead projector, 185
   overlays, 185
   transparencies, 185
"Overhead Projector—Use in Televising
   Geography," 186
Overlays, overhead projector, 185

Pacific Time Belt, 68, 69
Pakistan:
   area, 281
   population, 281
Panama Canal, 67
Paraguay, 107
Parallels, 35
   latitude, 58–59
Peanuts, 7
"Pegging-down" points, 96
Peninsula, defined, 117
Pepper, 197
Permafrost, 61
Perry, Commander Robert E., 182
Peru, 108
   climatic graph, 166–169
   topography, 166–169
Petroleum:
   producers, 278
   production by countries, 278
Philadelphia, Pa., 18
Phonograph, 182
   use, 182
Phonograph records, motivation, used for,
   182
Physical features, testing, 106
Physical geography, 6
Physical-political maps *see* Maps,
   physical-political
Pictographs, 157–160
   fishing, commercial (fig.), 160
   intermediate sequences, 157–160
   sample (fig.), 159
   symbols, 157–159
Pictorial maps, 87
Picture reading, 134
Picture reading skills:
   fifth sequence, 139
   fourth sequence, 138–139
   sequential development of, 138–139
   seventh sequence, 139
   sixth sequence, 139
Pictures, 129–139
   captions, 135
   criteria in selection, 132–133
   development of lesson plan, 136

Pictures (*Cont.*)
   lesson plan, development, 136
   lesson plan, motivation, 135–136
   lesson plan, used in testing, 137–138
   reading, 134–138
   selection, 132–138
   testing, sample test, 137–138
   testing by use of pictures, 137–138
   use, 129–139
   value, 129–132
"Pie" graphs *see* Graphs: circle
Pineapples, 17
Pittsburgh, Pa., 58, 59
   graphs, climatic (fig.), 165
   rainfall, measuring, illustration, 267
Planetary winds, arrangement (fig.), 247
Planning:
   teacher and pupil, 195–196
   teacher and pupil, activities, 233
Planning work, 187–214
   see also Plans
Plans:
   daily, 187, 206–214
      activities, 213
      concepts, 207–209
      improvement, 206–214
      motivation, 207
      relationships, 207–208
      summarizing, 213
   over-all, 187
   unit, 187–206
      appreciation, development, 194
      attitudes, development, 194
      background necessary, 189
      commercially prepared, 188
      development, 194–205
      development, activities, 201,
         202–204
      development, application, 204–205
      development, desired outcomes,
         201–204
      development, evaluation, 201,
         202–204
      development, summary, 204
      equipment, 189
      evaluation, 205–206
      format for geography, 189–190
      geography, defined, 188
      guidelines, 187
      India, development, 194–205
      India, motivation, 197–199
      India, objectives, 190–194
      motivation, 194–205

Plans (*Cont.*)
motivation, questions used for, 195
objectives, major, 191
objectives, specific, 191
objectives for geography, 190–194
objectives, statement of, 190
organization, 189
problem solving, 194, 199–204
purpose, 188
relationships, 192–193
summary, 204
teacher-pupil planning, 195–196
topic, 195
value, 188
vocabulary, 193–194
writing of, 188–206
writing of, preparation for, 188
Plant growth, temperature, 23
Plateau, defined, 89
Point Barrows, Alaska, 60
Pointed People, 28
Polar easterlies, 249
Polar regions, 52
Polar winds, 249
Political geography, 6
Population:
Connecticut, 84
Maine, 84
Massachusetts, 84
New Hampshire, 84
New Zealand (tab.), 148
Norway, 100
Rhode Island, 84
selected countries, 281
statistics, distribution shown by, 140
Vermont, 84
World, 281
Population figures, 84n
Population graphs *see* Graphs, population
Population map interpretations, U.S., 103–104
Population maps *see* Maps: population
Posters, 170–172
application work, 205
criteria, 172
value, 172
Potato Eaters, The, 13
Potatoes:
growing season, 269
producers, 269
production by countries, 269
rainfall required for, 269
Poultry houses, United States, 56

Precipitation, 246
Primary sequences:
Atlas, *Goode's World Atlas*, 102n
Beaufort scale, wind velocity, 218
charts, weather (fig.), 156
clouds, 219
direction, 216
direction, game, 123–124
geography readiness, 126, 215–220
globes, 216
globes, concepts, 35–53
globes, concepts, teaching suggestions, 41–43
globes, type, cradle, 35
globes, type, project, 35
graphs, 155–156
map game (fig.), 127
map reading readiness, 123
maps, 125, 216
maps, hypothetical, 115
maps, relationships, 124–128
maps, road, 87
memorization, 216
rain, appreciation, 219
rainfall concept, 219, 220
rainy day record, 219
seasonal change, 216, 220
sun position, 216
temperature, 218
thermometer, 218
weather, 216–220
weather calendar, 216–217
weather clock, 217
weather clothes line, 219–220
weather, concepts, 220
weather, effects, 217–218, 220
wind, effects, 218–219, 220
wind velocity, 218, 220
see also First sequence, Second sequence, Third sequence
Prime Meridian, 64, 65, 66
Printing, on maps, 112
Problem solving, 194, 200
unit on India, 199–204
Product graphs *see* Graphs: product
Production:
bibliography, 285
producers of essential products, 274–276
Production of goods, 18
Production Yearbook 1964, 161, 280n
Products:
maps of special products, 102–103

Products (*Cont.*)
New Zealand (tab.), 150
producers of essential products,
274–276
Profiles (fig.), 94, (fig.), 95
concept, 93–97
drawing, "pegging-down" points, 96
drawing, steps, 96
elevation, concept, 93–97
fifth sequence, 93
fourth sequence, 93
land use, 231
lesson plan, 94–97
Mystery Country (fig.), 168
"Pegging-down" points, 96
sixth sequence, 93
Providence, R.I., population (tab.), 141
Pupil-made maps *see* Maps: pupil-made
Pupils' work, acceptance of, 214

Questioning, as teaching method, 210–211
Questions, "trick," 34

Radiation, 246
Radio commercials, 243
Rain, 248
Rain, appreciation, primary sequences,
219
Rain forest, 18, 21, 30, 91
rainfall, 266
tropical, 259, 264
vegetation, 248
see also Brazil: Amazonia rain forest,
relationships
Rainfall, 17, 18, 21, 22, 23, 26, 27
Africa, 102
Alaska, 61
amount influenced by topography, 267
amount in various areas, 267
crops determined by, 272–273
distribution influenced by topography,
267
distribution, *Cont.*, 267
effects, agricultural, 246
equatorial region, 266
factors determining, 99
measuring, 266–267
measuring, illustrated, 267
Norway, 100
Rainfall, amount, fifth sequence, 266–267
Rainfall, concept:
fourth sequence, 266
intermediate sequences, 266–267
primary sequences, 219, 220

Rainfall, distribution, fifth sequence, 266,
267
Rainfall, monthly, climatic data for
selected cities, 264–265
Rainfall, chart, 267
Rainfall graphs *see* Graphs, rainfall
see also Graphs, climatic
Rainfall maps *see* Maps, rainfall
Rainy day record, primary sequences, 219
Readers' Guide to Periodical Literature,
189
Readiness *see* Geographic readiness
Recipe, weather clothes line, 220
Records, *see* Phonograph records
Region book, 244
Regional geography, 6
Relationships:
charts, shown by, 171
column form, 18, 19
cultural to cultural, 18
cultural to natural, 18, 27, 31, 32
development, 28
development in daily lesson, 207–208
fifth sequence, 30–31
fourth sequence, 29, 30
eighth sequence, 32
geographic, 16–32
India, 192, 193
matching exercise, 26–27
natural to natural, 17
one-step, 19, 29, 31, 32
planning, 22
primary sequences, 28
sentence form, 18
seventh sequence, 32
sixth sequence, 30, 31, 32
summarizing with, 30
teaching, reason for, 19–21
three-step, 19, 32
two-step, 19, 31, 32
use, 21
Relationships, and initiative, reasoning,
understanding, 20
Relationships, as summary, 204, 213
Relief maps *see* Maps, relief
Reports, 200–201
Republic of the Congo, Africa, climate,
102
Revolution, 46, 47
orbiting of space vehicles, 66, 67
teaching, 47–49
Revolution, and seasonal change, 45
Rhode Island:
area (tab.), 141

Rhode Island (*Cont.*)
  population, 84, (tab.), 141
  Providence, population (tab.), 141
Rice:
  growing season, 270
  producers, 270
  production by countries, 270
  rainfall required, 270
  relationships, 130–131
Rio de Janeiro, Brazil, 14
Rivers, Africa, 102
Road maps *see* Maps, road
Rotation, 39, (fig.), 40, 40, 41, 43, 46,
    67, 69, 248–249
  chart, 39, 40
  orbiting of space vehicles, 66, 67
  teaching, 39, 40
Rotation of crops, 250
Royal Greenwich Observatory, 65
Rubber, natural:
  producers, 275
  production by countries, 275
Russia:
  slides and phonograph records, 182
  see also Union of Soviet Socialist
    Republics
Ruwenzori Mountains, Africa, 101
Rye:
  growing season, 269
  producers, 269
  production by countries, 269
  rainfall required, 269

St. Lawrence Seaway, 99–100
Salisbury, Harrison, 182
San Diego, Calif., 60
Sand pan, 243
Sand table, 78, 89, 243
Sao Paulo, Brazil, 23, 24
  rainfall graph, 24
  temperature graph, 24
Satellite:
  Nimbus I, 33, 34
  Vanguard, 45
Savanna climate *see* Climate, Savanna
Scale of miles:
  distance determined, 85
  teaching, 80–82
  testing, 106, 226
Schuller, Charles F., 186
Scotland *see* United Kingdom
Seasonal change, 28, 29, 35, 36, 37, 46,
    48, 53
  primary sequences, 216, 220

Seasonal change (*Cont.*)
  revolution and inclination of earth as
    cause, 45
Season:
  length, 35
  sun position, 36, 37
  time, 35
Second sequence:
  cardinal directions, 37
  day, length, 36, 37
  field trip, 127–128
  map symbols, 128
  maps, 127–128
  seasonal change, 36, 37
  sun position, 36, 37
  see also Primary sequences
Semple, Ellen Churchill, 11n
Sequence, 3 *see also* First sequence,
    Primary sequence, etc.
Serra do Mar Mountains, 23
Seventh sequence, 32
  combination graph, 166
  globe study, 66–75
  picture reading skills, 139
  wind belts, 117
  see also Junior high school sequence
Shadow boxes, 243
Shadow stick, 37
Shadows, 37, 38
Shadows, children's, 37
Shareholders, 256
Sibelius, Jan, 13
Siberia, Yakutsk, 51
Sitka, Alaska, 61
Sixth sequence, 30, 31, 32
  globe study, 55–66
  graphs, bar, land use, 163
  graphs, rainfall, 267
  graphs, temperature, 267
  Great Circle Route, concept of, 56–57
  land use, bar graphs, 163
  latitude, 111
  longitude, 63–66, 111
  maps, enlarging, 109
  maps, hypothetical, 117
  maps, road, 87
  newspaper, pupil, 237–239
  picture reading skills, 139
  profile, 93–97
  rainfall maps, seasonal, 267
  statistics, 143
  see also Intermediate sequences
Sketch maps, 86–87
Sketches, 25, 26, 27

Sketching, 235–236
  application exercise, 236
  test, sketching used as, 236
Skills, geographic *see* Geographic
    education: skills, geographic
Skyscrapers, 28
Skyscrapers, 29
Slide projector, 183
Slides, 182
  used in development, 183
Smith, J. Russell, quotation, 194
Smog, 62
Social geography, 6
Social studies, 10, 11
  bibliography, 284
Soils, geography of, 6
Solar day, 75
Solar radiation, 51
Solstice:
  summer, 47, 48
  winter, 47, 48
South America:
  climatic regions (map), 262
  landscape imagery, sample test,
    106–108
  rain forest, 18
  see also country
South American Handbook, The, 140,
    169
South Pole, 41, 42, 43, 44, 45
Soy beans:
  producers, 275
  production by countries, 275
Space vehicle, orbiting, 66, 67
Spain, 56
Spyri, Johanna, 93
Statesman's Year-book, The, 86, 140,
    145, 147, 150, 169, 271n, 274n
*Statistical Abstract of the United States,
    The*, 86, 103, 140, 141, 142, 158, 169
Statistical table, use of, example,
    142–143
Statistical Yearbook, 86
*Statistical Yearbook of the United
    Nations, The*, 169
Statistics, 86, 139–154
  almanacs, 103
  bibliography, 285
  census, 86
  criteria for use, 144
  distribution shown by, climate, 140
  distribution shown by, crop production,
    140

Statistics (*Cont.*)
  distribution shown by, minerals, 140
  distribution shown by, population, 140
  distribution shown by, trade movement,
    140
  fifth sequence, 140–143
  fourth sequence, 140
  interpretation, 140–154
  Junior high school sequences, 143–154
  lesson plan, development, 146–147
  lesson plan, motivation, 144–146
  lesson plan, motivation, sample, 145
  lesson plan, use in, 144–148
  "Mystery Country," 148–154
  reading, 140–154
  sixth sequence, 143
  teaching with, 139–154
  testing with, 148, 226
  value, 139–140
Steel:
  producers, 277
  production by countries, 277
  United States, 154
Steel mills, 17
Steppes, 264
  see also Low latitude steppes
Steppes *see* Middle latitude steppes
Stevenson, Robert Louis, 37
Stockholders, 256
*Story of the United States Through
    Maps, The*, 103
Straw, 251
Student newspaper, *see* Newspaper,
    student
Subarctic climate—forested lands *see*
    Climate, subarctic
Subtropical climate *see* Climate,
    subtropical
Sugar, 197
  producers, 276
  production by countries, 276
Sugar, cane:
  growing season, 271
  producers, 271
  production by countries, 271
  rainfall required, 271
Sugar cane, Cuba, 18
Summarizing, with relationships, 30
Summary:
  charts used in, 171
  desk mural used as, 236–237
  lesson plan, maps used in, 103–104
  maps used in, 103–104

Summer solstice *see* Solstice, summer
Sun:
  behavior, 56
  position, 28, 29, 35, 46, 53
  position, concept, 36, 37, 38, 39
  position, primary sequences, 216
  rays, dispersion by the atmosphere
    (fig.), 38
  rays, slanting, 51
  rays, vertical, 51
Sun, midnight, 49, (fig.), 49, 50, (fig.),
  50
Sundial *see* Analemma
Sunlight, 246
  amount, 246
Sunlines, 50, 52
Sunrise *see* Sun chart
Sunset *see* Sun chart
Surface, 88
Swiss Plateau, Switzerland, 90, 92
Switzerland:
  Alps, 90, 92
  border countries, 92
  dairying, 20
  elevation, 88, 90–93
  elevation, effect, 187
  Jura Mountains, 90, 92
  land use data, 280
  layouts, 239–240, (fig.), 242
  profile (fig.), 91
Switzerland, Swiss plateau, 90, 92
Symbols:
  city represented by, 79–80
  nonpictorial, 79
  pictographs, 157–159
  semipictorial, 79
Symbols, map *see* Map symbols

Taiwan:
  area, 281
  population, 281
Tape recorders, 182–183
Tasting party, 243
Tea, 197
  producers, 276
  production by countries, 276
Teaching of Geography, The (Thralls),
  36n, 216n
Television commercials, 243
Tempera paint map *see* Maps: tempera
  paint
Temperature:
  primary sequences, 218

Temperature (*Cont.*)
  mean, 246
  monthly, climatic data for selected
    cities, 264–265
Temperature graphs *see* also Graphs,
  climatic
Temperature graphs *see* Graphs,
  temperature
Temperature inversion, 62
Temperature variations, 246
Test construction, 221–229
Testing, 221–229
  arrow statements, 26, 27, 28
  construction of tests for map reading
    skills, 105–109
  cultural and natural features, 225
  direction, sample test, 105
  geographic imagery, 228
  geographic skills, 225–229
  geographic thinking, 228
  key words, 222
  landscape imagery, 105, 106–108
  latitude, use, 226
  location, ability to use longitude and
    latitude, 226
  location skills, 105
  longitude, 226
  map interpretation, 105, 227
  map making, 226
  map reading, 227
  map reading skills, 105–106
  map reading skills with hypothetical
    map, 108–109
  maps used, 105–109
  physical features, 106
  pictures, sample test, 137–138
  pictures used in, 137–138
  relationship-matching, 26, 27
  relationships, reason for use, 22
  sample tests, 105–109
  scale of miles, 106
    use of, 226
  sketching used as, 236
  statistics used in, 148, 226
Tests, criteria, 221
Tests:
  association, lesson plan, 104–105
  completion, 224–225
  essay, 28, 222–223
    use, 221–222
  matching, 224
  multiple-choice, 224

Tests (*Cont.*)
  objective, 223–225
    use, 222
  open book, 228–229
Textbooks, geography, 172–181
  criteria for selection, 178–181
  reading made meaningful, 176–178
  relationships, lack, 174
  tool, used as, 174–178
  use, 172–178
Thailand, slides and phonograph records, 182
Thermometer, primary sequences, 218
Third sequence:
  day, length, graph, 156
  day, time, 37
  direction, 37
  elevation, 88
  graphs, 156–157
  map reading readiness, 123
  seasons, 37
  shadows, 37
  sun position, 38
  temperature, 38
  wind, 218–219, 220
  see also Primary sequences
Thomas, Lowell, 182
Thralls, Zoe A., 36n, 216n
Three-step relationships *see* Relationships: three-step
Tidal wave, 17
Tilt of the earth *see* Earth: inclination of
Time, analemma, 73–75
Time belts (fig.), 69
  application work, 70
  concept, 68
  establishment, 68
  International Date Line, 70–71
  lesson plan, 68–70
  need, 68, 69
Time limits, 234
Time systems, prior to 1883, 68, 69
Timetables, 68
Tin:
  producers, 278
  production by countries, 278
Tobacco:
  producers, 276
  production by countries, 276
Tom Sawyer, 13
Tool subject *see* Geographic education: tool subject
Topography:
  Africa, 101–102

Topography (*Cont.*)
  climate, affected by, 247
  Norway, 100
  Peru, 166–169
  rainfall, amount and distribution influenced by, 267
  water supply, 99
Trade, statistics, distribution shown by, 140
Trade winds, 121, 248
  crops determined by elevation, latitude, and rainfall, 273
Transparencies, overhead projector, 185
Transportation facilities, maps, 102–103
Trapping:
  Alaska, 61
  California, 61
Travel, Great Circle Route, 56–57, 67
Travel folders, 244
  hypothetical countries, 116, 122
"Trend" graph *see* Graphs, line
Tropic of Cancer, 52, 53, 73, 75
  drawing, 48
  India, 197
Tropic of Capricorn, 52, 53, 73
  drawing, 47–48
Tropical rain forest *see* Rain forest: tropical
Trowbridge, John Townsend, 37
Truck farming, 251–252
  factors affecting, 251–252
  location, 251, 252
Truck gardening:
  Alaska, 61
  California, 61
Tschaikowsky, 13
Tundra:
  rainfall, monthly for Barrow, Alaska, 265
  temperature, monthly for Barrow, Alaska, 265
Tungsten:
  producers, 279
  production by countries, 279
Two-step relationships *see* Relationships: two-step

Understandings, major geographic, 188, 190
Union of Soviet Socialist Republics:
  area, 281
  land use data, 280
  population, 281
Union of Soviet Socialist Republics, Moscow, 70

Unit plans *see* Plans: unit
United Kingdom:
  area, 281
  land use data, 280
  population, 281
United States:
  aid to Brazil, 21
  almanacs, statistics, 103
  area, 281
  fifth sequence, studies in, 55
  fish, 154
  foreign policy, 7–9, 21
  global leadership, 8
  iron, 154
  land use data, 280
  lesson plan, summary, 103–104
  population, 281
  population, compared with India (fig.), 198
  population map interpretation, 103–104
  poultry houses, 56
  statistics, almanacs, 103
  steel, 154
  wheat, 56
United States Geological Survey, 34
Units of work, 9
"Up," concept, 42, 43
Uruguay, 107

Van Gogh, 12, 13
Vanguard, 45
Vegetable growing, commercial *see* Truck farming
Vegetables, 18
Vegetation:
  affected by elevation in low latitudes, 272
  affected by elevation in middle latitudes, 272
Vegetation, type, rainfall in various areas, 267
Venezuela, 107
  iron ore, 17
Vermont:
  area (tab.), 141
  population, 84, (tab.), 141
Vernal equinox *see* Equinox, vernal
Vietnam:
  area, 281
  population, 281
Vineyards *see* Viniculture
Viniculture, 254–255
  climate, 254–255

Viniculture (*Cont.*)
  location, 254–255
  temperature, 254–255
Vocabulary *see* Geographic vocabulary

Wales *see* United Kingdom
Washington, latitude effects, 62
Washington, D.C., 64
Washington Meridian Conference, 64
Water current *see* North Atlantic Drift
Water resources, lesson plan, motivation, 99
Water supply, 99
  determined by topography, 99
Waterbury, Conn., population (tab.), 141
Weather, 28
  primary sequences, 216–220
Weather concepts, primary sequences, 220
Weather effects, primary sequences, 217–218, 220
Weather calendar, primary sequences, 216–217
Weather calendar, monthly, graphs, 155–156
Weather chart *see* Charts, weather
Weather clock, illustrated (fig.), 217
  primary sequences, 217
Weather clothes line, primary sequences, 219–220
West Germany *see* Germany, west
Westerlies, 121, 248–249
  crops determined by elevation, latitude, and rainfall, 273
  Eurasia, 266
Wheat:
  growing season, 268
  producers, 268
  production by countries, 268
  rainfall required, 268
  spring, 56
Wind, third sequence, 218–219, 220
Wind, effects, primary sequences, 218–219, 220
Wind belts, 117, 247–249
  effects, 248–249
  see also Calm belts
Wind system, 247–249
Wind velocity:
  Beaufort scale, 218
  primary sequences, 218, 220
Winds, 246
  cause, 248

Winds (*Cont.*)
  direction determined by, 248
  strength, how determined, 248
  planetary, 247n
  polar *see* Polar winds
  trade *see* Trade winds
Winter solstice *see* Solstice: winter
Wisconsin, dairying, 18, 20
Wittich, Walter A., 186
Wool:
  producers, 276
  production by countries, 276

Worcester, Mass., population (tab.), 141
Work habits, 234
Work sheets, individual, 234
World Almanac and Book of Facts, 84n, 86, 116, 169, 276n, 281n

Yakutsk, Siberia *see* Siberia, Yakutsk
Yearbook of Agriculture, 86
Yukon Basin *see* Alaska, Arctic
Yukon Standard Time Belt, 69
Yukon Territory, Canada *see* Canada: Yukon Territory